ROCKO'S MODERN LIFE ™

VOLUME TWO

kaboom!™

COVER BY
JORGE MONLONGO

SERIES DESIGNER
MICHELLE ANKLEY

COLLECTION DESIGNER
KARA LEOPARD

EDITOR
MATTHEW LEVINE

SPECIAL THANKS TO JOAN HILTY, LINDA LEE,
JAMES SALERNO, ALEXANDRA MAURER
AND THE WONDERFUL TEAM AT NICKELODEON

ROSS RICHIE ....CEO & Founder
JOY HUFFMAN.. CFO
MATT GAGNON...Editor-in-Chief
FILIP SABLIK ....President , Publishing & Marketing
STEPHEN CHRISTY.............................President, Development
LANCE KREITER...........Vice President, Licensing & Merchandising
PHIL BARBARO......... Vice President, Finance & Human Resources
ARUNE SINGH..Vice President, Marketing
BRYCE CARLSON ...... Vice President, Editorial & Creative Strategy
SCOTT NEWMAN.......................... Manager, Production Design
KATE HENNING... Manager, Operations
SPENCER SIMPSON .... Manager, Sales
SIERRA HAHN...Executive Editor
JEANINE SCHAEFER...Executive Editor
DAFNA PLEBAN .... Senior Editor
SHANNON WATTERS .... Senior Editor
ERIC HARBURN... Senior Editor
WHITNEY LEOPARD...Editor
CAMERON CHITTOCK...Editor
CHRIS ROSA ....Editor
MATTHEW LEVINE ....Editor
SOPHIE PHILIPS-ROBERTS......................... Assistant Editor
GAVIN GRONENTHAL................................... Assistant Editor
MICHAEL MOCCIO .... Assistant Editor
AMANDA LaFRANCO ....Executive Assistant
JILLIAN CRAB ....Design Coordinator
MICHELLE ANKLEY...............................Design Coordinator
KARA LEOPARD......................................Production Designer
MARIE KRUPINA ....Production Designer
GRACE PARK .... Production Design Assistant
CHELSEA ROBERTS.....................Production Design Assistant
SAMANTHA KNAPP....................Production Design Assistant
ELIZABETH LOUGHRIDGE.......................Accounting Coordinator
STEPHANIE HOCUTT ....Social Media Coordinator
JOSÉ MEZA ....Event Coordinator
HOLLY AITCHISON.................................Operations Coordinator
MEGAN CHRISTOPHER.............................Operations Assistant
RODRIGO HERNANDEZ.................................Mailroom Assistant
MORGAN PERRY.............................. Direct Market Representative
CAT O'GRADY......................................Marketing Assistant
BREANNA SARPY.................................Executive Assistant

ROCKO'S MODERN LIFE Volume Two, March 2019. Published by KaBOOM!,
a division of Boom Entertainment, Inc., 5670 Wilshire Boulevard, Suite 400, Los
Angeles, CA 90036-5679. © 2019 Viacom International Inc. All Rights Reserved.
Nickelodeon, ROCKO'S MODERN LIFE and all related titles, logos, and characters
are trademarks of Viacom International Inc. Originally published in single magazine
form as ROCKO'S MODERN LIFE No. 5-8. © 2018 Viacom International Inc. Created Joe
Murray. KaBOOM!™ and the KaBOOM! logo are trademarks of Boom Entertainment,
Inc., registered in various countries and categories. All characters, events, and
institutions depicted herein are fictional. Any similarity between any of the names,
characters, persons, events, and/or institutions in this publication to actual names,
characters, and persons, whether living or dead, events, and/or institutions is
unintended and purely coincidental. KaBOOM! does not read or accept unsolicited
submissions of ideas, stories, or artwork.

BOOM! Studios, 5670 Wilshire Boulevard, Suite 400, Los Angeles, CA 90036-5679.
Printed in China. First Printing.

ISBN: 978-1-68415-271-1, eISBN: 978-1-64144-133-9

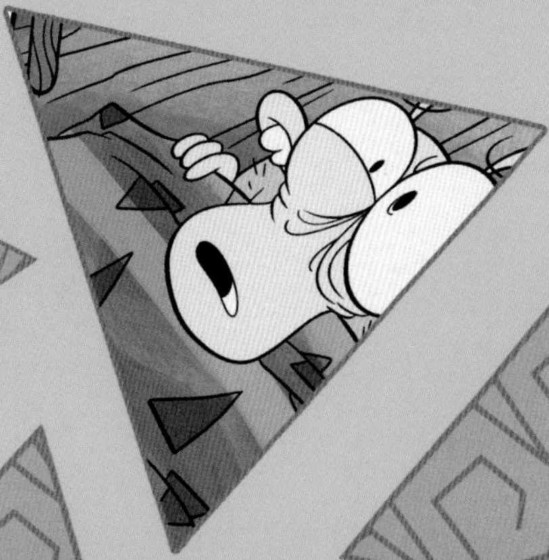

CREATED BY
JOE MURRAY

WRITTEN BY
RYAN FERRIER

ILLUSTRATED BY
IAN MCGINTY

COLORS BY
FRED C. STRESING

LETTERS BY
JIM CAMPBELL

"TRASIG"

WRITTEN & ILLUSTRATED BY
MARIE ENGER

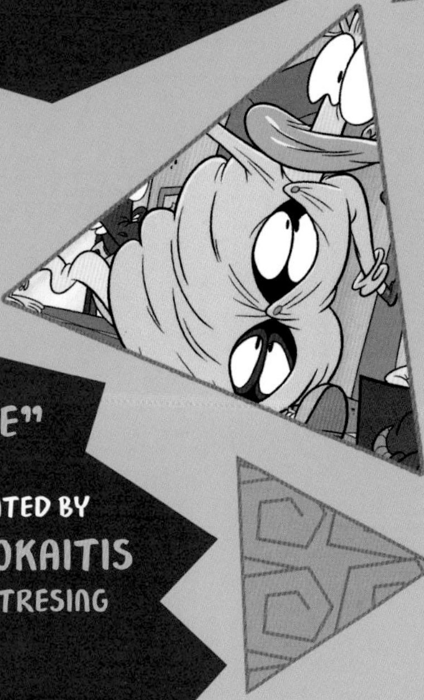

"MONSTER MOWER"

WRITTEN & ILLUSTRATED BY
DAVID DEGRAND

"G'DAY CAFE"

WRITTEN & ILLUSTRATED BY
PRANAS T. NAUJOKAITIS
COLORS BY FRED C. STRESING

LETTERS BY
JIM CAMPBELL

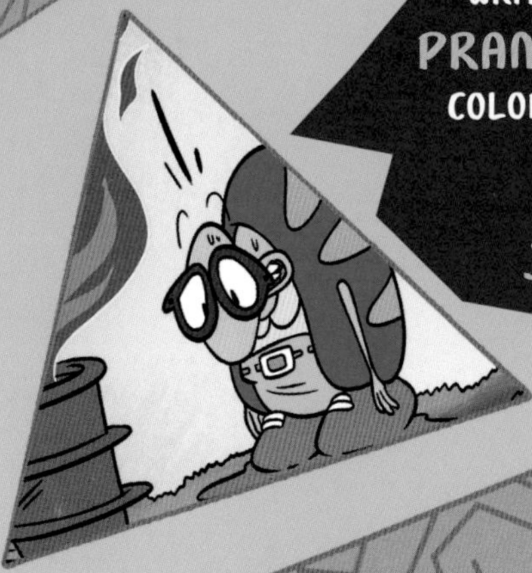

"MATRIMOANY"

WRITTEN & ILLUSTRATED BY
LUCIE EBREY

CHAPTER
FIVE

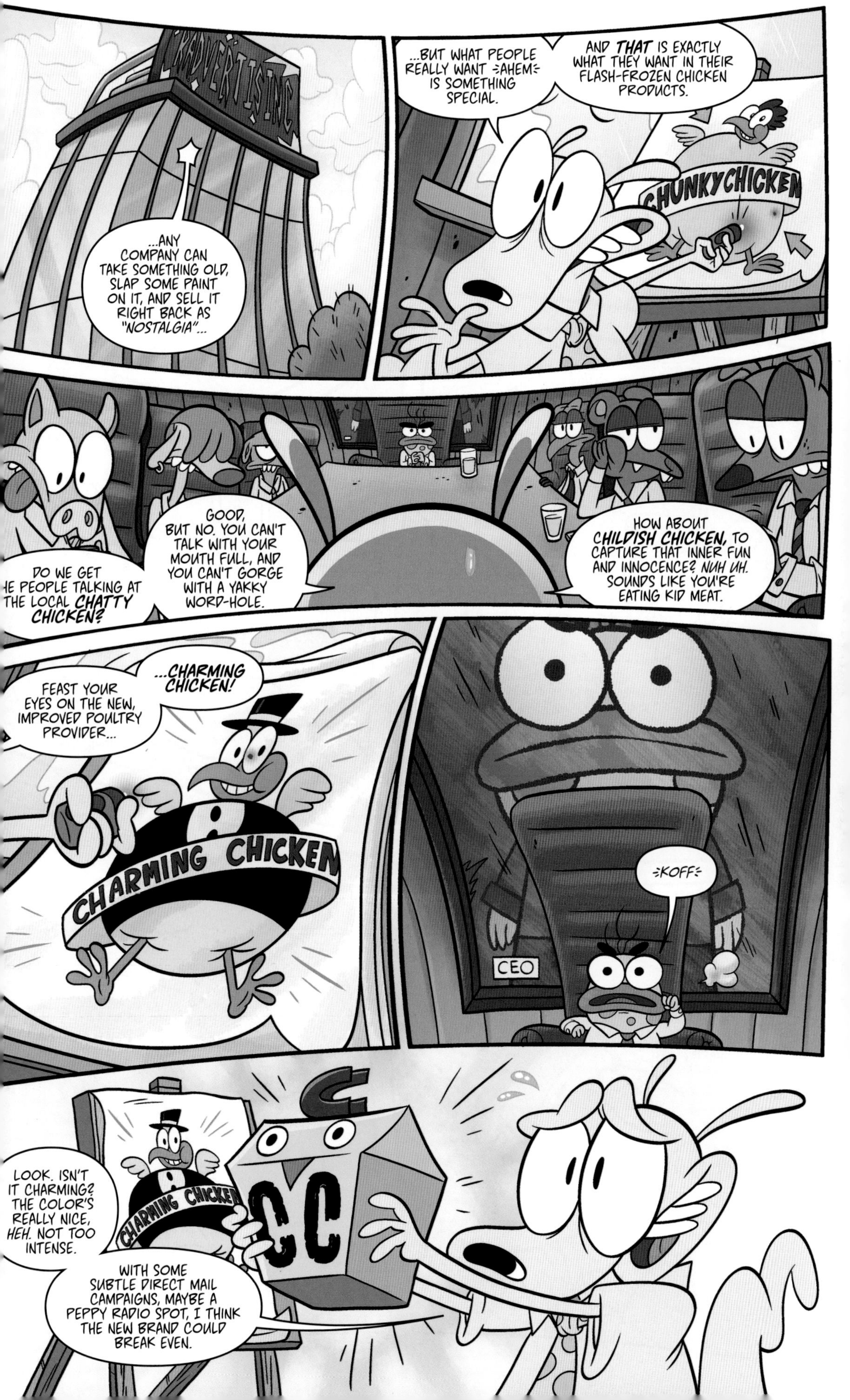

CRADVERTISING INC
...ANY COMPANY CAN TAKE SOMETHING OLD, SLAP SOME PAINT ON IT, AND SELL IT RIGHT BACK AS "NOSTALGIA"...
...BUT WHAT PEOPLE REALLY WANT =AHEM= IS SOMETHING SPECIAL.
AND THAT IS EXACTLY WHAT THEY WANT IN THEIR FLASH-FROZEN CHICKEN PRODUCTS.
CHUNKY CHICKEN
...DO WE GET THE PEOPLE TALKING AT THE LOCAL CHATTY CHICKEN?
GOOD, BUT NO. YOU CAN'T TALK WITH YOUR MOUTH FULL, AND YOU CAN'T GORGE WITH A YAKKY WORD-HOLE.
HOW ABOUT CHILDISH CHICKEN, TO CAPTURE THAT INNER FUN AND INNOCENCE? NUH UH. SOUNDS LIKE YOU'RE EATING KID MEAT.
FEAST YOUR EYES ON THE NEW, IMPROVED POULTRY PROVIDER...
...CHARMING CHICKEN!
CHARMING CHICKEN
=KOFF=
CEO
LOOK. ISN'T IT CHARMING? THE COLOR'S REALLY NICE, HEH. NOT TOO INTENSE.
CHARMING CHICKEN
CC
WITH SOME SUBTLE DIRECT MAIL CAMPAIGNS, MAYBE A PEPPY RADIO SPOT, I THINK THE NEW BRAND COULD BREAK EVEN.

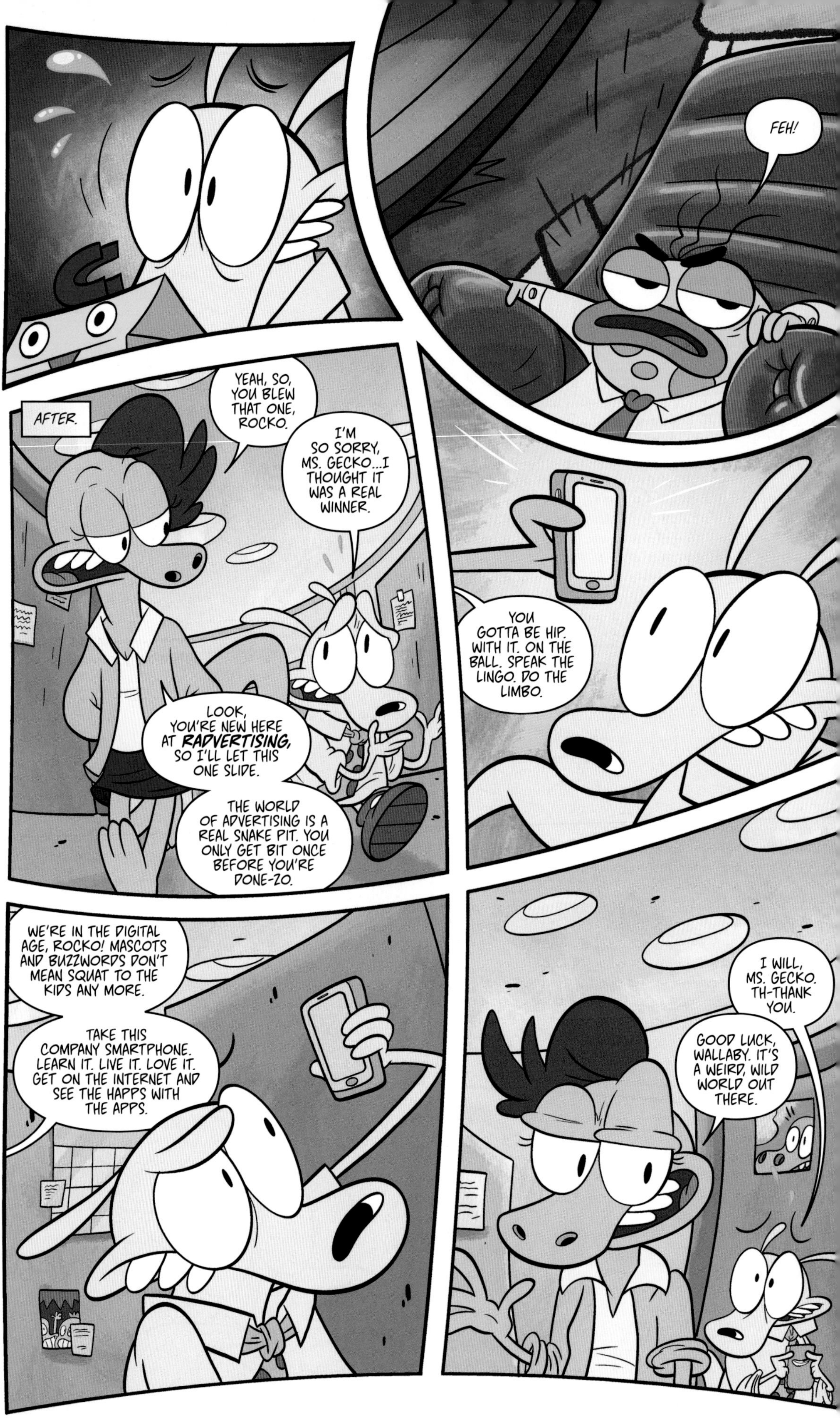
FEH!
AFTER.
YEAH, SO, YOU BLEW THAT ONE, ROCKO.
I'M SO SORRY, MS. GECKO...I THOUGHT IT WAS A REAL WINNER.
LOOK, YOU'RE NEW HERE AT RADVERTISING, SO I'LL LET THIS ONE SLIDE.
THE WORLD OF ADVERTISING IS A REAL SNAKE PIT. YOU ONLY GET BIT ONCE BEFORE YOU'RE DONE-ZO.
YOU GOTTA BE HIP. WITH IT. ON THE BALL. SPEAK THE LINGO. DO THE LIMBO.
WE'RE IN THE DIGITAL AGE, ROCKO! MASCOTS AND BUZZWORDS DON'T MEAN SQUAT TO THE KIDS ANY MORE.
TAKE THIS COMPANY SMARTPHONE. LEARN IT. LIVE IT. LOVE IT. GET ON THE INTERNET AND SEE THE HAPPS WITH THE APPS.
GOOD LUCK, WALLABY. IT'S A WEIRD, WILD WORLD OUT THERE.
I WILL, MS. GECKO. TH-THANK YOU.

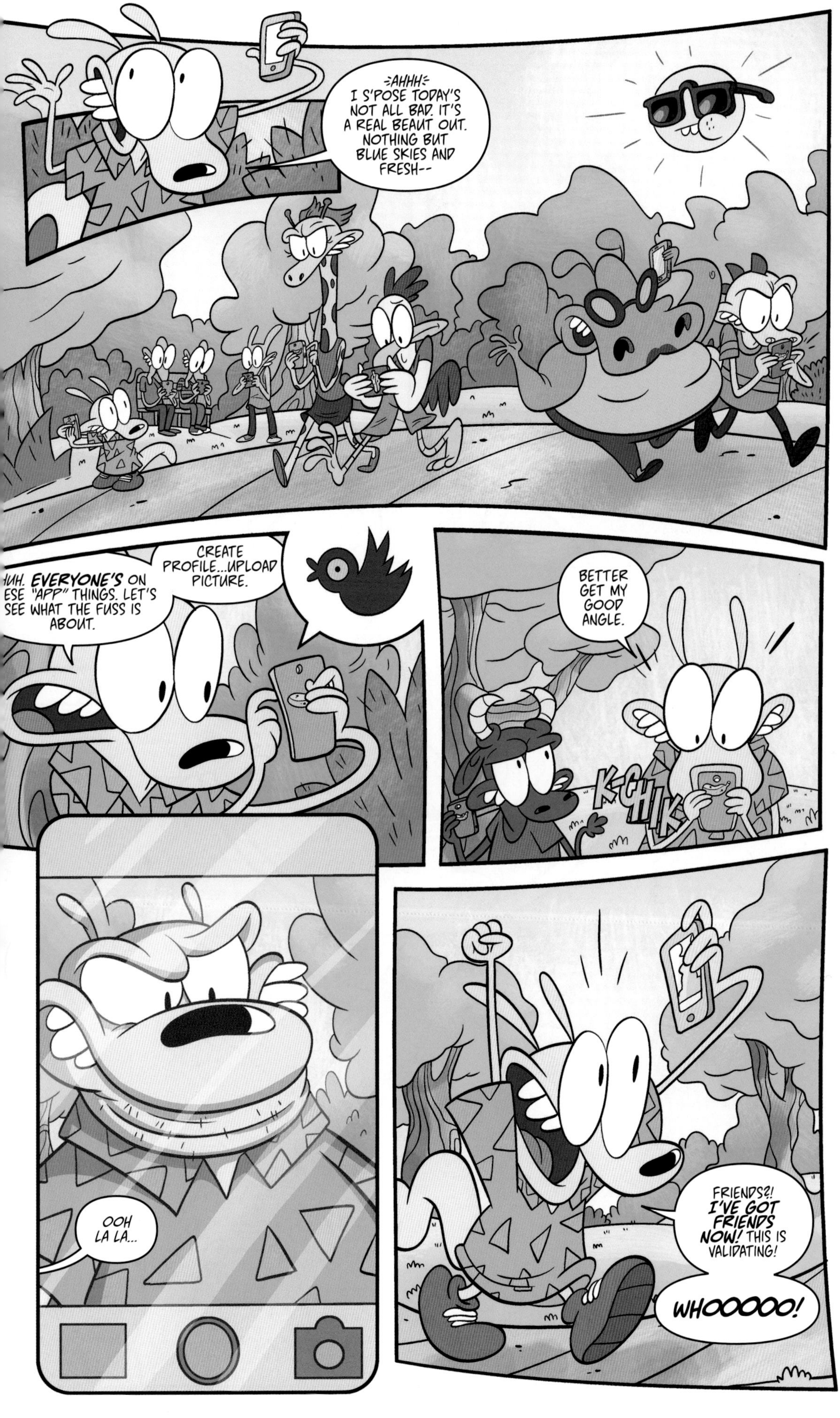

AHHH
I S'POSE TODAY'S NOT ALL BAD. IT'S A REAL BEAUT OUT. NOTHING BUT BLUE SKIES AND FRESH--
HUH. EVERYONE'S ON ESE "APP" THINGS. LET'S SEE WHAT THE FUSS IS ABOUT.
CREATE PROFILE...UPLOAD PICTURE.
BETTER GET MY GOOD ANGLE.
K-CHIK
OOH LA LA...
FRIENDS?! I'VE GOT FRIENDS NOW! THIS IS VALIDATING!
WHOOOOO!

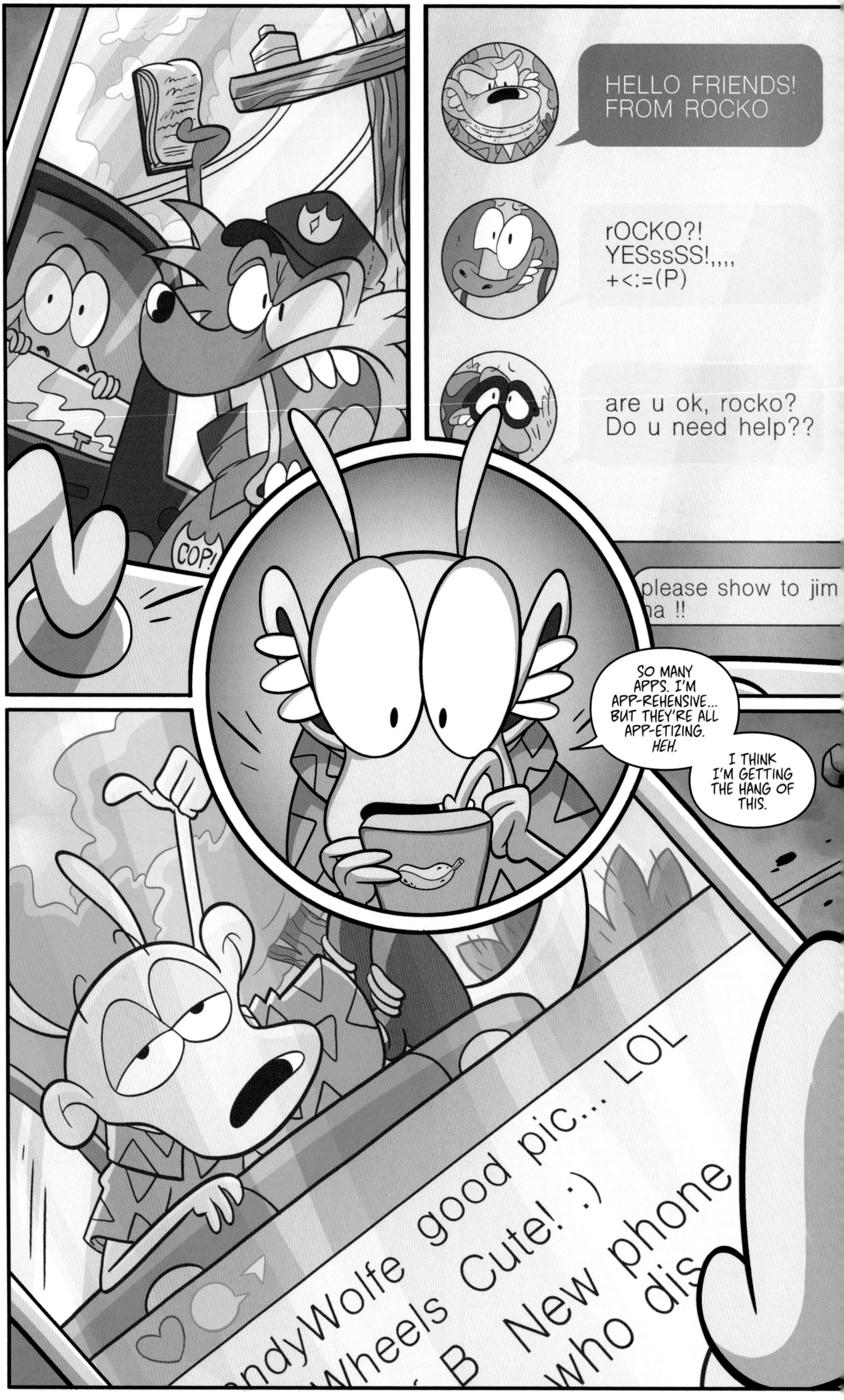
COP!
HELLO FRIENDS!
FROM ROCKO
rOCKO?!
YESssSS!,,,,
+<:=(P)
are u ok, rocko?
Do u need help??
please show to jim
ha !!
SO MANY APPS. I'M APP-REHENSIVE... BUT THEY'RE ALL APP-ETIZING. HEH.
I THINK I'M GETTING THE HANG OF THIS.
ndyWolfe good pic... LOL
Wheels Cute! :)
B New phone
who dis

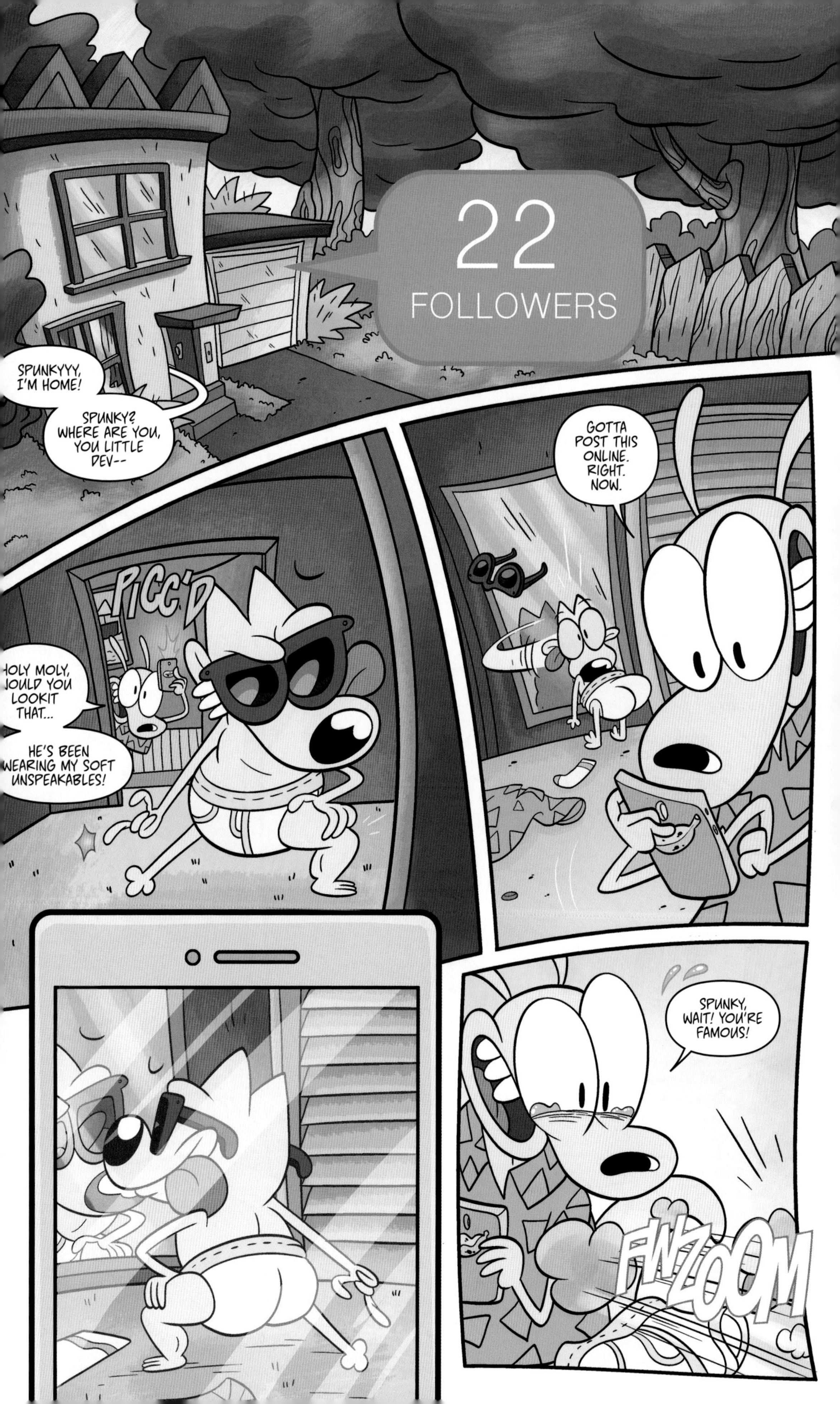
22
FOLLOWERS
SPUNKYYY, I'M HOME!
SPUNKY? WHERE ARE YOU, YOU LITTLE DEV--
PICC'D
HOLY MOLY, WOULD YOU LOOKIT THAT...
HE'S BEEN WEARING MY SOFT UNSPEAKABLES!
GOTTA POST THIS ONLINE. RIGHT. NOW.
SPUNKY, WAIT! YOU'RE FAMOUS!
FWZOOM

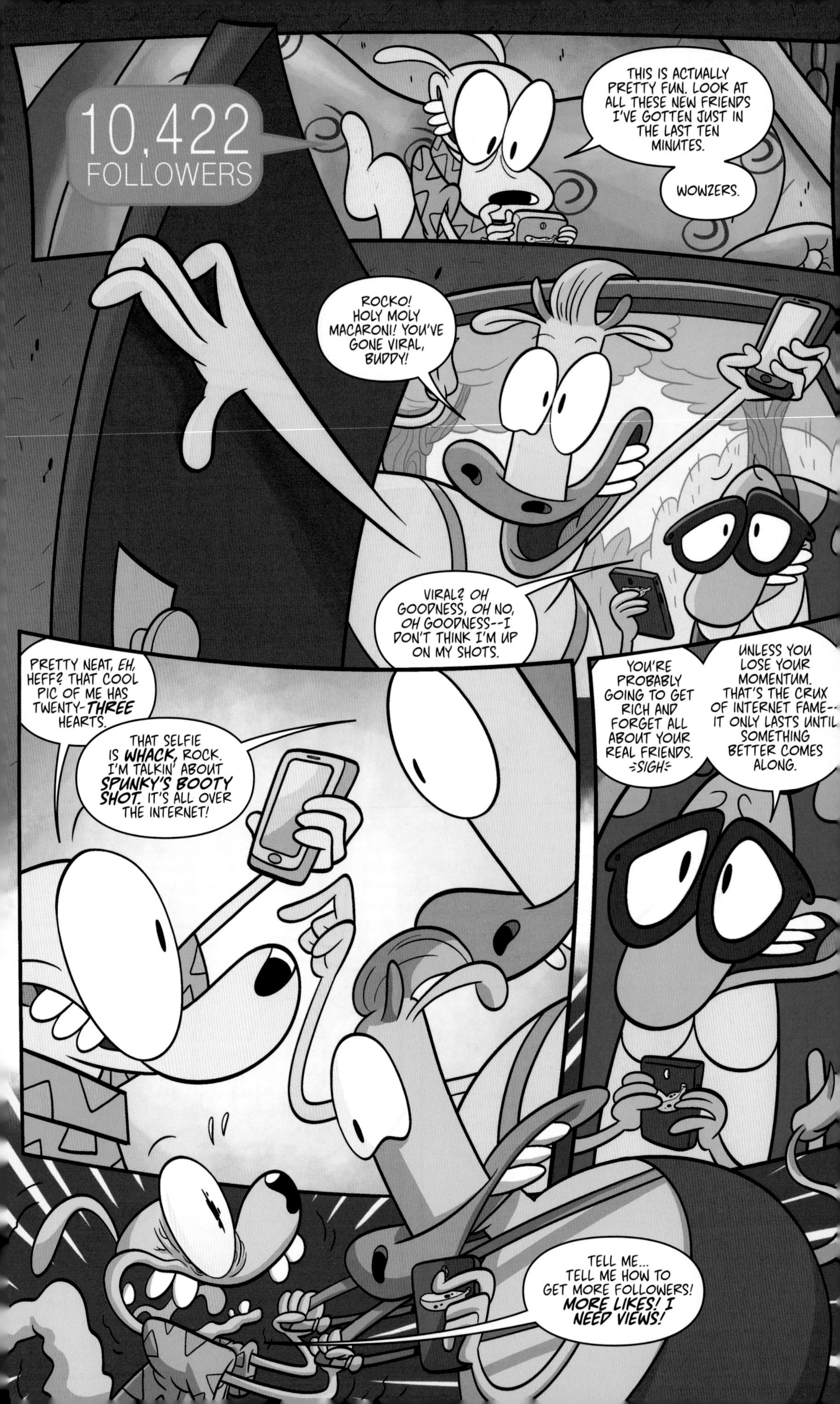
10,422 FOLLOWERS
THIS IS ACTUALLY PRETTY FUN. LOOK AT ALL THESE NEW FRIENDS I'VE GOTTEN JUST IN THE LAST TEN MINUTES.
WOWZERS.
ROCKO! HOLY MOLY MACARONI! YOU'VE GONE VIRAL, BUDDY!
VIRAL? OH GOODNESS, OH NO, OH GOODNESS--I DON'T THINK I'M UP ON MY SHOTS.
PRETTY NEAT, EH, HEFF? THAT COOL PIC OF ME HAS TWENTY-THREE HEARTS.
THAT SELFIE IS WHACK, ROCK. I'M TALKIN' ABOUT SPUNKY'S BOOTY SHOT. IT'S ALL OVER THE INTERNET!
YOU'RE PROBABLY GOING TO GET RICH AND FORGET ALL ABOUT YOUR REAL FRIENDS. =SIGH=
UNLESS YOU LOSE YOUR MOMENTUM. THAT'S THE CRUX OF INTERNET FAME--IT ONLY LASTS UNTIL SOMETHING BETTER COMES ALONG.
TELL ME... TELL ME HOW TO GET MORE FOLLOWERS! MORE LIKES! I NEED VIEWS!

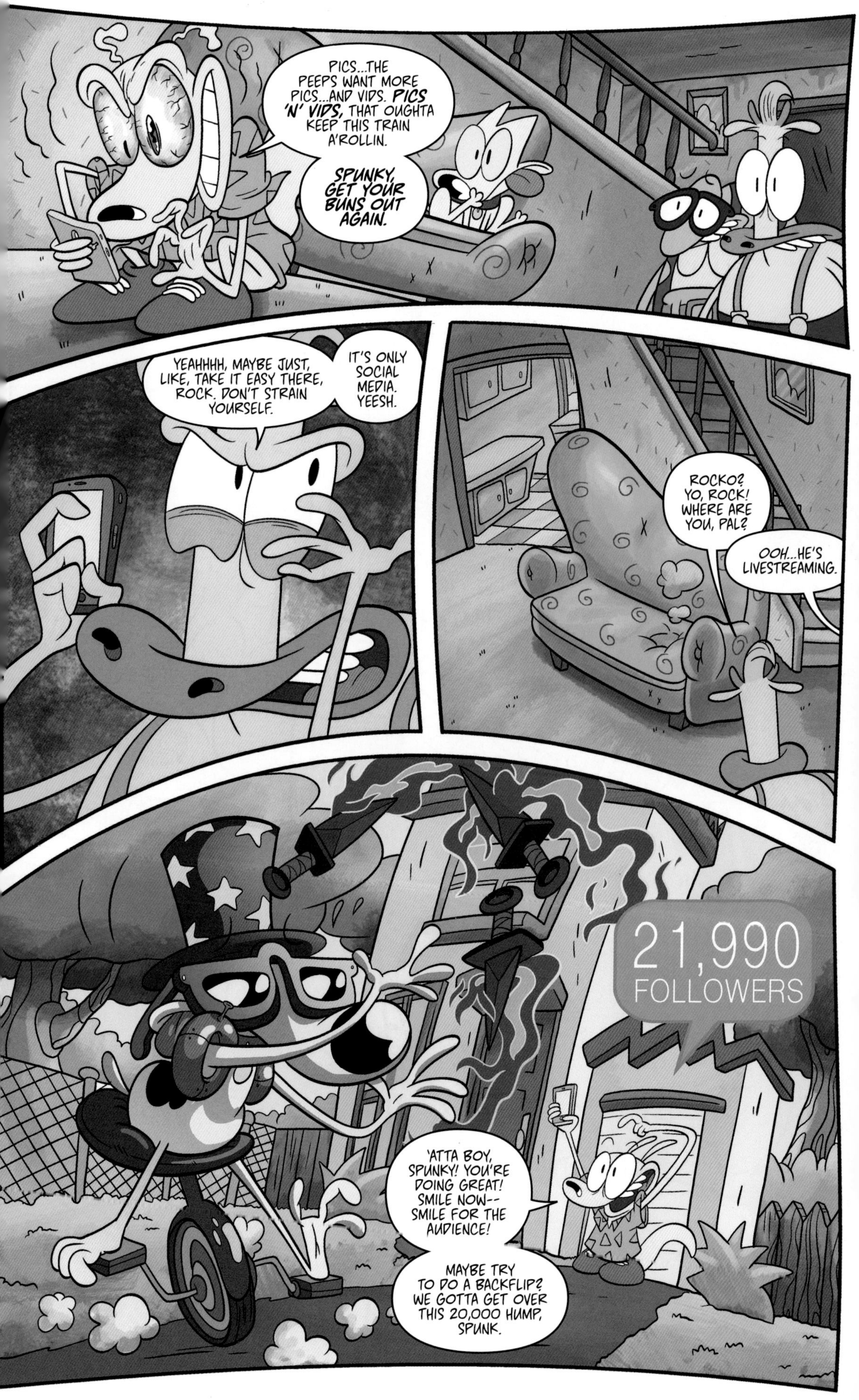
PICS...THE PEEPS WANT MORE PICS...AND VIDS. PICS 'N' VIDS, THAT OUGHTA KEEP THIS TRAIN A'ROLLIN.
SPUNKY, GET YOUR BUNS OUT AGAIN.
YEAHHHH, MAYBE JUST, LIKE, TAKE IT EASY THERE, ROCK. DON'T STRAIN YOURSELF.
IT'S ONLY SOCIAL MEDIA. YEESH.
ROCKO? YO, ROCK! WHERE ARE YOU, PAL?
OOH...HE'S LIVESTREAMING.
21,990 FOLLOWERS
'ATTA BOY, SPUNKY! YOU'RE DOING GREAT! SMILE NOW-- SMILE FOR THE AUDIENCE!
MAYBE TRY TO DO A BACKFLIP? WE GOTTA GET OVER THIS 20,000 HUMP, SPUNK.

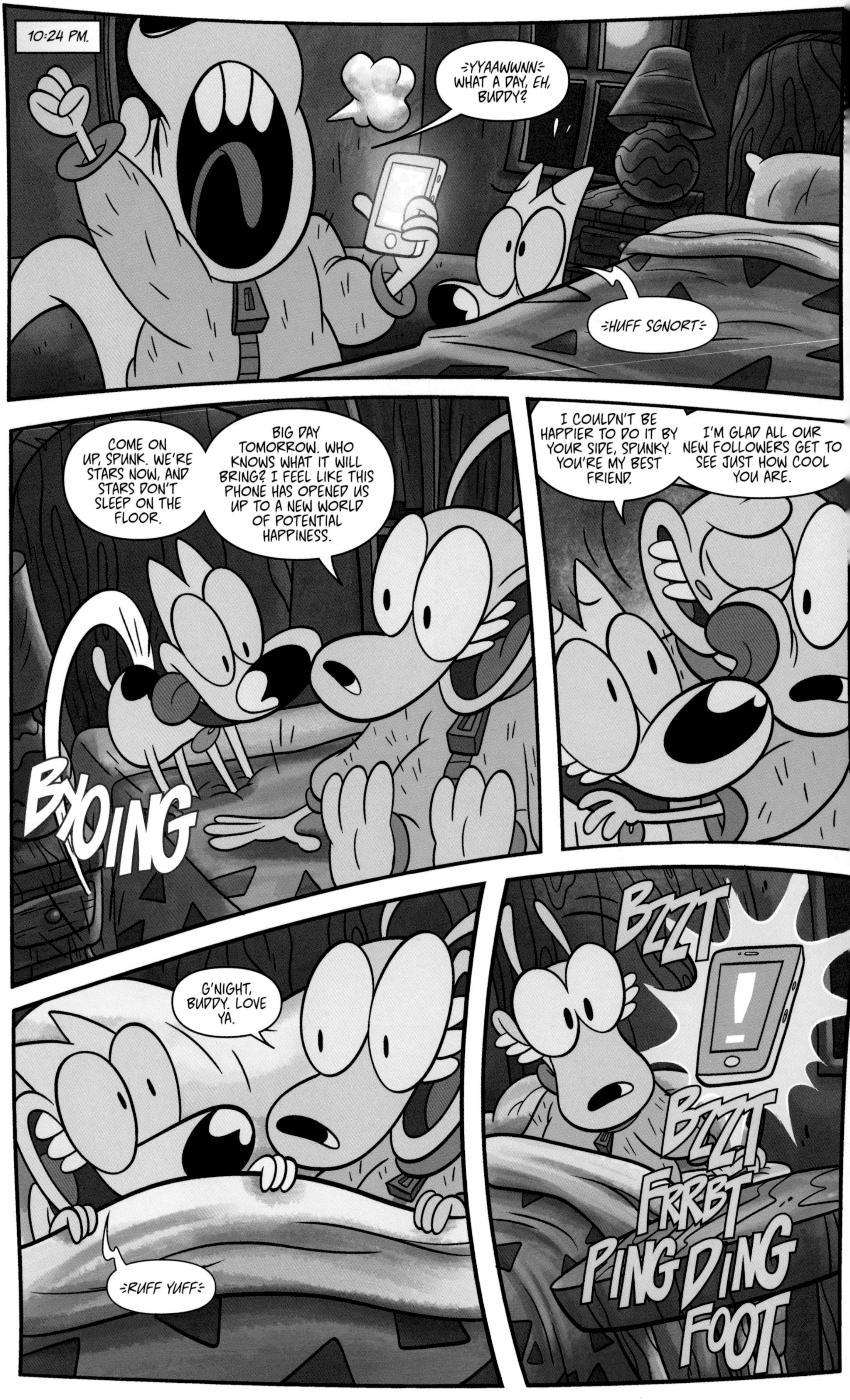
10:24 PM.
=YYAAWWNN= WHAT A DAY, EH, BUDDY?
=HUFF SGNORT=
COME ON UP, SPUNK. WE'RE STARS NOW, AND STARS DON'T SLEEP ON THE FLOOR.
BIG DAY TOMORROW. WHO KNOWS WHAT IT WILL BRING? I FEEL LIKE THIS PHONE HAS OPENED US UP TO A NEW WORLD OF POTENTIAL HAPPINESS.
BYOING
I COULDN'T BE HAPPIER TO DO IT BY YOUR SIDE, SPUNKY. YOU'RE MY BEST FRIEND.
I'M GLAD ALL OUR NEW FOLLOWERS GET TO SEE JUST HOW COOL YOU ARE.
G'NIGHT, BUDDY. LOVE YA.
=RUFF YUFF=
BZZT
BZZT
FRRBT
PING DING
FOOT

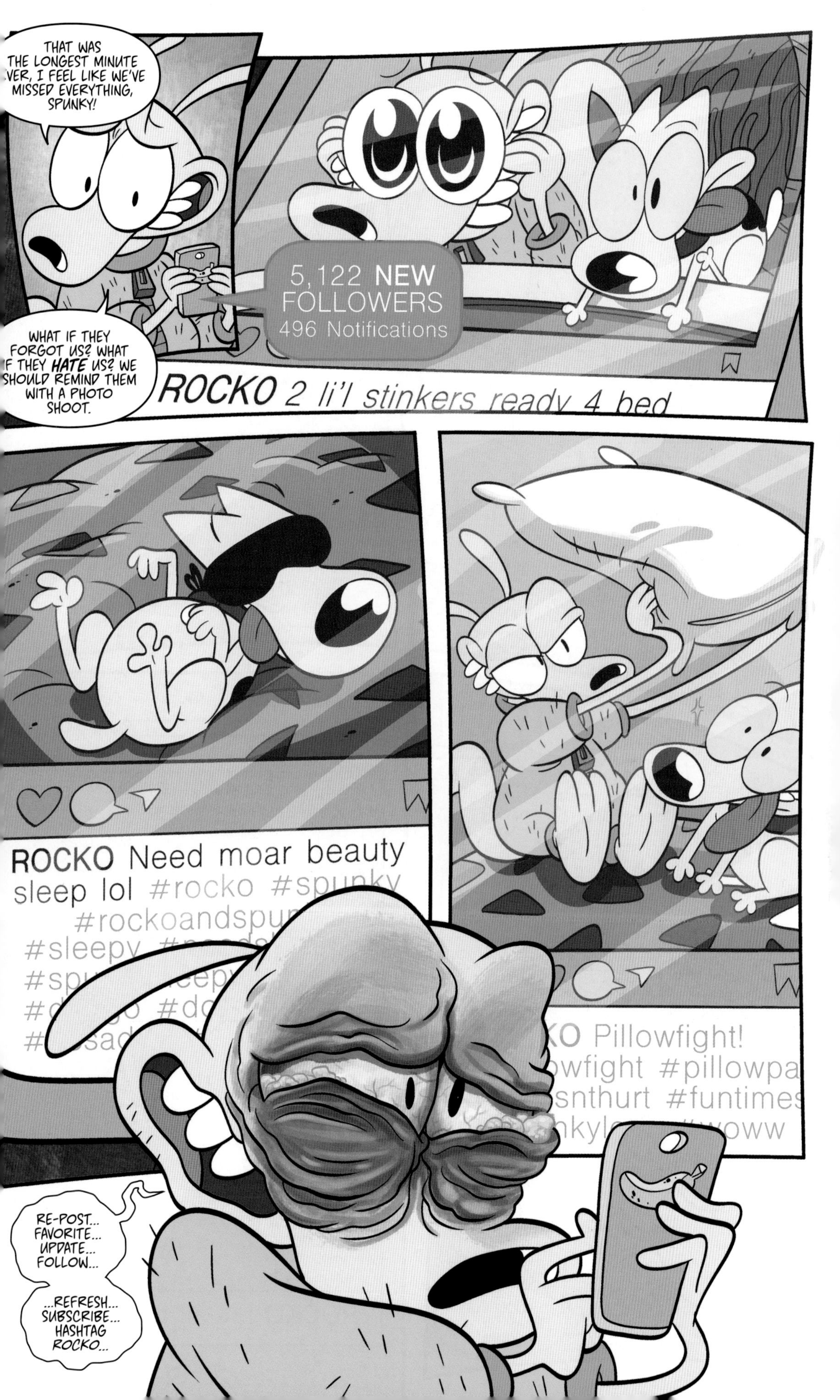

THAT WAS THE LONGEST MINUTE EVER, I FEEL LIKE WE'VE MISSED EVERYTHING, SPUNKY!
WHAT IF THEY FORGOT US? WHAT IF THEY **HATE** US? WE SHOULD REMIND THEM WITH A PHOTO SHOOT.
5,122 NEW FOLLOWERS
496 Notifications
ROCKO 2 li'l stinkers ready 4 bed
ROCKO Need moar beauty sleep lol #rocko #spunky
KO Pillowfight!
RE-POST... FAVORITE... UPDATE... FOLLOW...
...REFRESH... SUBSCRIBE... HASHTAG ROCKO...

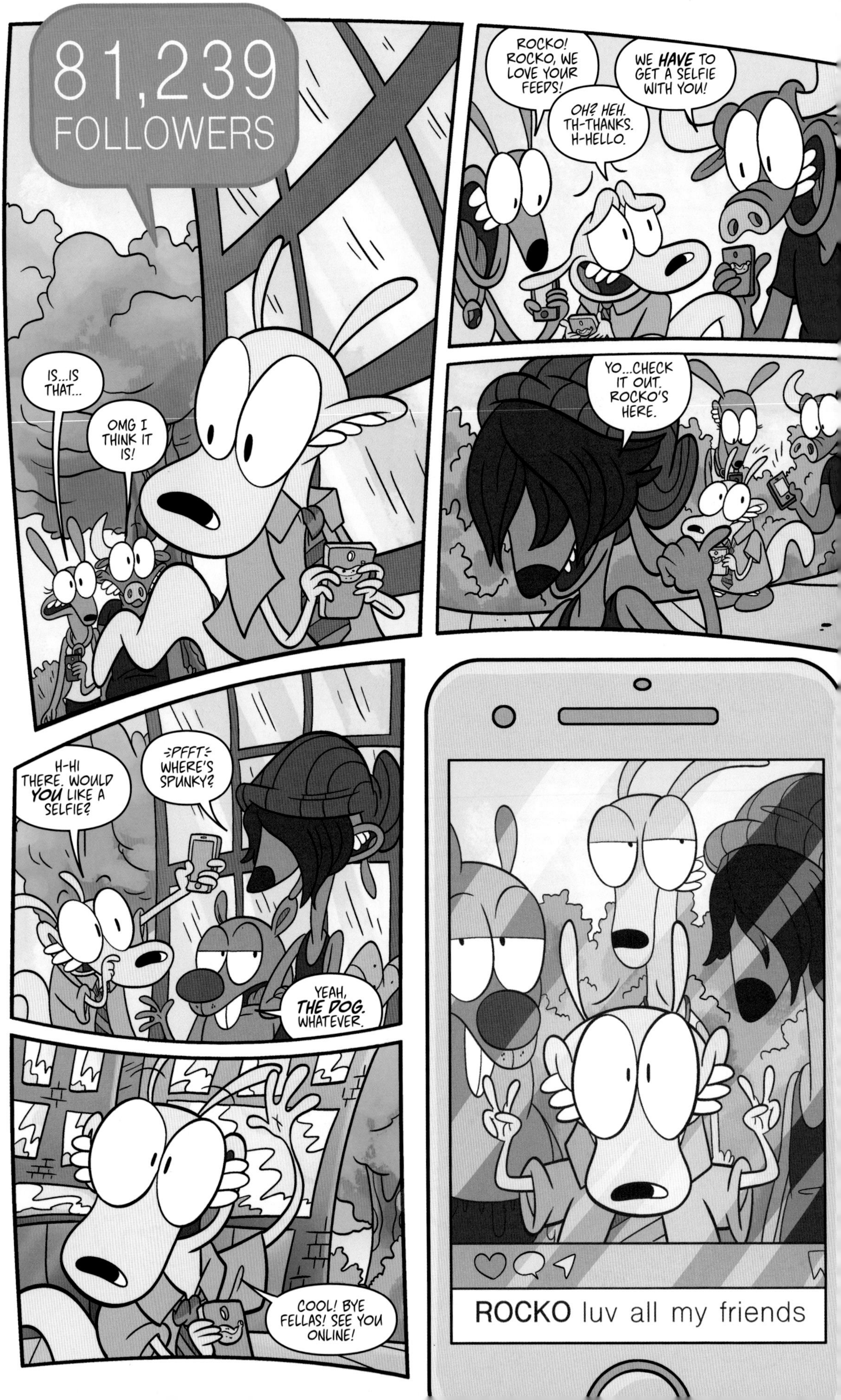
81,239 FOLLOWERS
IS...IS THAT...
OMG I THINK IT IS!
ROCKO! ROCKO, WE LOVE YOUR FEEDS!
OH? HEH. TH-THANKS. H-HELLO.
WE HAVE TO GET A SELFIE WITH YOU!
YO...CHECK IT OUT. ROCKO'S HERE.
H-HI THERE. WOULD YOU LIKE A SELFIE?
PFFT. WHERE'S SPUNKY?
YEAH, THE DOG. WHATEVER.
COOL! BYE FELLAS! SEE YOU ONLINE!
ROCKO luv all my friends

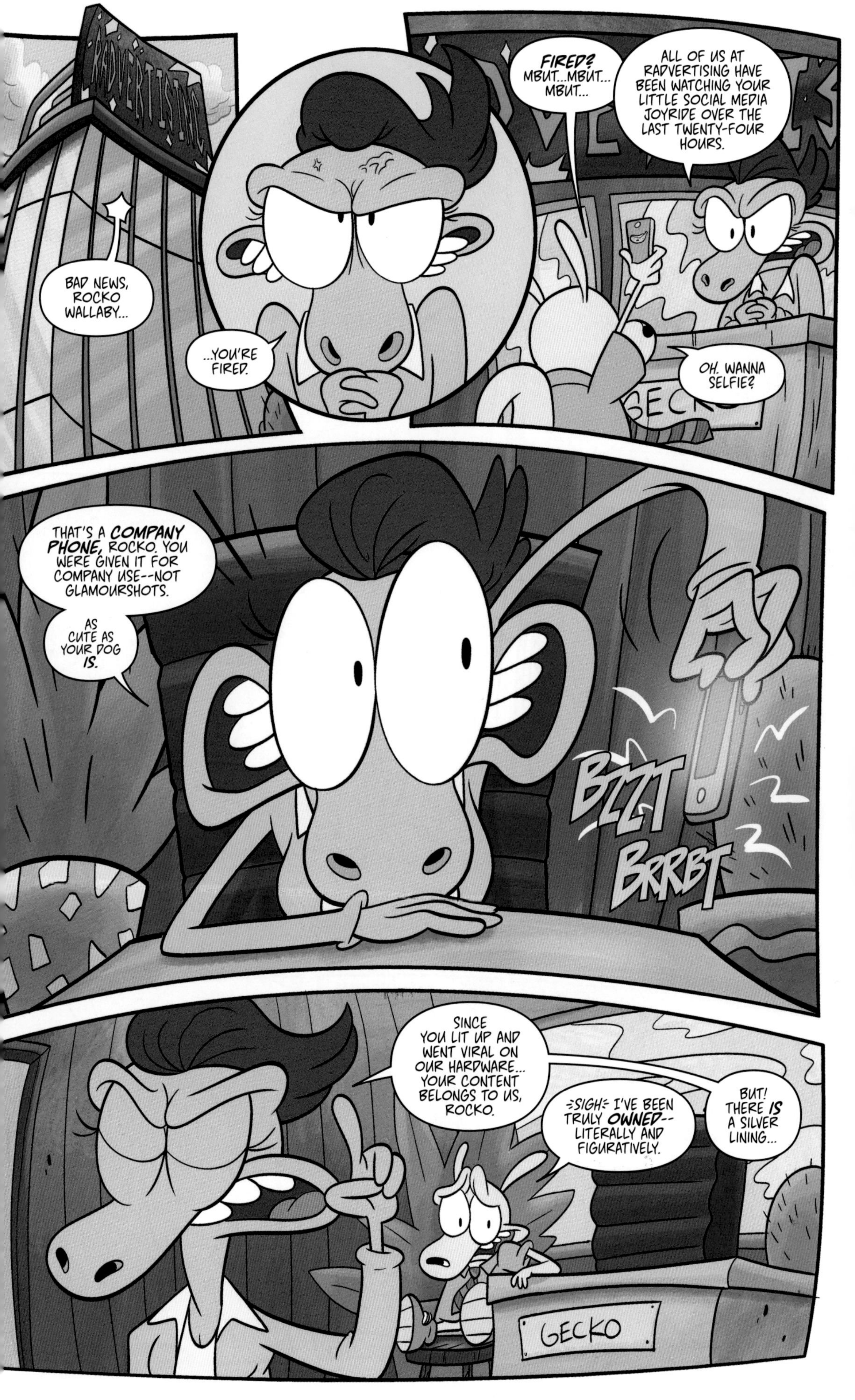

RADVERTISING
BAD NEWS, ROCKO WALLABY...
...YOU'RE FIRED.
FIRED? MBUT...MBUT... MBUT...
ALL OF US AT RADVERTISING HAVE BEEN WATCHING YOUR LITTLE SOCIAL MEDIA JOYRIDE OVER THE LAST TWENTY-FOUR HOURS.
OH. WANNA SELFIE?
THAT'S A COMPANY PHONE, ROCKO. YOU WERE GIVEN IT FOR COMPANY USE--NOT GLAMOURSHOTS.
AS CUTE AS YOUR DOG IS.
BZZT
BRRBT
SINCE YOU LIT UP AND WENT VIRAL ON OUR HARDWARE... YOUR CONTENT BELONGS TO US, ROCKO.
=SIGH= I'VE BEEN TRULY OWNED-- LITERALLY AND FIGURATIVELY.
BUT! THERE IS A SILVER LINING...
GECKO

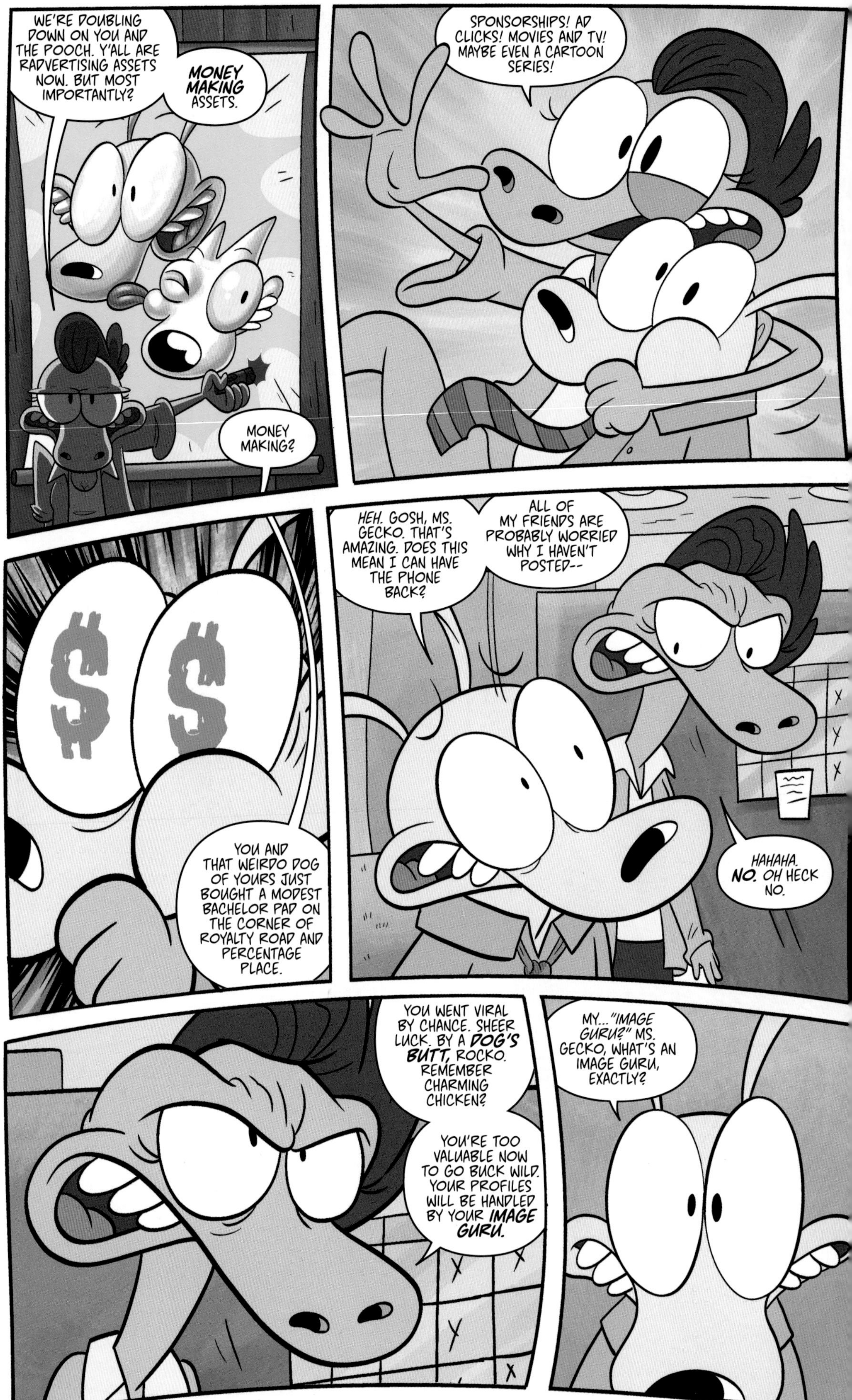

WE'RE DOUBLING DOWN ON YOU AND THE POOCH. Y'ALL ARE RADVERTISING ASSETS NOW. BUT MOST IMPORTANTLY?
MONEY MAKING ASSETS.
MONEY MAKING?
SPONSORSHIPS! AD CLICKS! MOVIES AND TV! MAYBE EVEN A CARTOON SERIES!
YOU AND THAT WEIRDO DOG OF YOURS JUST BOUGHT A MODEST BACHELOR PAD ON THE CORNER OF ROYALTY ROAD AND PERCENTAGE PLACE.
HEH. GOSH, MS. GECKO. THAT'S AMAZING. DOES THIS MEAN I CAN HAVE THE PHONE BACK?
ALL OF MY FRIENDS ARE PROBABLY WORRIED WHY I HAVEN'T POSTED--
HAHAHA. **NO.** OH HECK NO.
YOU WENT VIRAL BY CHANCE. SHEER LUCK. BY A ***DOG'S BUTT,*** ROCKO. REMEMBER CHARMING CHICKEN?
YOU'RE TOO VALUABLE NOW TO GO BUCK WILD. YOUR PROFILES WILL BE HANDLED BY YOUR ***IMAGE GURU.***
MY... "IMAGE GURU?" MS. GECKO, WHAT'S AN IMAGE GURU, EXACTLY?

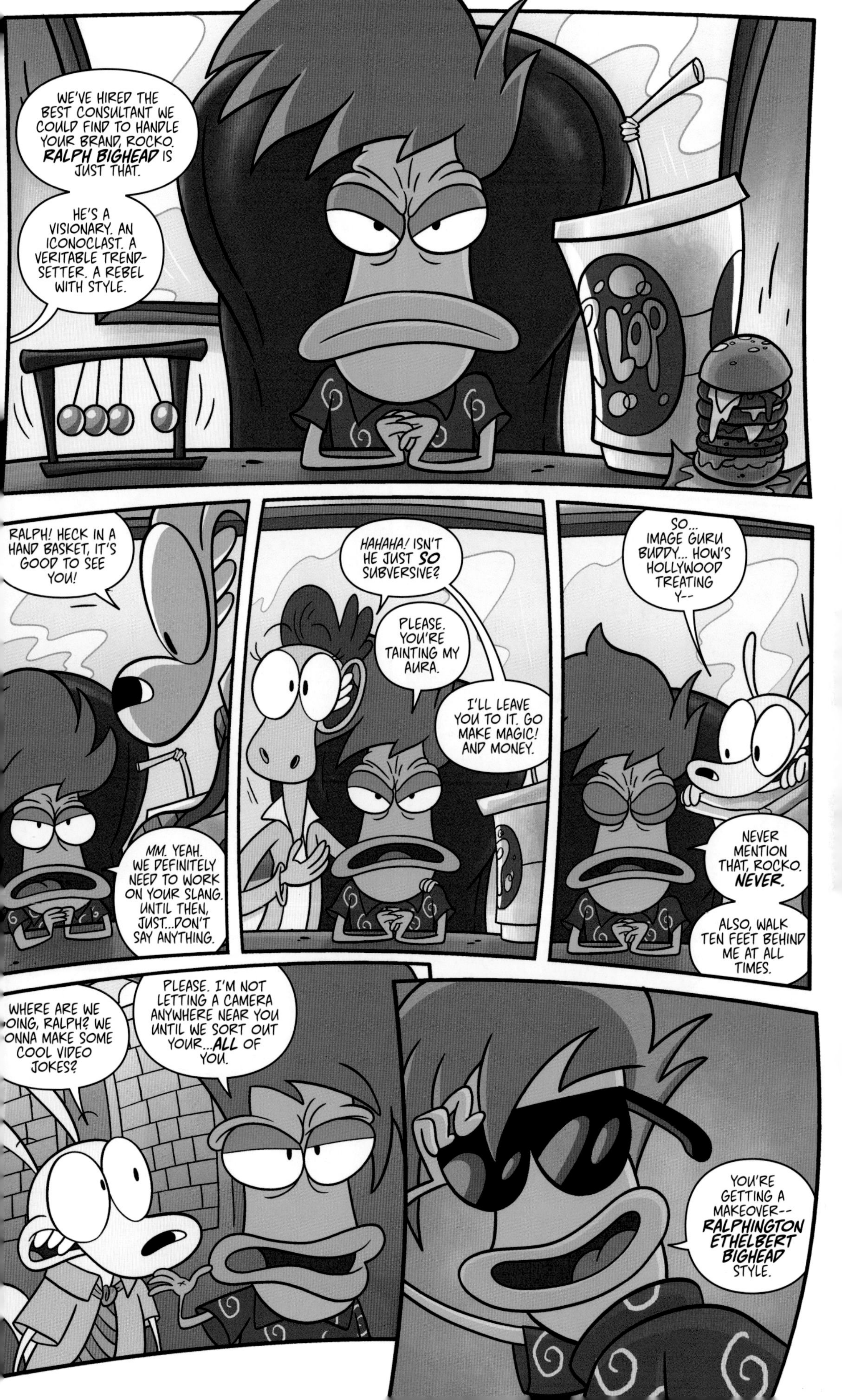

WE'VE HIRED THE BEST CONSULTANT WE COULD FIND TO HANDLE YOUR BRAND, ROCKO. **RALPH BIGHEAD** IS JUST THAT.
HE'S A VISIONARY. AN ICONOCLAST. A VERITABLE TREND-SETTER. A REBEL WITH STYLE.
RALPH! HECK IN A HAND BASKET, IT'S GOOD TO SEE YOU!
MM. YEAH. WE DEFINITELY NEED TO WORK ON YOUR SLANG. UNTIL THEN, JUST...DON'T SAY ANYTHING.
HAHAHA! ISN'T HE JUST ***SO*** SUBVERSIVE?
PLEASE. YOU'RE TAINTING MY AURA.
I'LL LEAVE YOU TO IT. GO MAKE MAGIC! AND MONEY.
SO... IMAGE GURU BUDDY... HOW'S HOLLYWOOD TREATING Y--
NEVER MENTION THAT, ROCKO. ***NEVER.***
ALSO, WALK TEN FEET BEHIND ME AT ALL TIMES.
WHERE ARE WE OING, RALPH? WE ONNA MAKE SOME COOL VIDEO JOKES?
PLEASE. I'M NOT LETTING A CAMERA ANYWHERE NEAR YOU UNTIL WE SORT OUT YOUR...***ALL*** OF YOU.
YOU'RE GETTING A MAKEOVER-- **RALPHINGTON ETHELBERT BIGHEAD** STYLE.

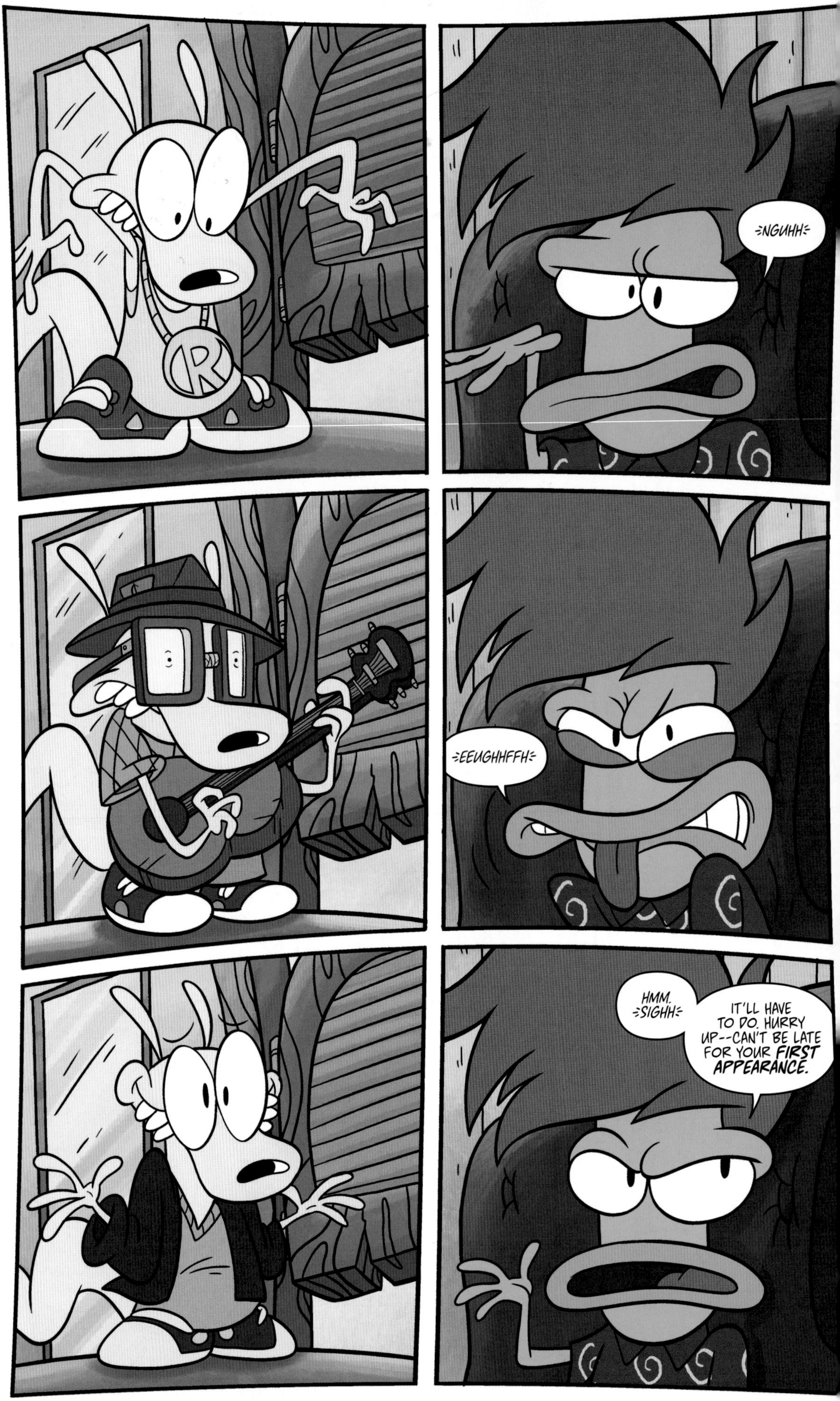
=NGUHH=
=EEUGHHFFH=
HMM. =SIGHH=
IT'LL HAVE TO DO. HURRY UP--CAN'T BE LATE FOR YOUR **FIRST APPEARANCE**.

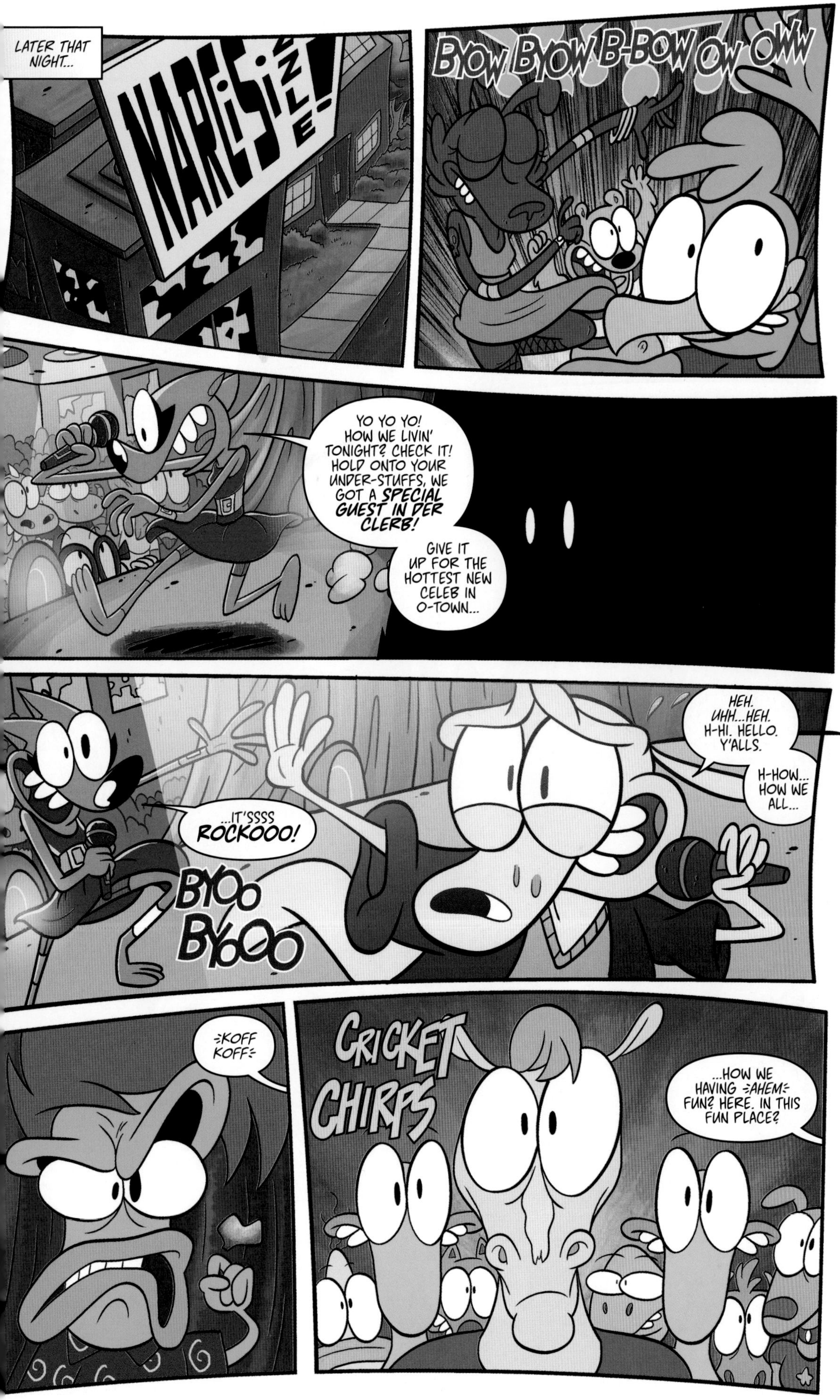

LATER THAT NIGHT...
NARCISSIZZLE!
BYOW BYOW B-BOW OW OWW
YO YO YO! HOW WE LIVIN' TONIGHT? CHECK IT! HOLD ONTO YOUR UNDER-STUFFS, WE GOT A SPECIAL GUEST IN DER CLERB!
GIVE IT UP FOR THE HOTTEST NEW CELEB IN O-TOWN...
...IT'SSSS ROCKOOO!
BYOO BYOOO
HEH. UHH...HEH. H-HI. HELLO. Y'ALLS.
H-HOW... HOW WE ALL...
=KOFF KOFF=
CRICKET CHIRPS
...HOW WE HAVING =AHEM= FUN? HERE. IN THIS FUN PLACE?

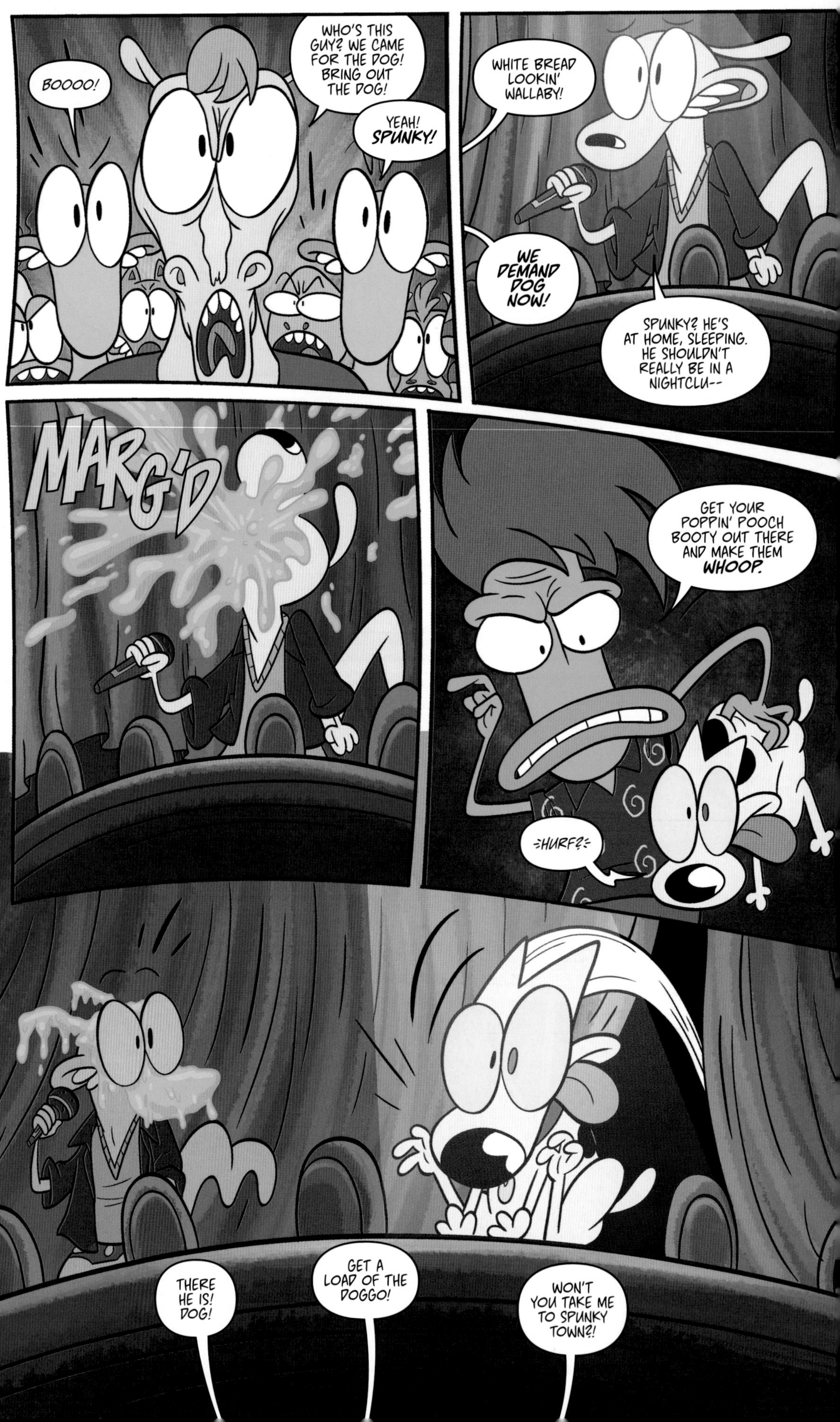
BOOOO!
WHO'S THIS GUY? WE CAME FOR THE DOG! BRING OUT THE DOG!
YEAH! SPUNKY!
WHITE BREAD LOOKIN' WALLABY!
WE DEMAND DOG NOW!
SPUNKY? HE'S AT HOME, SLEEPING. HE SHOULDN'T REALLY BE IN A NIGHTCLU--
MARG'D
GET YOUR POPPIN' POOCH BOOTY OUT THERE AND MAKE THEM WHOOP.
HURF?
THERE HE IS! DOG!
GET A LOAD OF THE DOGGO!
WON'T YOU TAKE ME TO SPUNKY TOWN?!

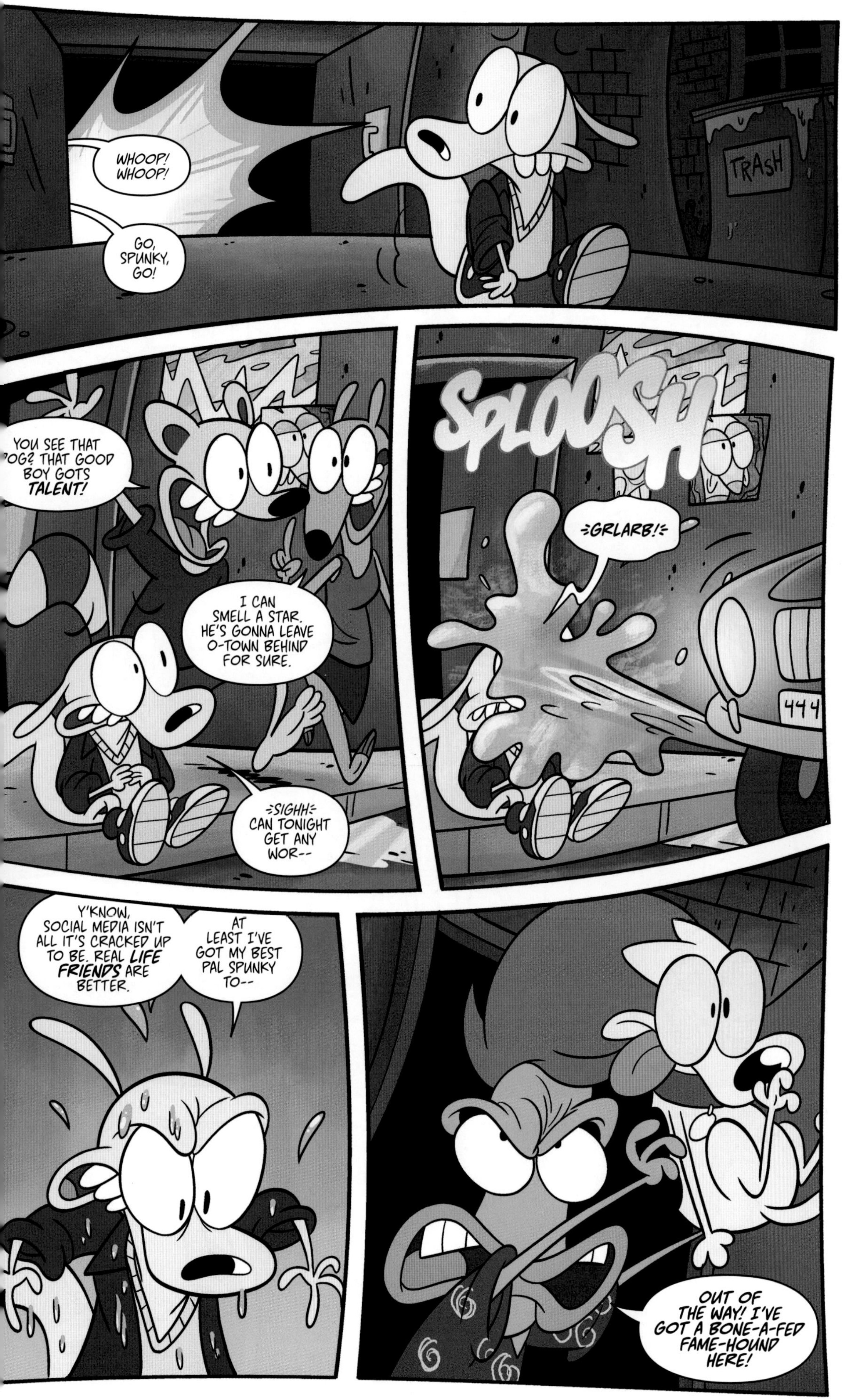
WHOOP! WHOOP!
GO, SPUNKY, GO!
TRASH
YOU SEE THAT DOG? THAT GOOD BOY GOTS TALENT!
I CAN SMELL A STAR. HE'S GONNA LEAVE O-TOWN BEHIND FOR SURE.
SIGHH CAN TONIGHT GET ANY WOR--
SPLOOSH
GRLARB!
444
Y'KNOW, SOCIAL MEDIA ISN'T ALL IT'S CRACKED UP TO BE. REAL LIFE FRIENDS ARE BETTER.
AT LEAST I'VE GOT MY BEST PAL SPUNKY TO--
OUT OF THE WAY! I'VE GOT A BONE-A-FED FAME-HOUND HERE!

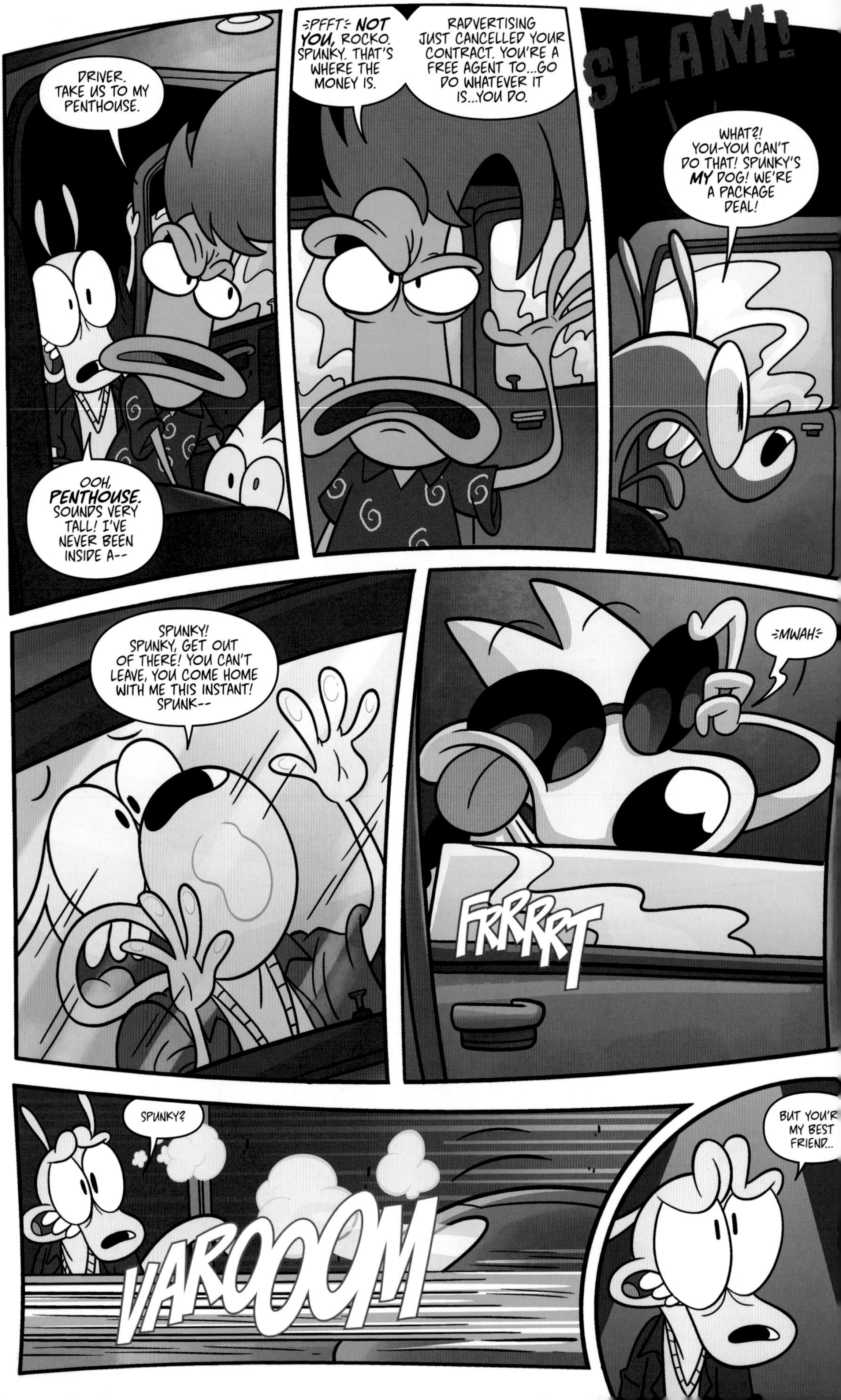
DRIVER. TAKE US TO MY PENTHOUSE.
OOH, PENTHOUSE. SOUNDS VERY TALL! I'VE NEVER BEEN INSIDE A--
=PFFT= NOT YOU, ROCKO. SPUNKY. THAT'S WHERE THE MONEY IS.
RADVERTISING JUST CANCELLED YOUR CONTRACT. YOU'RE A FREE AGENT TO...GO DO WHATEVER IT IS...YOU DO.
SLAM!
WHAT?! YOU-YOU CAN'T DO THAT! SPUNKY'S MY DOG! WE'RE A PACKAGE DEAL!
SPUNKY! SPUNKY, GET OUT OF THERE! YOU CAN'T LEAVE, YOU COME HOME WITH ME THIS INSTANT! SPUNK--
=MWAH=
FRRRRT
SPUNKY?
VAROOOM
BUT YOU'R MY BEST FRIEND...

CHAPTER
SIX

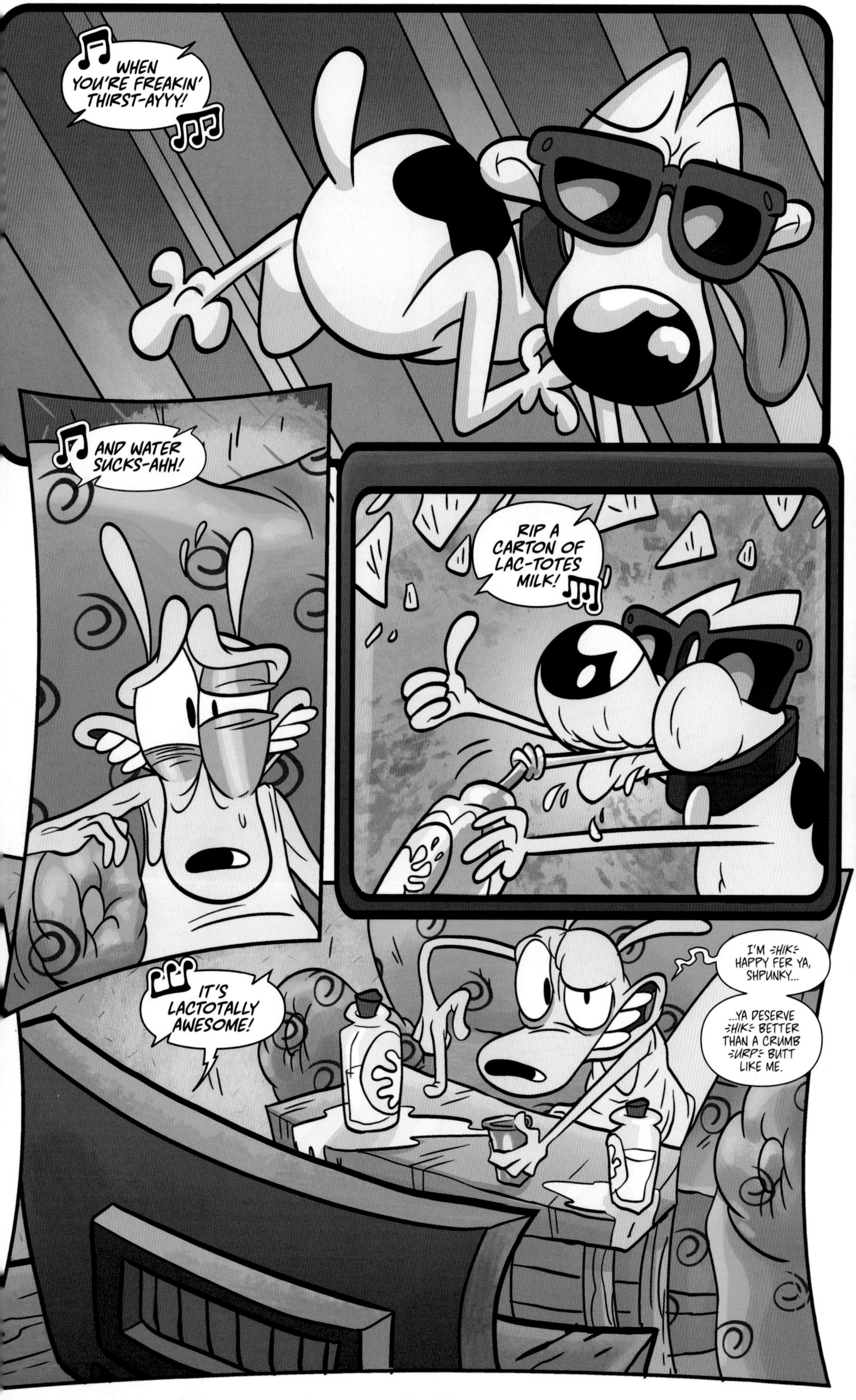
WHEN YOU'RE FREAKIN' THIRST-AYYY!
AND WATER SUCKS-AHH!
RIP A CARTON OF LAC-TOTES MILK!
IT'S LACTOTALLY AWESOME!
I'M =HIK= HAPPY FER YA, SHPUNKY...
...YA DESERVE =HIK= BETTER THAN A CRUMB =URP= BUTT LIKE ME.

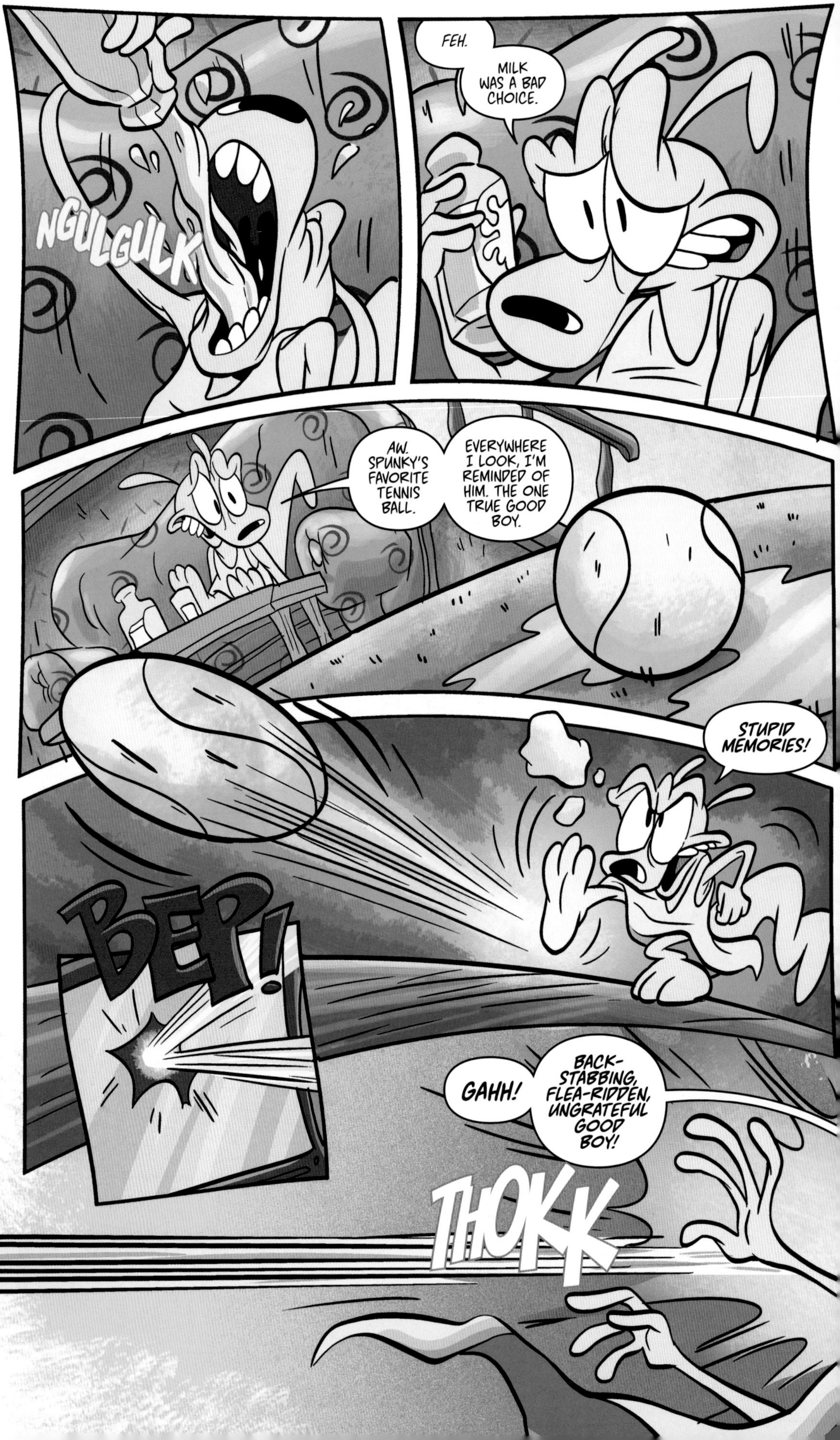
NGULGULK
FEH.
MILK WAS A BAD CHOICE.
AW. SPUNKY'S FAVORITE TENNIS BALL.
EVERYWHERE I LOOK, I'M REMINDED OF HIM. THE ONE TRUE GOOD BOY.
STUPID MEMORIES!
BEP!
GAHH!
BACK-STABBING, FLEA-RIDDEN, UNGRATEFUL GOOD BOY!
THOKK

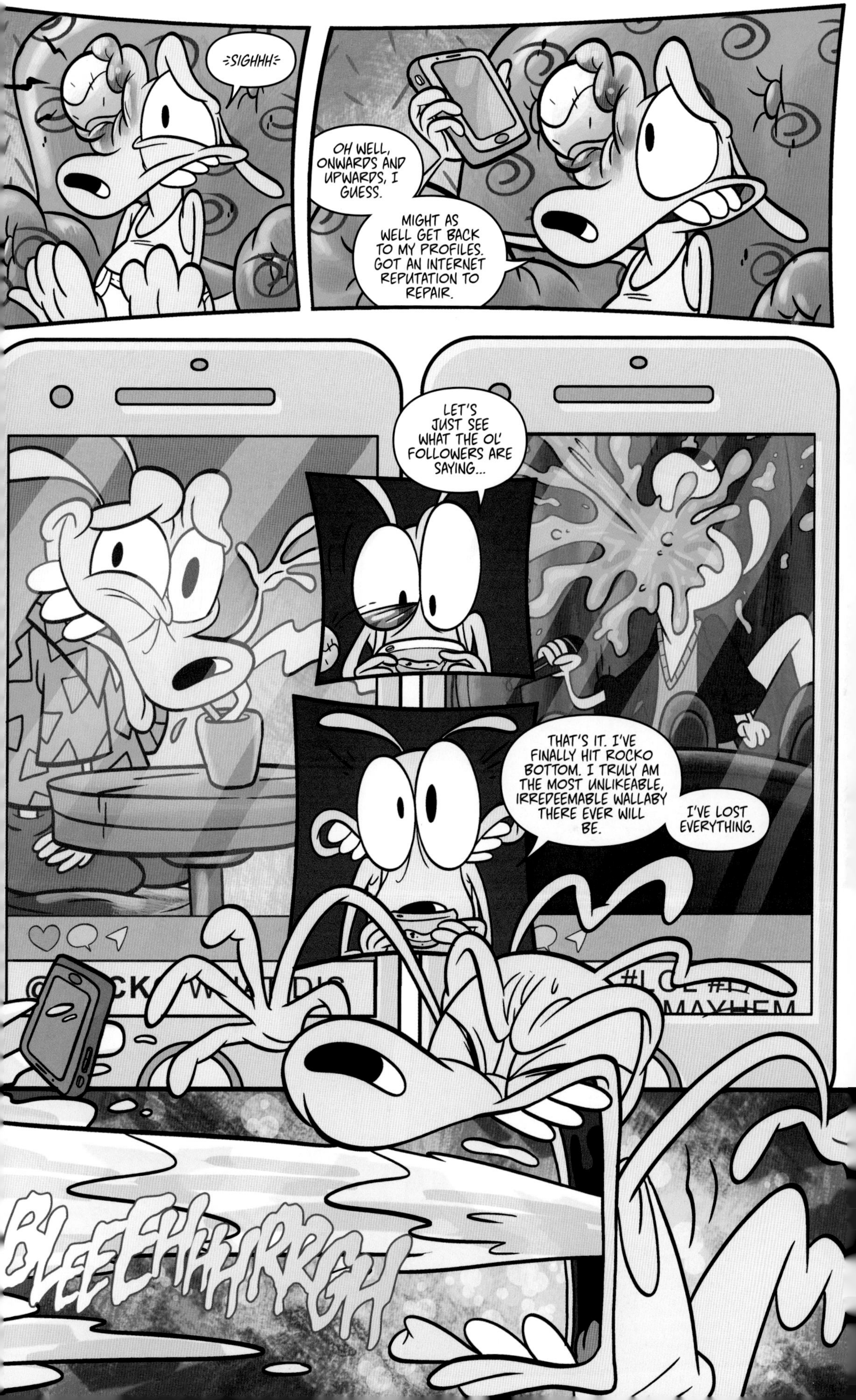
SIGHHH
OH WELL, ONWARDS AND UPWARDS, I GUESS.
MIGHT AS WELL GET BACK TO MY PROFILES. GOT AN INTERNET REPUTATION TO REPAIR.
LET'S JUST SEE WHAT THE OL' FOLLOWERS ARE SAYING...
THAT'S IT. I'VE FINALLY HIT ROCKO BOTTOM. I TRULY AM THE MOST UNLIKEABLE, IRREDEEMABLE WALLABY THERE EVER WILL BE.
I'VE LOST EVERYTHING.
BLEECHHHRRRGH

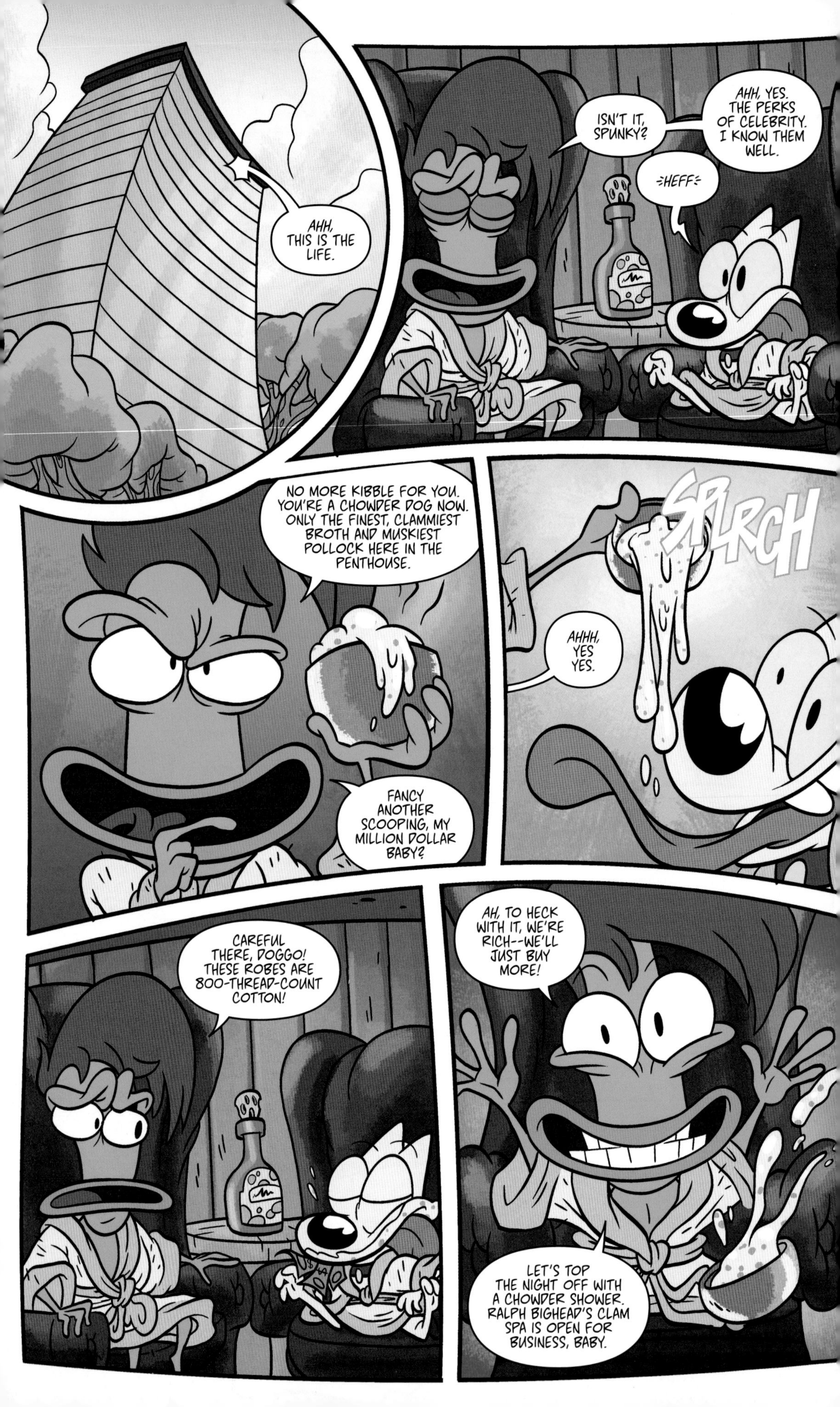
AHH, THIS IS THE LIFE.
ISN'T IT, SPUNKY?
AHH, YES. THE PERKS OF CELEBRITY. I KNOW THEM WELL.
HEFF
NO MORE KIBBLE FOR YOU. YOU'RE A CHOWDER DOG NOW. ONLY THE FINEST, CLAMMIEST BROTH AND MUSKIEST POLLOCK HERE IN THE PENTHOUSE.
FANCY ANOTHER SCOOPING, MY MILLION DOLLAR BABY?
SPLRCH
AHHH, YES YES.
CAREFUL THERE, DOGGO! THESE ROBES ARE 800-THREAD-COUNT COTTON!
AH, TO HECK WITH IT, WE'RE RICH--WE'LL JUST BUY MORE!
LET'S TOP THE NIGHT OFF WITH A CHOWDER SHOWER. RALPH BIGHEAD'S CLAM SPA IS OPEN FOR BUSINESS, BABY.

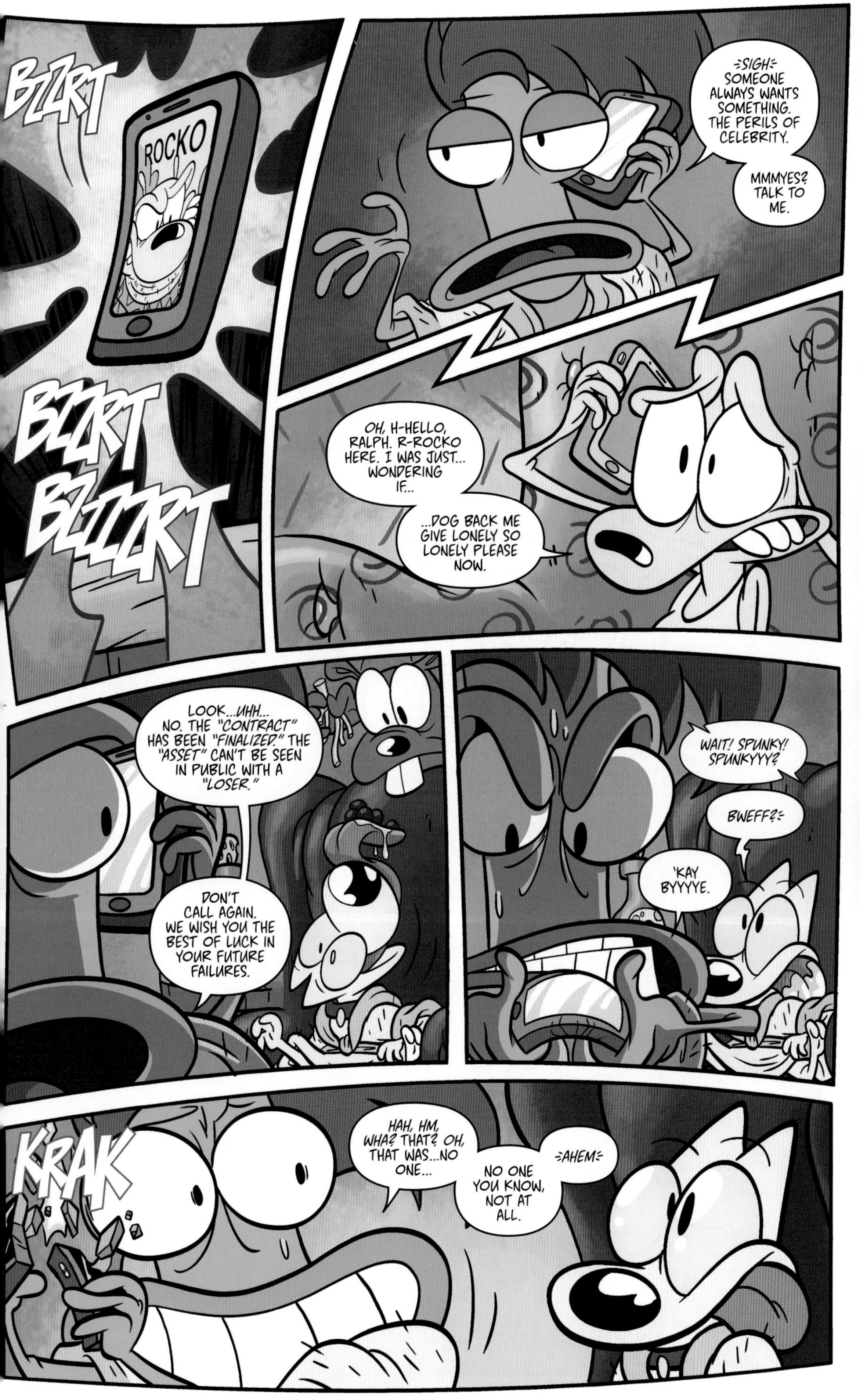

BZZRT
ROCKO
BZZRT
BZZZRT
BZZZZRT
≈SIGH≈ SOMEONE ALWAYS WANTS SOMETHING. THE PERILS OF CELEBRITY.
MMMYES? TALK TO ME.
OH, H-HELLO, RALPH. R-ROCKO HERE. I WAS JUST... WONDERING IF...
...DOG BACK ME GIVE LONELY SO LONELY PLEASE NOW.
LOOK...UHH... NO. THE "CONTRACT" HAS BEEN "FINALIZED." THE "ASSET" CAN'T BE SEEN IN PUBLIC WITH A "LOSER."
DON'T CALL AGAIN. WE WISH YOU THE BEST OF LUCK IN YOUR FUTURE FAILURES.
WAIT! SPUNKY! SPUNKYYY?
BWEFF?
'KAY BYYYYE.
KRAK
HAH, HM, WHA? THAT? OH, THAT WAS...NO ONE...
≈AHEM≈
NO ONE YOU KNOW, NOT AT ALL.

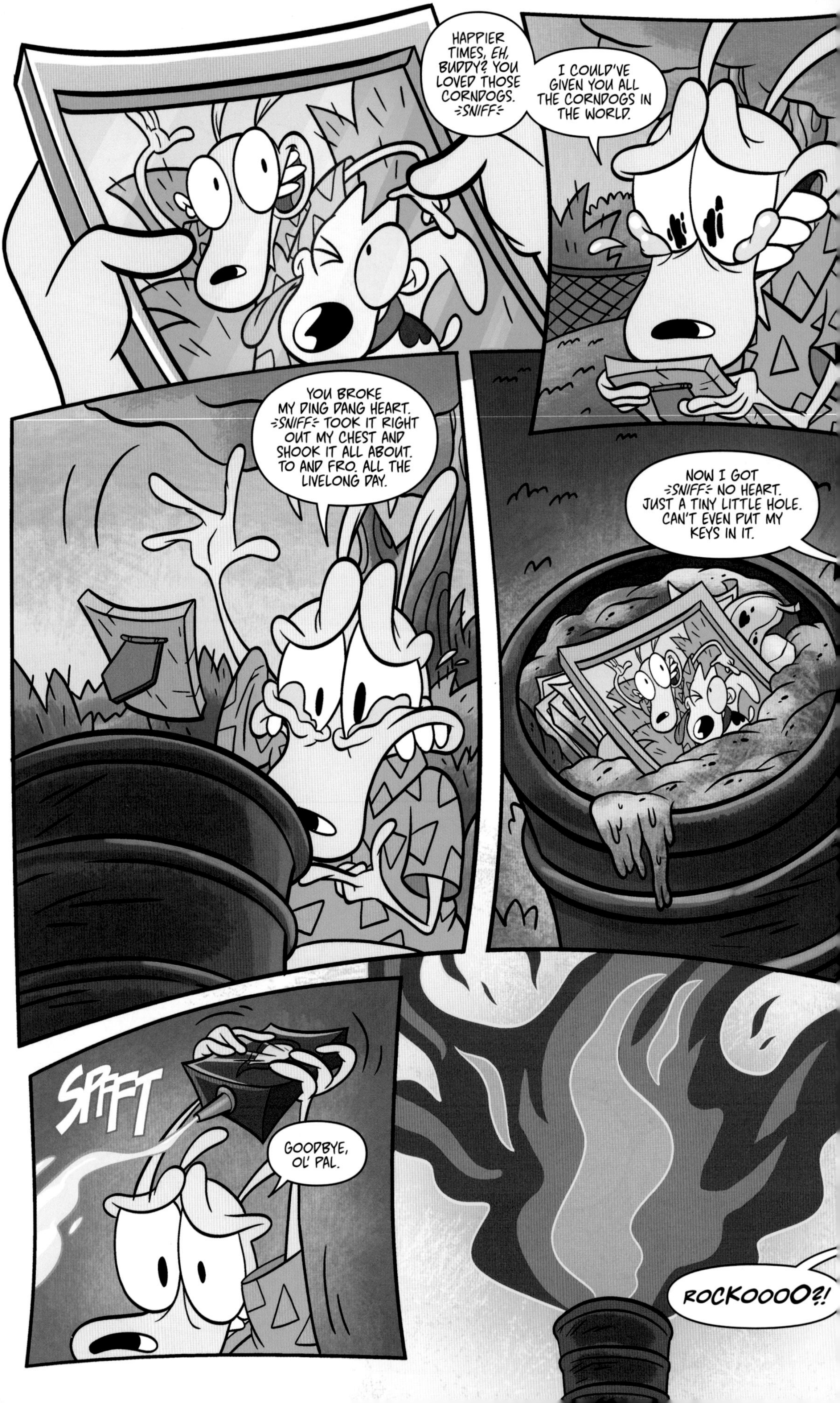

HAPPIER TIMES, EH, BUDDY? YOU LOVED THOSE CORNDOGS. =SNIFF=
I COULD'VE GIVEN YOU ALL THE CORNDOGS IN THE WORLD.
YOU BROKE MY DING DANG HEART. =SNIFF= TOOK IT RIGHT OUT MY CHEST AND SHOOK IT ALL ABOUT. TO AND FRO. ALL THE LIVELONG DAY.
NOW I GOT =SNIFF= NO HEART. JUST A TINY LITTLE HOLE. CAN'T EVEN PUT MY KEYS IN IT.
SPFFT
GOODBYE, OL' PAL.
ROCKOOOO?!

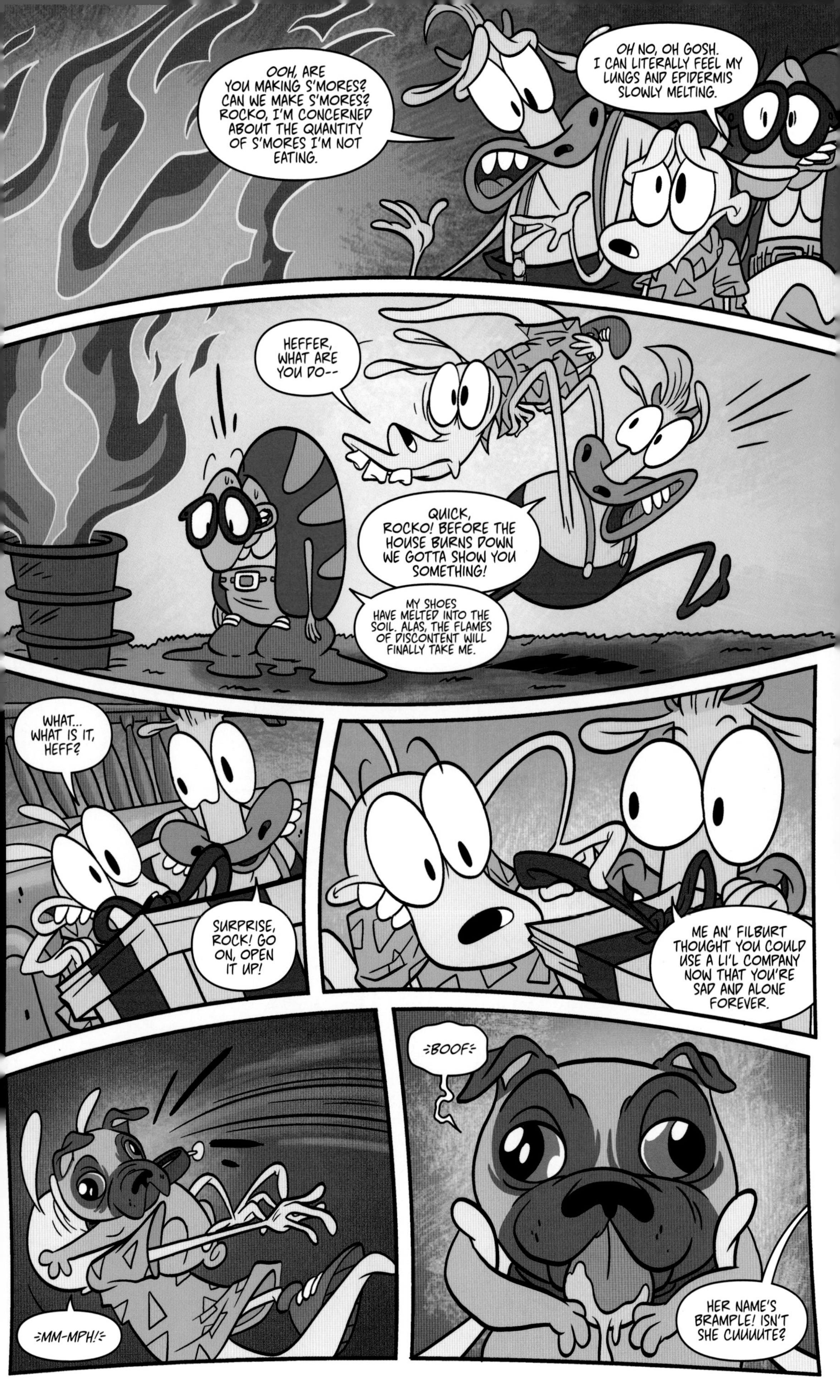

OOH, ARE YOU MAKING S'MORES? CAN WE MAKE S'MORES? ROCKO, I'M CONCERNED ABOUT THE QUANTITY OF S'MORES I'M NOT EATING.
OH NO, OH GOSH. I CAN LITERALLY FEEL MY LUNGS AND EPIDERMIS SLOWLY MELTING.
HEFFER, WHAT ARE YOU DO--
QUICK, ROCKO! BEFORE THE HOUSE BURNS DOWN WE GOTTA SHOW YOU SOMETHING!
MY SHOES HAVE MELTED INTO THE SOIL. ALAS, THE FLAMES OF DISCONTENT WILL FINALLY TAKE ME.
WHAT... WHAT IS IT, HEFF?
SURPRISE, ROCK! GO ON, OPEN IT UP!
ME AN' FILBURT THOUGHT YOU COULD USE A LI'L COMPANY NOW THAT YOU'RE SAD AND ALONE FOREVER.
=MM-MPH!=
=BOOF=
HER NAME'S BRAMPLE! ISN'T SHE CUUUUTE?

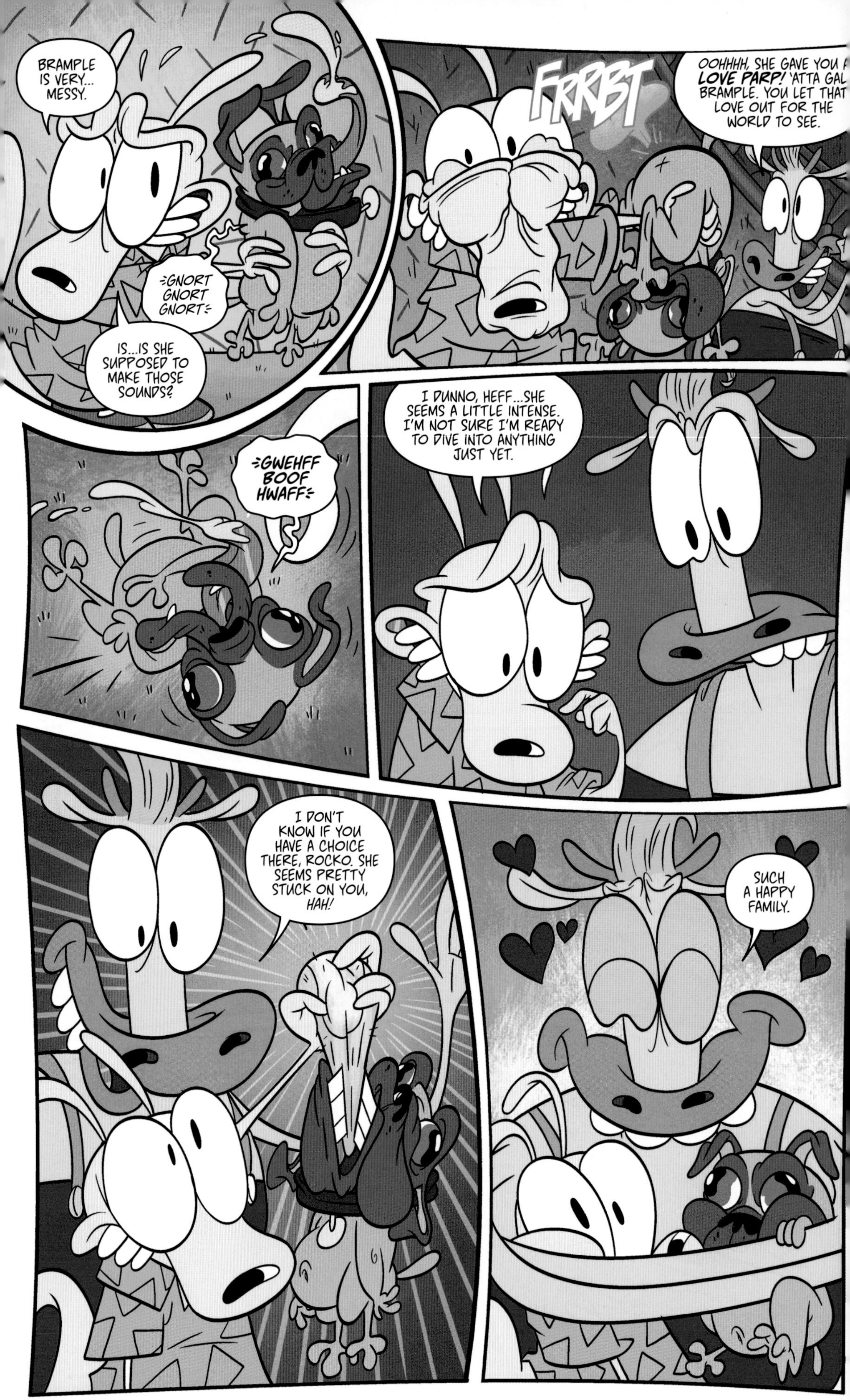
BRAMPLE IS VERY... MESSY.
GNORT GNORT GNORT
IS...IS SHE SUPPOSED TO MAKE THOSE SOUNDS?
FRRBT
OOHHHH, SHE GAVE YOU A LOVE PARP! 'ATTA GAL BRAMPLE. YOU LET THAT LOVE OUT FOR THE WORLD TO SEE.
GWEHFF BOOF HWAFF
I DUNNO, HEFF...SHE SEEMS A LITTLE INTENSE. I'M NOT SURE I'M READY TO DIVE INTO ANYTHING JUST YET.
I DON'T KNOW IF YOU HAVE A CHOICE THERE, ROCKO. SHE SEEMS PRETTY STUCK ON YOU, HAH!
SUCH A HAPPY FAMILY.

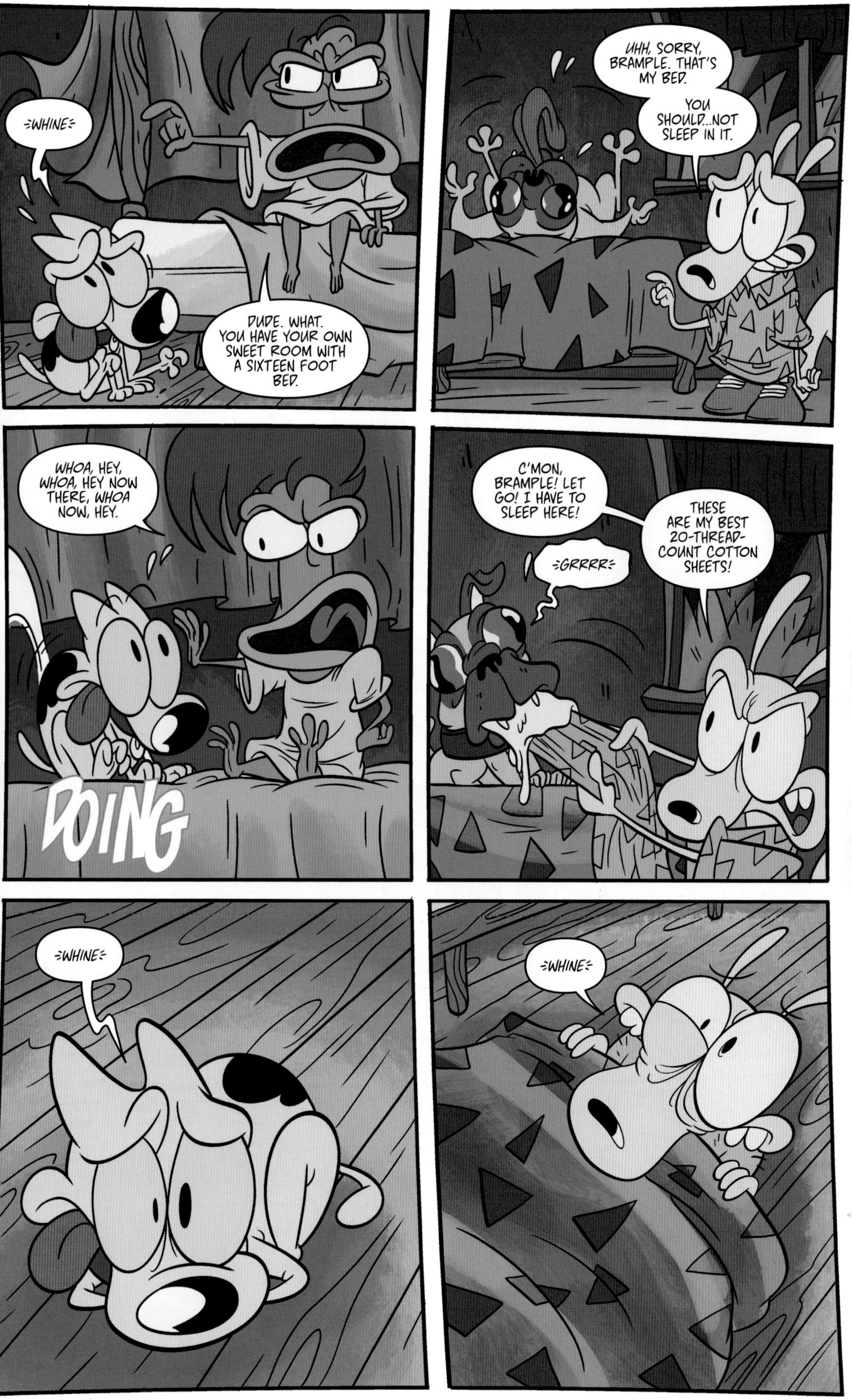

=WHINE=
DUDE. WHAT. YOU HAVE YOUR OWN SWEET ROOM WITH A SIXTEEN FOOT BED.
UHH, SORRY, BRAMPLE. THAT'S MY BED.
YOU SHOULD...NOT SLEEP IN IT.
WHOA, HEY, WHOA, HEY NOW THERE, WHOA NOW, HEY.
DOING
C'MON, BRAMPLE! LET GO! I HAVE TO SLEEP HERE!
=GRRRR=
THESE ARE MY BEST 20-THREAD-COUNT COTTON SHEETS!
=WHINE=
=WHINE=

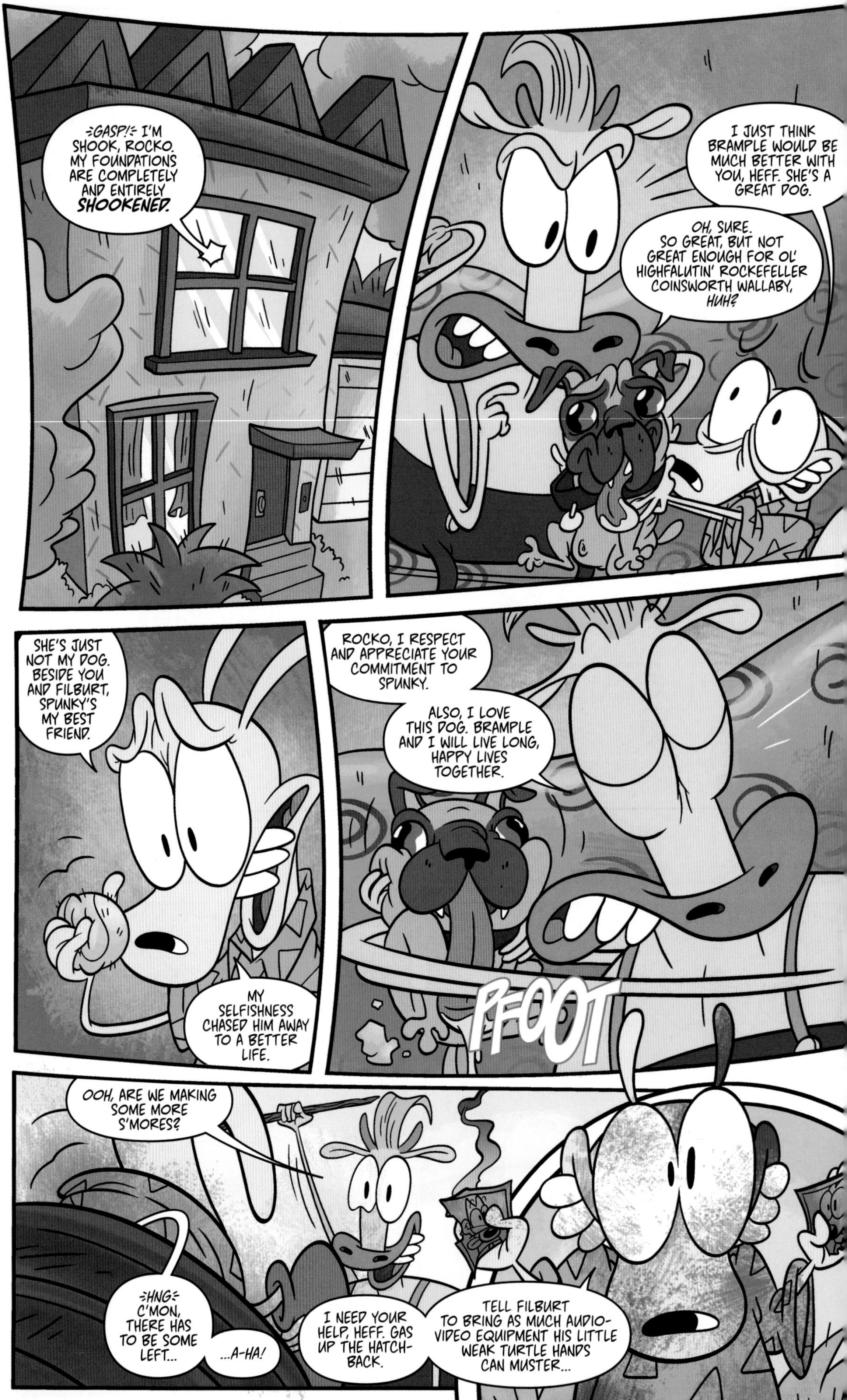

=GASP!= I'M SHOOK, ROCKO. MY FOUNDATIONS ARE COMPLETELY AND ENTIRELY SHOOKENED.
I JUST THINK BRAMPLE WOULD BE MUCH BETTER WITH YOU, HEFF. SHE'S A GREAT DOG.
OH, SURE. SO GREAT, BUT NOT GREAT ENOUGH FOR OL' HIGHFALUTIN' ROCKEFELLER COINSWORTH WALLABY, HUH?
SHE'S JUST NOT MY DOG. BESIDE YOU AND FILBURT, SPUNKY'S MY BEST FRIEND.
MY SELFISHNESS CHASED HIM AWAY TO A BETTER LIFE.
ROCKO, I RESPECT AND APPRECIATE YOUR COMMITMENT TO SPUNKY.
ALSO, I LOVE THIS DOG. BRAMPLE AND I WILL LIVE LONG, HAPPY LIVES TOGETHER.
PFOOT
OOH, ARE WE MAKING SOME MORE S'MORES?
=HNG= C'MON, THERE HAS TO BE SOME LEFT...
...A-HA!
I NEED YOUR HELP, HEFF. GAS UP THE HATCH-BACK.
TELL FILBURT TO BRING AS MUCH AUDIO-VIDEO EQUIPMENT HIS LITTLE WEAK TURTLE HANDS CAN MUSTER...

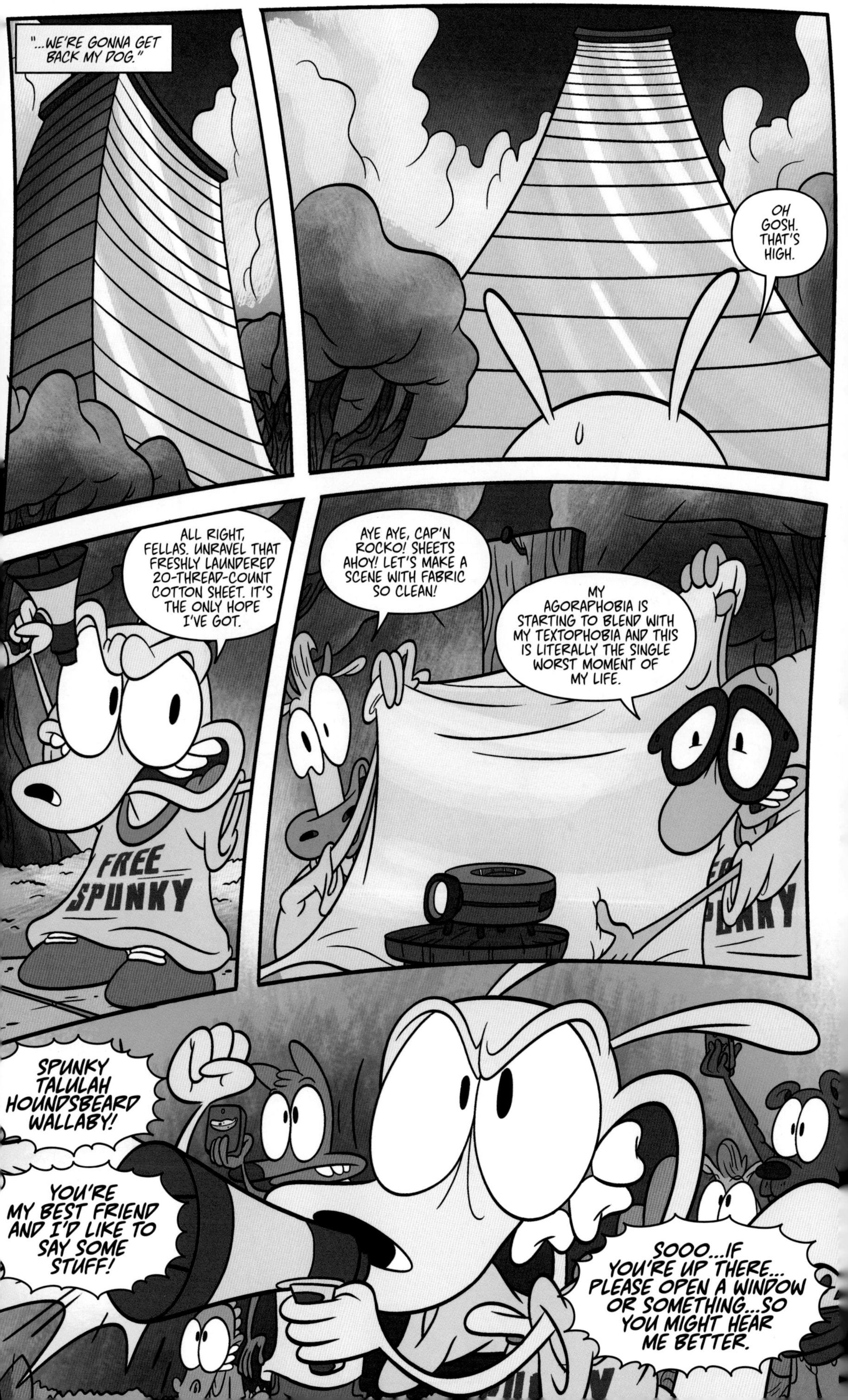
"...WE'RE GONNA GET BACK MY DOG."
OH GOSH. THAT'S HIGH.
ALL RIGHT, FELLAS. UNRAVEL THAT FRESHLY LAUNDERED 20-THREAD-COUNT COTTON SHEET. IT'S THE ONLY HOPE I'VE GOT.
FREE SPUNKY
AYE AYE, CAP'N ROCKO! SHEETS AHOY! LET'S MAKE A SCENE WITH FABRIC SO CLEAN!
MY AGORAPHOBIA IS STARTING TO BLEND WITH MY TEXTOPHOBIA AND THIS IS LITERALLY THE SINGLE WORST MOMENT OF MY LIFE.
SPUNKY TALULAH HOUNDSBEARD WALLABY!
YOU'RE MY BEST FRIEND AND I'D LIKE TO SAY SOME STUFF!
SOOO...IF YOU'RE UP THERE... PLEASE OPEN A WINDOW OR SOMETHING...SO YOU MIGHT HEAR ME BETTER.

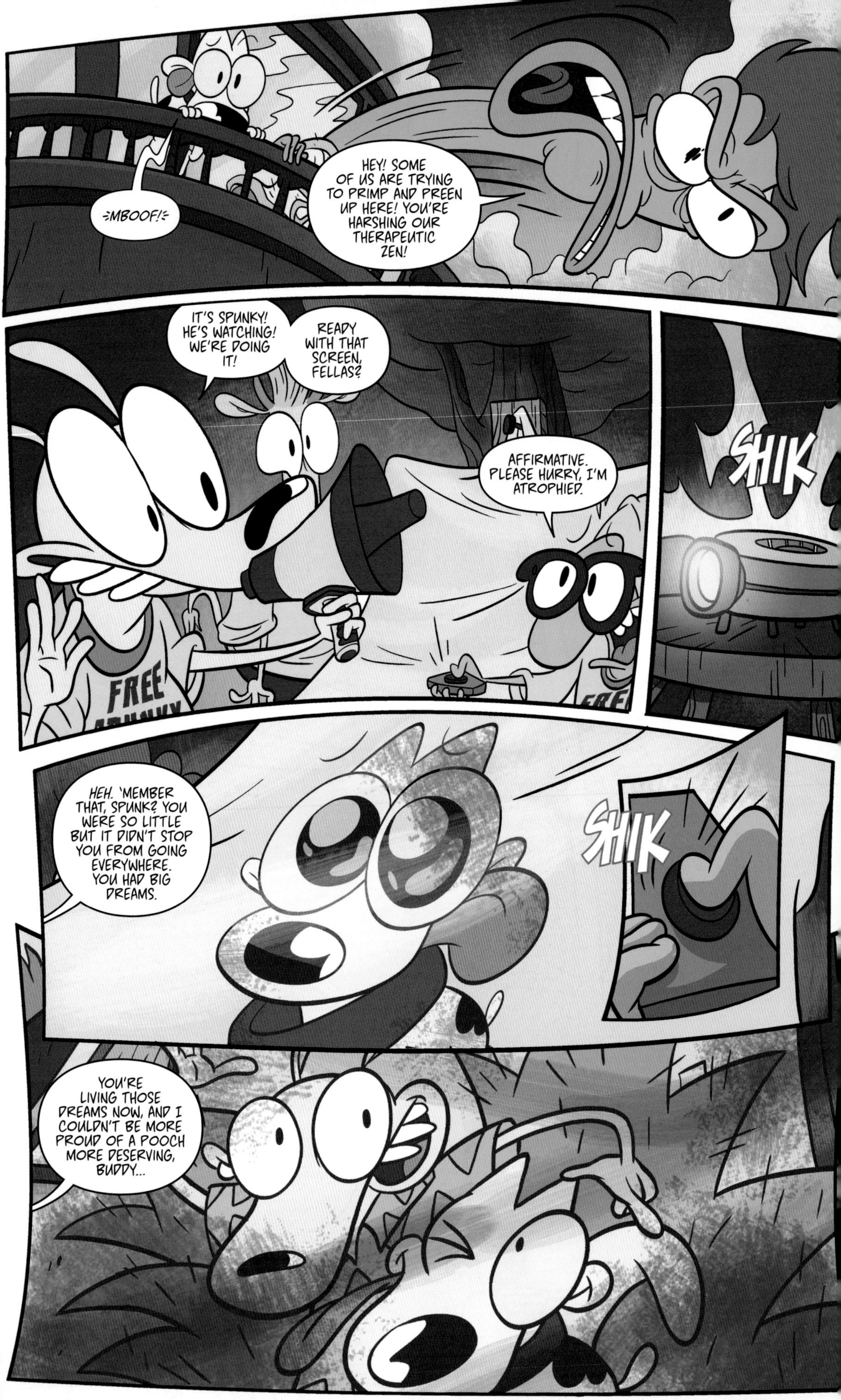

-MBOOF!-
HEY! SOME OF US ARE TRYING TO PRIMP AND PREEN UP HERE! YOU'RE HARSHING OUR THERAPEUTIC ZEN!
IT'S SPUNKY! HE'S WATCHING! WE'RE DOING IT!
READY WITH THAT SCREEN, FELLAS?
AFFIRMATIVE. PLEASE HURRY, I'M ATROPHIED.
FREE
SHIK
HEH. 'MEMBER THAT, SPUNK? YOU WERE SO LITTLE BUT IT DIDN'T STOP YOU FROM GOING EVERYWHERE. YOU HAD BIG DREAMS.
SHIK
YOU'RE LIVING THOSE DREAMS NOW, AND I COULDN'T BE MORE PROUD OF A POOCH MORE DESERVING, BUDDY...

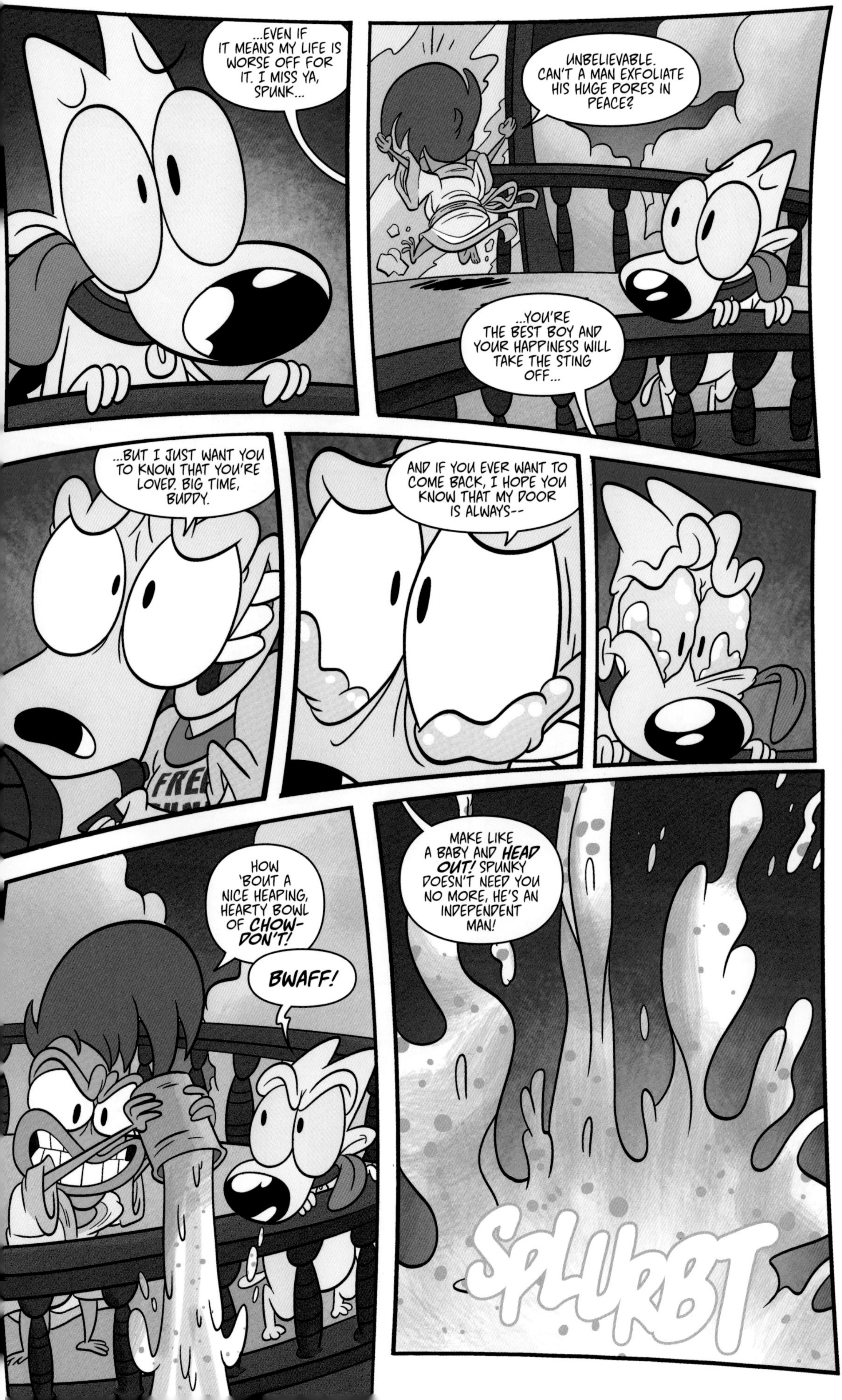
...EVEN IF IT MEANS MY LIFE IS WORSE OFF FOR IT. I MISS YA, SPUNK...
UNBELIEVABLE. CAN'T A MAN EXFOLIATE HIS HUGE PORES IN PEACE?
...YOU'RE THE BEST BOY AND YOUR HAPPINESS WILL TAKE THE STING OFF...
...BUT I JUST WANT YOU TO KNOW THAT YOU'RE LOVED. BIG TIME, BUDDY.
AND IF YOU EVER WANT TO COME BACK, I HOPE YOU KNOW THAT MY DOOR IS ALWAYS--
HOW 'BOUT A NICE HEAPING, HEARTY BOWL OF CHOW-DON'T!
BWAFF!
MAKE LIKE A BABY AND HEAD OUT! SPUNKY DOESN'T NEED YOU NO MORE, HE'S AN INDEPENDENT MAN!
SPLURBT

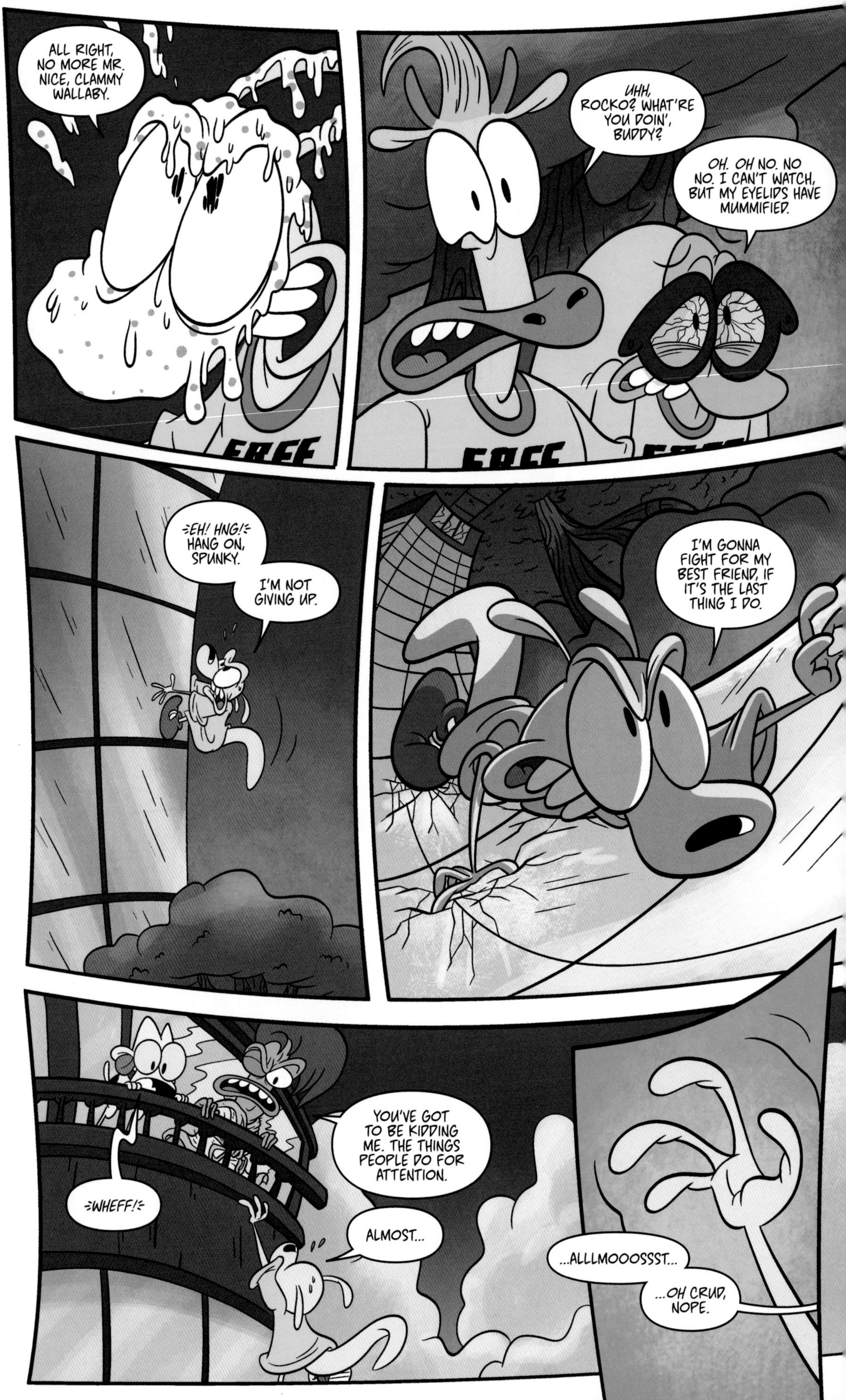
ALL RIGHT, NO MORE MR. NICE, CLAMMY WALLABY.
UHH, ROCKO? WHAT'RE YOU DOIN', BUDDY?
OH. OH NO. NO NO. I CAN'T WATCH, BUT MY EYELIDS HAVE MUMMIFIED.
FREE
FREE
=EH! HNG!= HANG ON, SPUNKY.
I'M NOT GIVING UP.
I'M GONNA FIGHT FOR MY BEST FRIEND, IF IT'S THE LAST THING I DO.
YOU'VE GOT TO BE KIDDING ME. THE THINGS PEOPLE DO FOR ATTENTION.
=WHEFF!=
ALMOST...
...ALLLMOOOSSST...
...OH CRUD, NOPE.

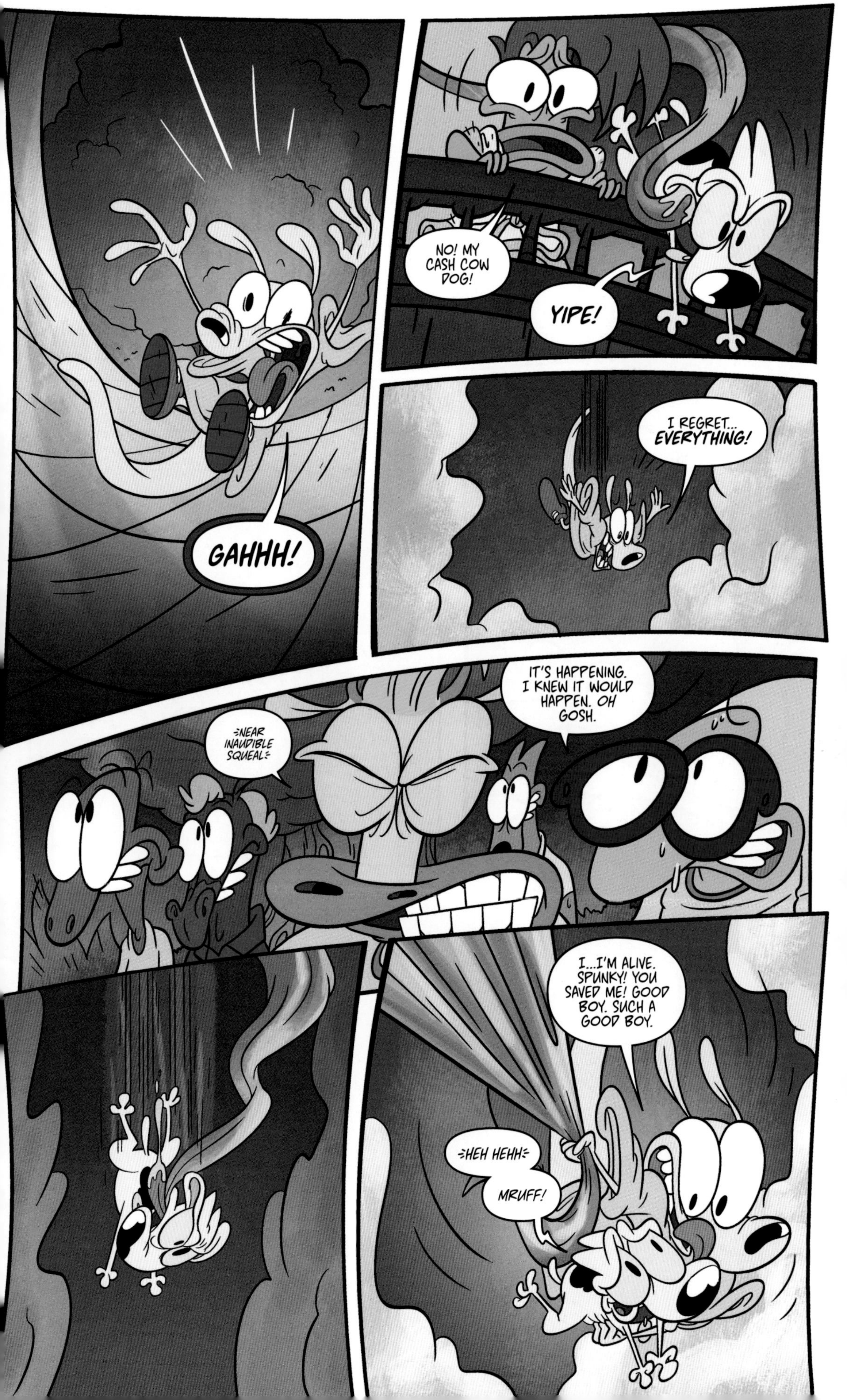
GAHHH!
NO! MY CASH COW DOG!
YIPE!
I REGRET... EVERYTHING!
=NEAR INAUDIBLE SQUEAL=
IT'S HAPPENING. I KNEW IT WOULD HAPPEN. OH GOSH.
I...I'M ALIVE. SPUNKY! YOU SAVED ME! GOOD BOY. SUCH A GOOD BOY.
=HEH HEHH=
MRUFF!

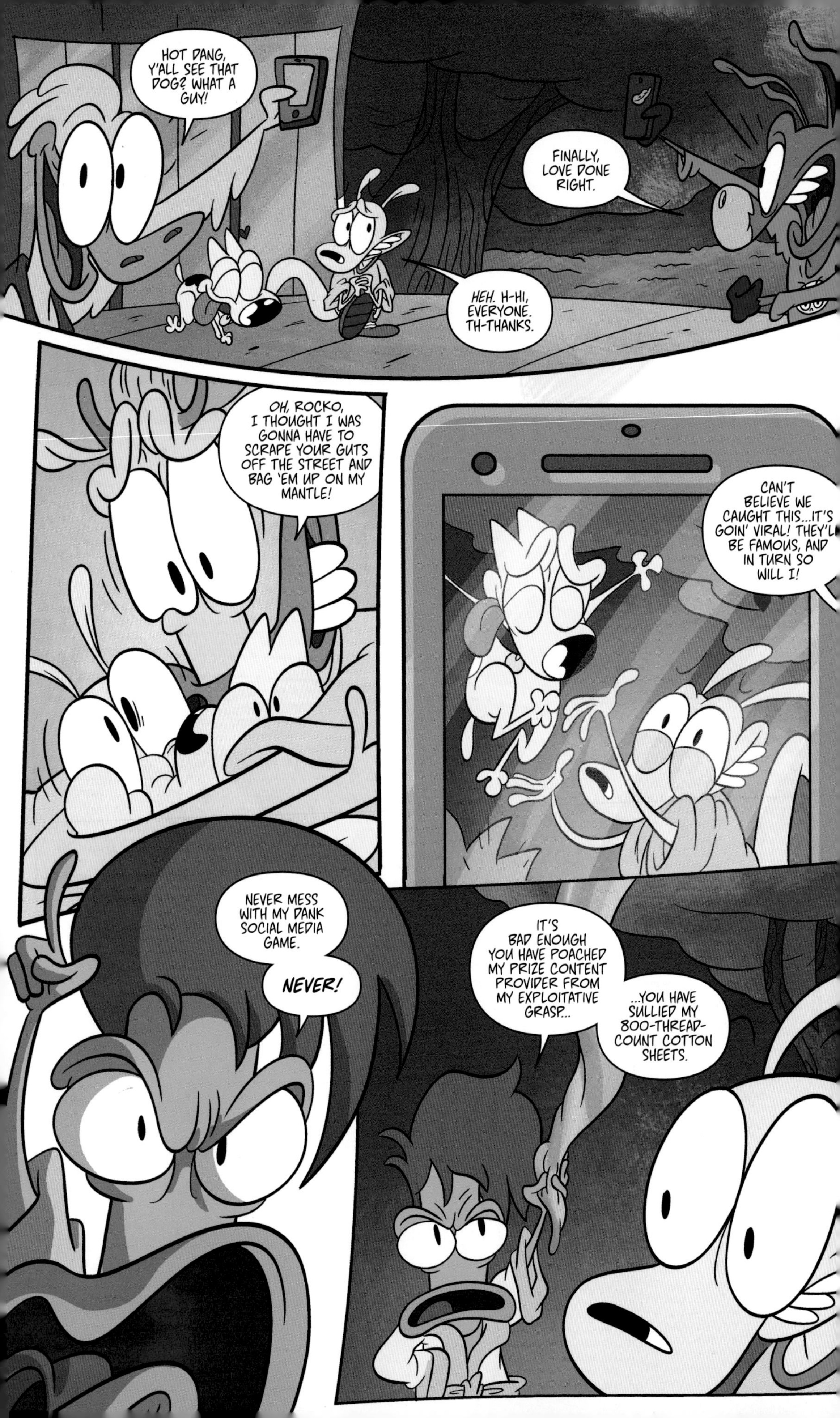
HOT DANG, Y'ALL SEE THAT DOG? WHAT A GUY!
FINALLY, LOVE DONE RIGHT.
HEH. H-HI, EVERYONE. TH-THANKS.
OH, ROCKO, I THOUGHT I WAS GONNA HAVE TO SCRAPE YOUR GUTS OFF THE STREET AND BAG 'EM UP ON MY MANTLE!
CAN'T BELIEVE WE CAUGHT THIS...IT'S GOIN' VIRAL! THEY'LL BE FAMOUS, AND IN TURN SO WILL I!
NEVER MESS WITH MY DANK SOCIAL MEDIA GAME.
NEVER!
IT'S BAD ENOUGH YOU HAVE POACHED MY PRIZE CONTENT PROVIDER FROM MY EXPLOITATIVE GRASP...
...YOU HAVE SULLIED MY 800-THREAD-COUNT COTTON SHEETS.

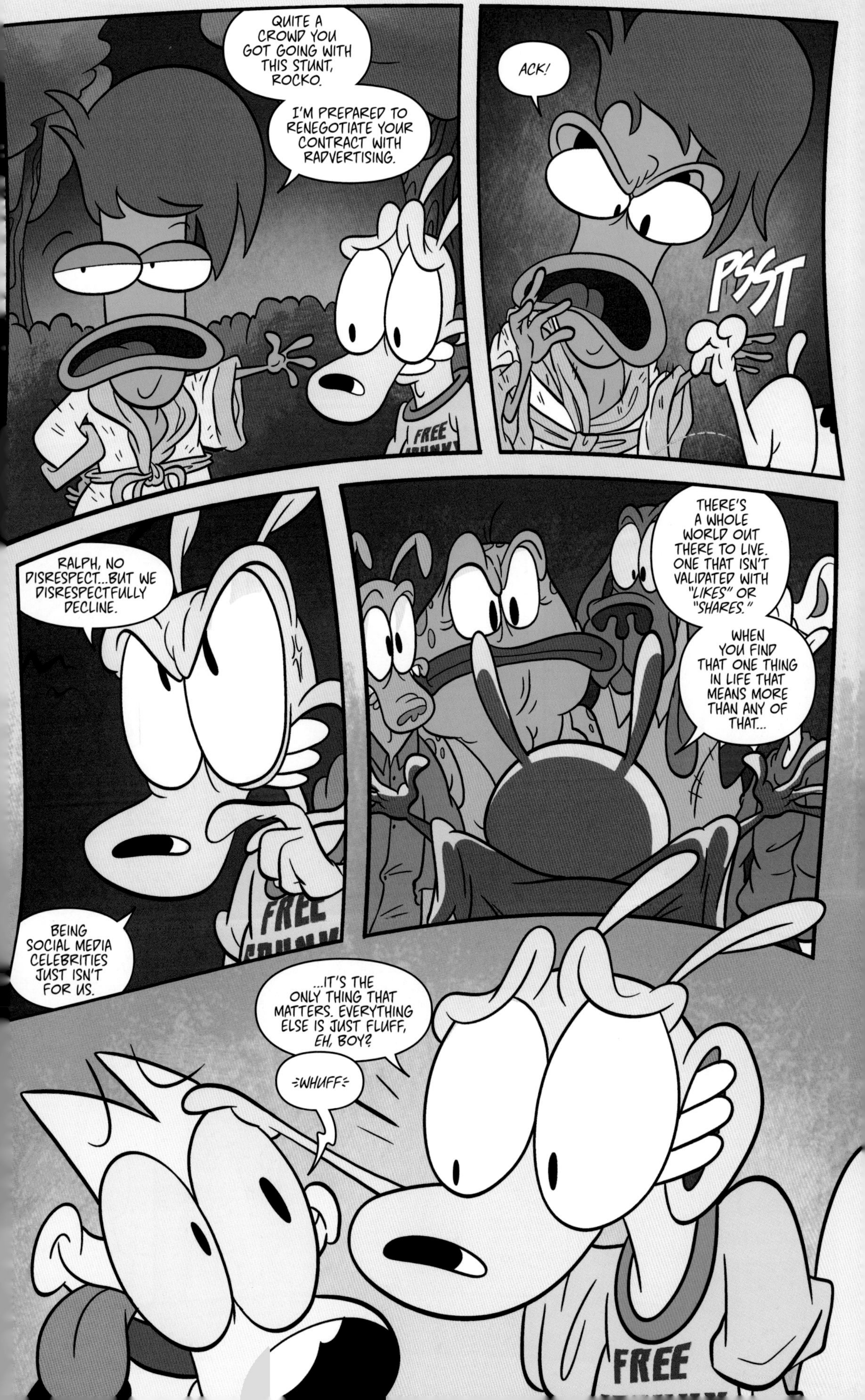
QUITE A CROWD YOU GOT GOING WITH THIS STUNT, ROCKO.
I'M PREPARED TO RENEGOTIATE YOUR CONTRACT WITH RADVERTISING.
FREE
ACK!
PSST
RALPH, NO DISRESPECT...BUT WE DISRESPECTFULLY DECLINE.
BEING SOCIAL MEDIA CELEBRITIES JUST ISN'T FOR US.
FREE
THERE'S A WHOLE WORLD OUT THERE TO LIVE. ONE THAT ISN'T VALIDATED WITH "LIKES" OR "SHARES."
WHEN YOU FIND THAT ONE THING IN LIFE THAT MEANS MORE THAN ANY OF THAT...
...IT'S THE ONLY THING THAT MATTERS. EVERYTHING ELSE IS JUST FLUFF, EH, BOY?
=WHUFF=
FREE

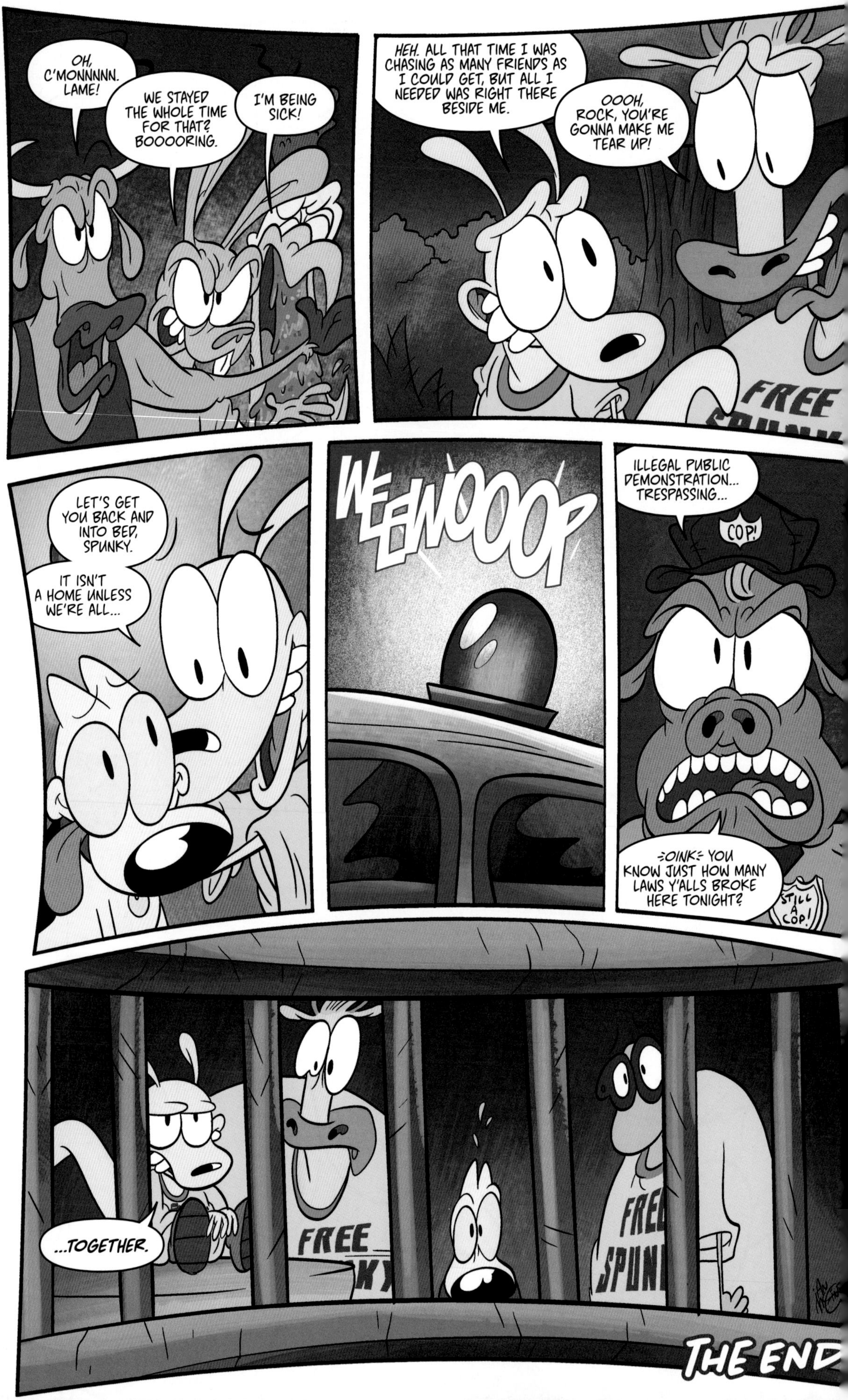
OH, C'MONNNNN. LAME!
WE STAYED THE WHOLE TIME FOR THAT? BOOOORING.
I'M BEING SICK!
HEH. ALL THAT TIME I WAS CHASING AS MANY FRIENDS AS I COULD GET, BUT ALL I NEEDED WAS RIGHT THERE BESIDE ME.
OOOH, ROCK, YOU'RE GONNA MAKE ME TEAR UP!
FREE
LET'S GET YOU BACK AND INTO BED, SPUNKY.
IT ISN'T A HOME UNLESS WE'RE ALL...
WEEWOOOP
ILLEGAL PUBLIC DEMONSTRATION... TRESPASSING...
COP!
=OINK= YOU KNOW JUST HOW MANY LAWS Y'ALLS BROKE HERE TONIGHT?
STILL A COP!
...TOGETHER.
FREE
FREE SPUN
THE END

CHAPTER
SEVEN

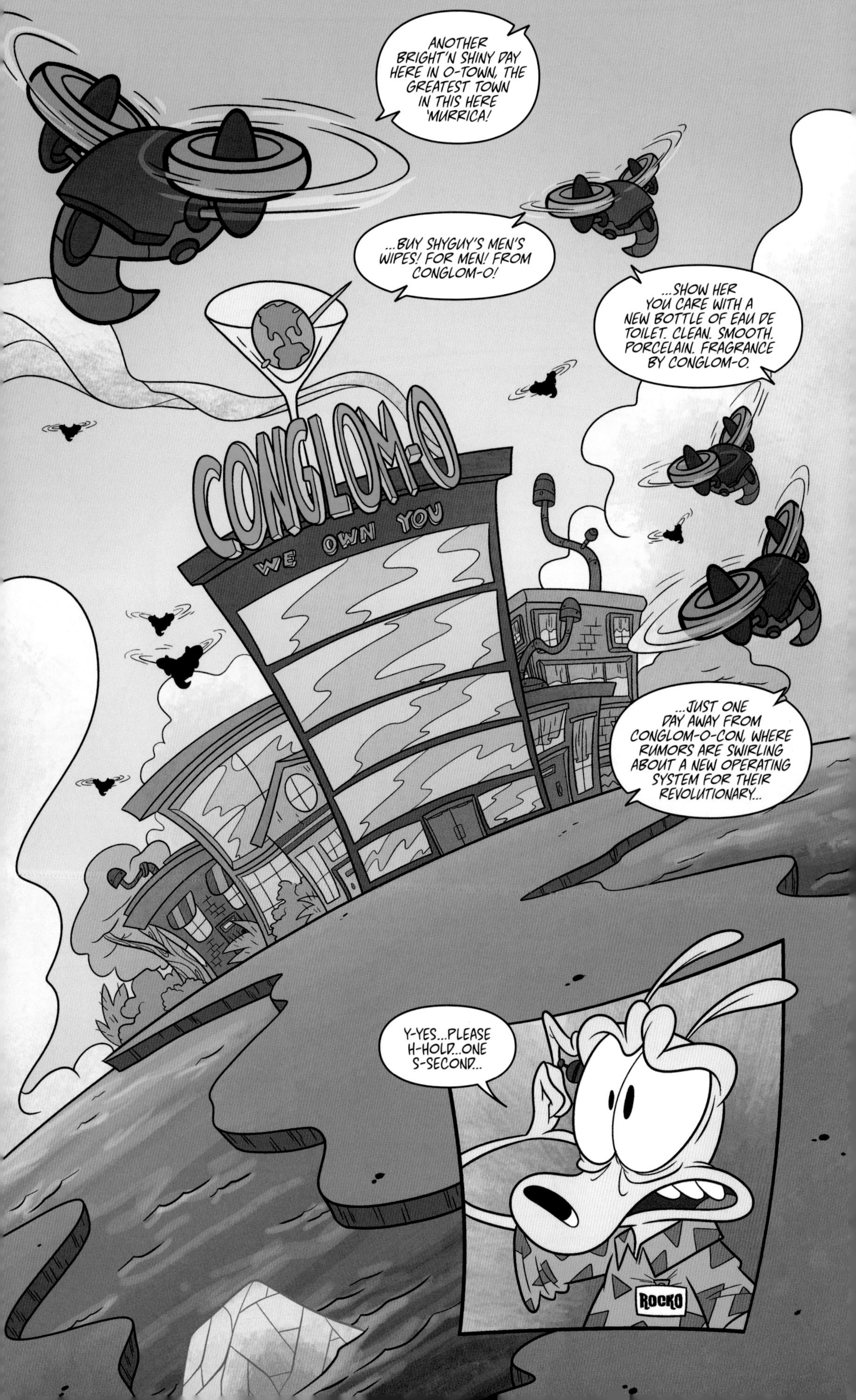
ANOTHER BRIGHT'N SHINY DAY HERE IN O-TOWN, THE GREATEST TOWN IN THIS HERE 'MURRICA!
...BUY SHYGUY'S MEN'S WIPES! FOR MEN! FROM CONGLOM-O!
...SHOW HER YOU CARE WITH A NEW BOTTLE OF EAU DE TOILET. CLEAN. SMOOTH. PORCELAIN. FRAGRANCE BY CONGLOM-O.
CONGLOM-O
WE OWN YOU
...JUST ONE DAY AWAY FROM CONGLOM-O-CON, WHERE RUMORS ARE SWIRLING ABOUT A NEW OPERATING SYSTEM FOR THEIR REVOLUTIONARY...
Y-YES...PLEASE H-HOLD...ONE S-SECOND...
ROCKO

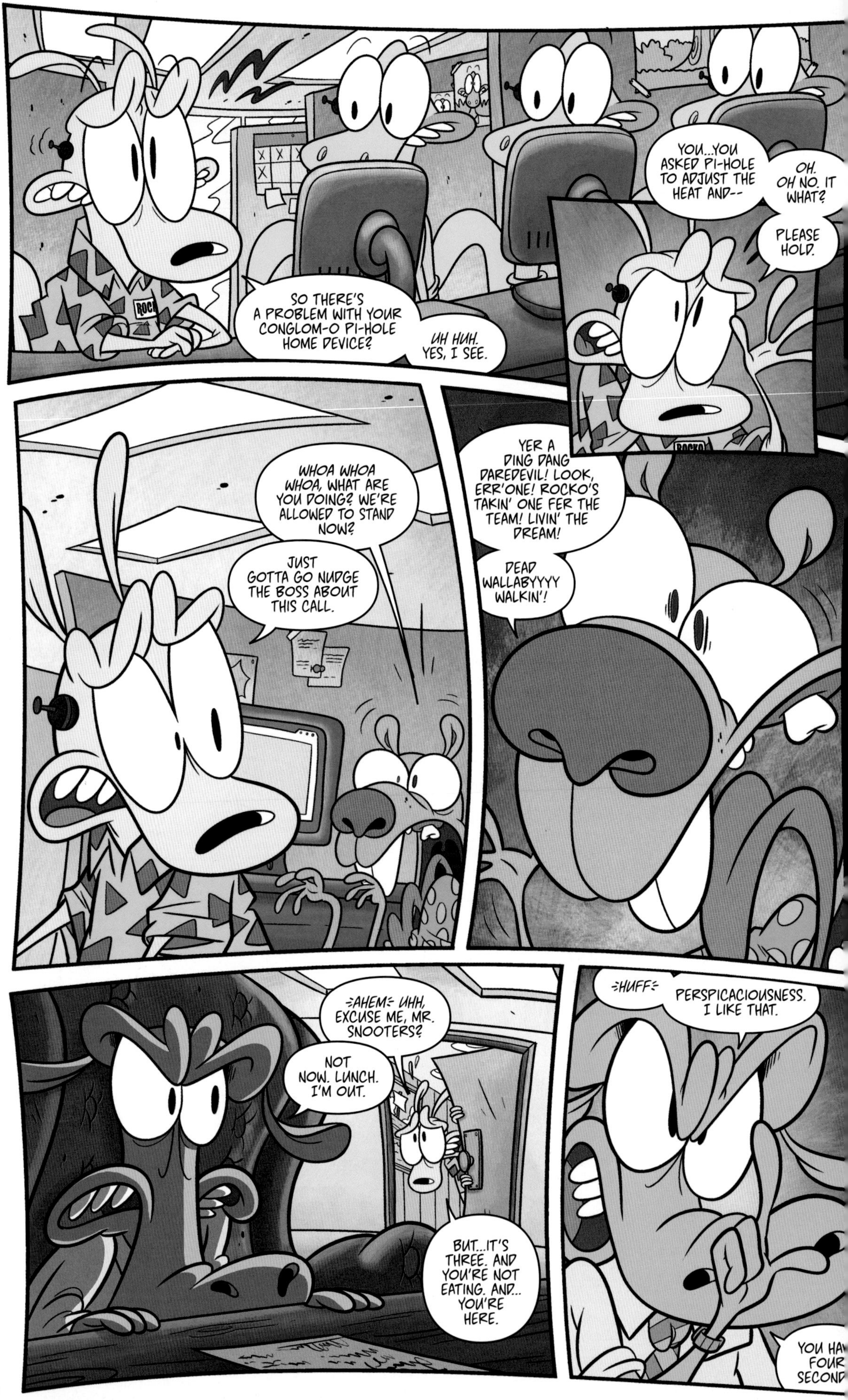

SO THERE'S A PROBLEM WITH YOUR CONGLOM-O PI-HOLE HOME DEVICE?
UH HUH. YES, I SEE.
YOU...YOU ASKED PI-HOLE TO ADJUST THE HEAT AND--
OH. OH NO. IT WHAT?
PLEASE HOLD.
ROCKO
WHOA WHOA WHOA, WHAT ARE YOU DOING? WE'RE ALLOWED TO STAND NOW?
JUST GOTTA GO NUDGE THE BOSS ABOUT THIS CALL.
YER A DING DANG DAREDEVIL! LOOK, ERR'ONE! ROCKO'S TAKIN' ONE FER THE TEAM! LIVIN' THE DREAM!
DEAD WALLABYYYY WALKIN'!
=AHEM= UHH, EXCUSE ME, MR. SNOOTERS?
NOT NOW. LUNCH. I'M OUT.
BUT...IT'S THREE. AND YOU'RE NOT EATING. AND... YOU'RE HERE.
=HUFF=
PERSPICACIOUSNESS. I LIKE THAT.
YOU HA FOUR SECOND

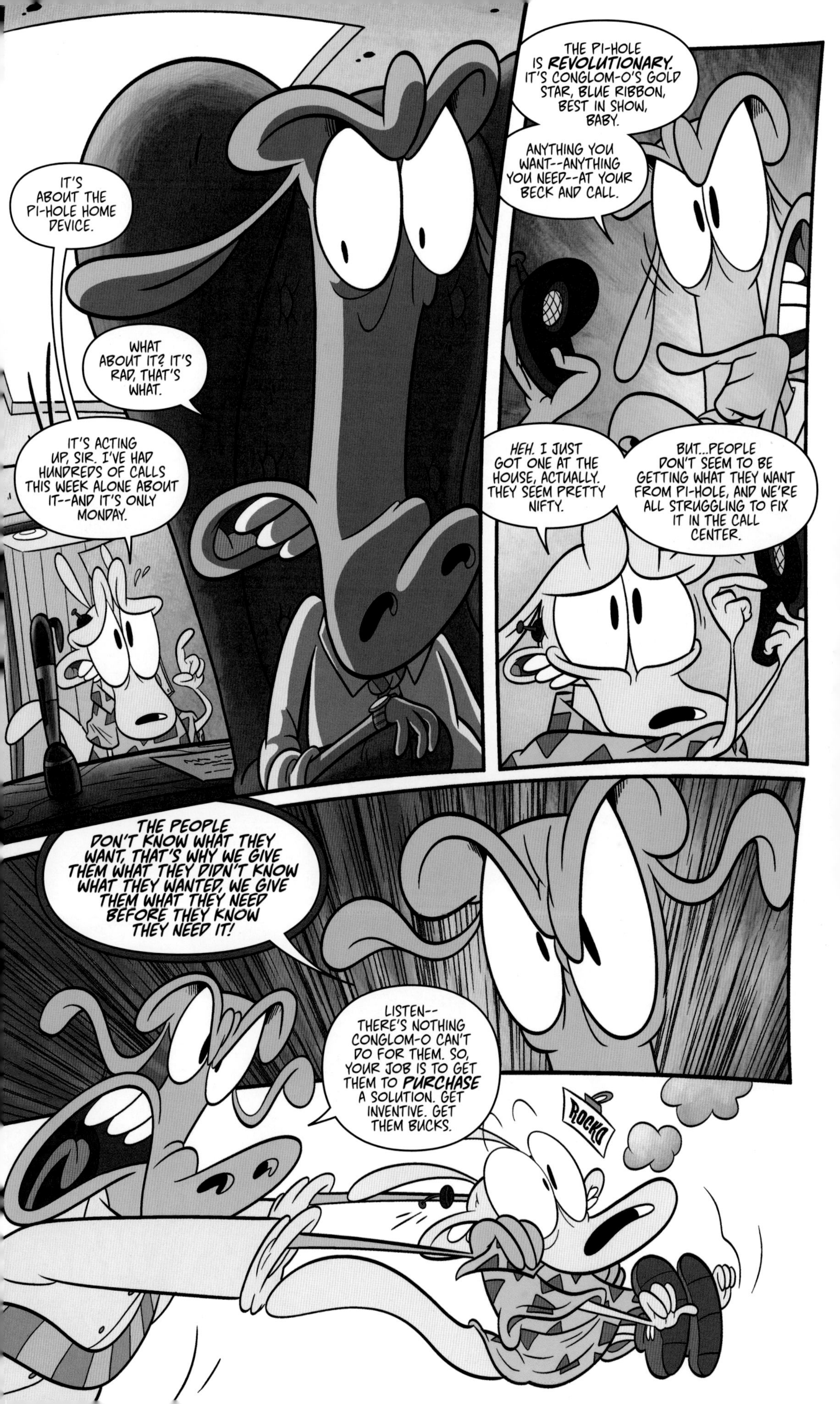
IT'S ABOUT THE PI-HOLE HOME DEVICE.
WHAT ABOUT IT? IT'S RAD, THAT'S WHAT.
IT'S ACTING UP, SIR. I'VE HAD HUNDREDS OF CALLS THIS WEEK ALONE ABOUT IT--AND IT'S ONLY MONDAY.
THE PI-HOLE IS **REVOLUTIONARY.** IT'S CONGLOM-O'S GOLD STAR, BLUE RIBBON, BEST IN SHOW, BABY.
ANYTHING YOU WANT--ANYTHING YOU NEED--AT YOUR BECK AND CALL.
HEH. I JUST GOT ONE AT THE HOUSE, ACTUALLY. THEY SEEM PRETTY NIFTY.
BUT...PEOPLE DON'T SEEM TO BE GETTING WHAT THEY WANT FROM PI-HOLE, AND WE'RE ALL STRUGGLING TO FIX IT IN THE CALL CENTER.
THE PEOPLE DON'T KNOW WHAT THEY WANT, THAT'S WHY WE GIVE THEM WHAT THEY DIDN'T KNOW WHAT THEY WANTED, WE GIVE THEM WHAT THEY NEED BEFORE THEY KNOW THEY NEED IT!
LISTEN-- THERE'S NOTHING CONGLOM-O CAN'T DO FOR THEM. SO, YOUR JOB IS TO GET THEM TO ***PURCHASE*** A SOLUTION. GET INVENTIVE. GET THEM BUCKS.
ROCKO

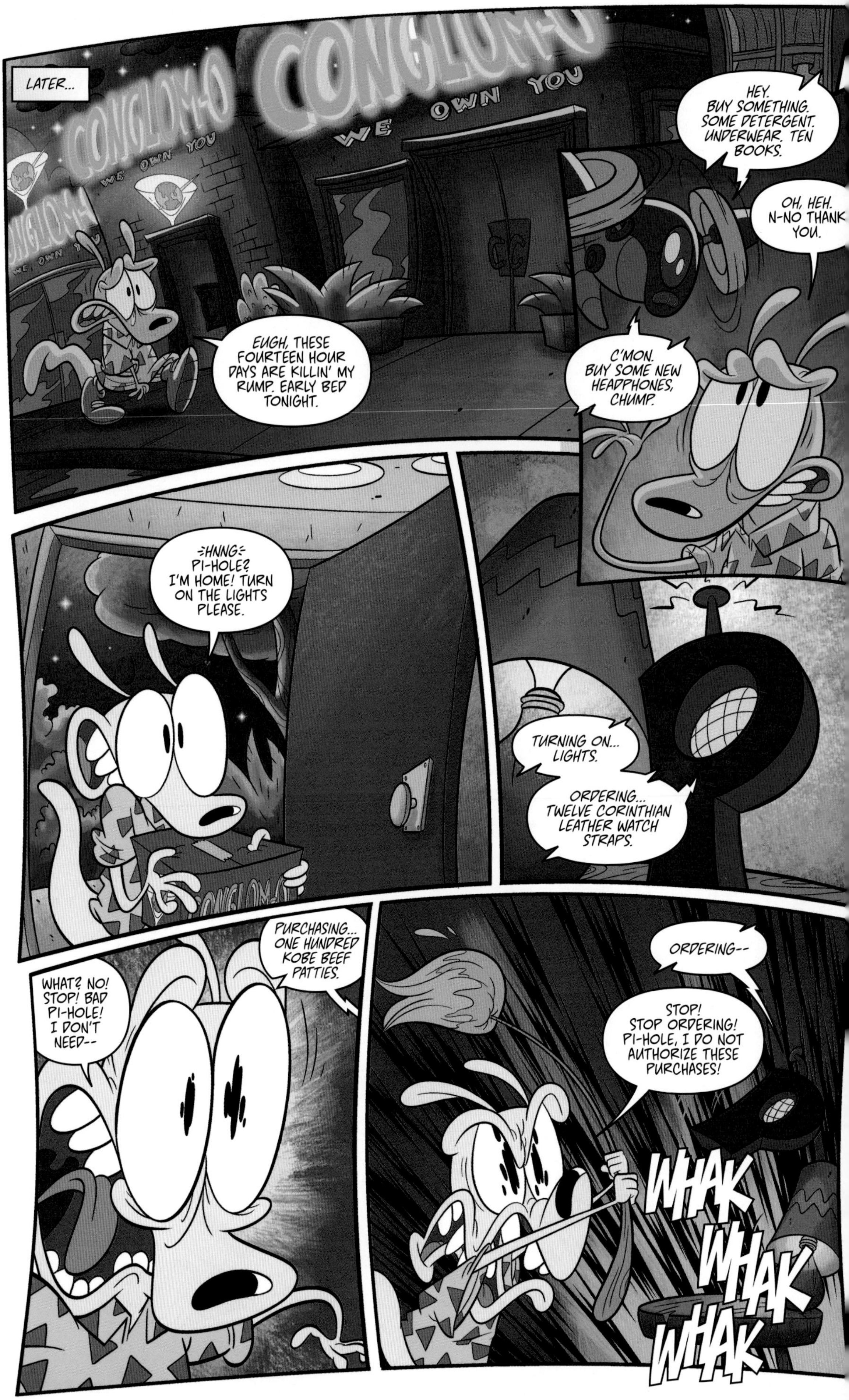
LATER...
CONGLOM-O
WE OWN YOU
EUGH, THESE FOURTEEN HOUR DAYS ARE KILLIN' MY RUMP. EARLY BED TONIGHT.
HEY. BUY SOMETHING. SOME DETERGENT. UNDERWEAR. TEN BOOKS.
OH, HEH. N-NO THANK YOU.
C'MON. BUY SOME NEW HEADPHONES, CHUMP.
=HNNG= PI-HOLE? I'M HOME! TURN ON THE LIGHTS PLEASE.
CONGLOM-O
TURNING ON... LIGHTS.
ORDERING... TWELVE CORINTHIAN LEATHER WATCH STRAPS.
PURCHASING... ONE HUNDRED KOBE BEEF PATTIES.
WHAT? NO! STOP! BAD PI-HOLE! I DON'T NEED--
ORDERING--
STOP! STOP ORDERING! PI-HOLE, I DO NOT AUTHORIZE THESE PURCHASES!
WHAK
WHAK
WHAK

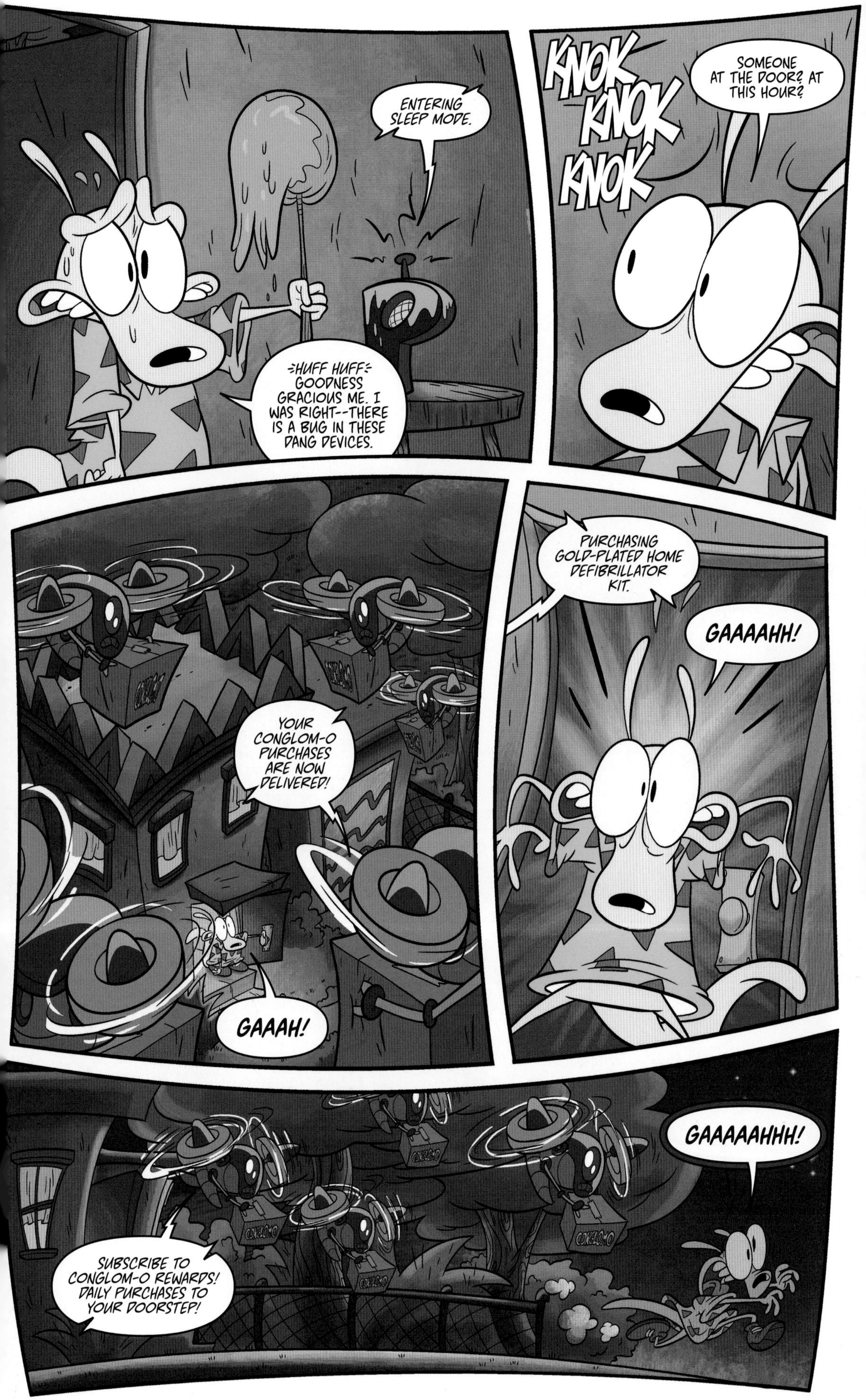
ENTERING SLEEP MODE.
=HUFF HUFF= GOODNESS GRACIOUS ME. I WAS RIGHT--THERE IS A BUG IN THESE DANG DEVICES.
KNOK KNOK KNOK
SOMEONE AT THE DOOR? AT THIS HOUR?
YOUR CONGLOM-O PURCHASES ARE NOW DELIVERED!
GAAAH!
PURCHASING GOLD-PLATED HOME DEFIBRILLATOR KIT.
GAAAAHH!
SUBSCRIBE TO CONGLOM-O REWARDS! DAILY PURCHASES TO YOUR DOORSTEP!
GAAAAAHHH!

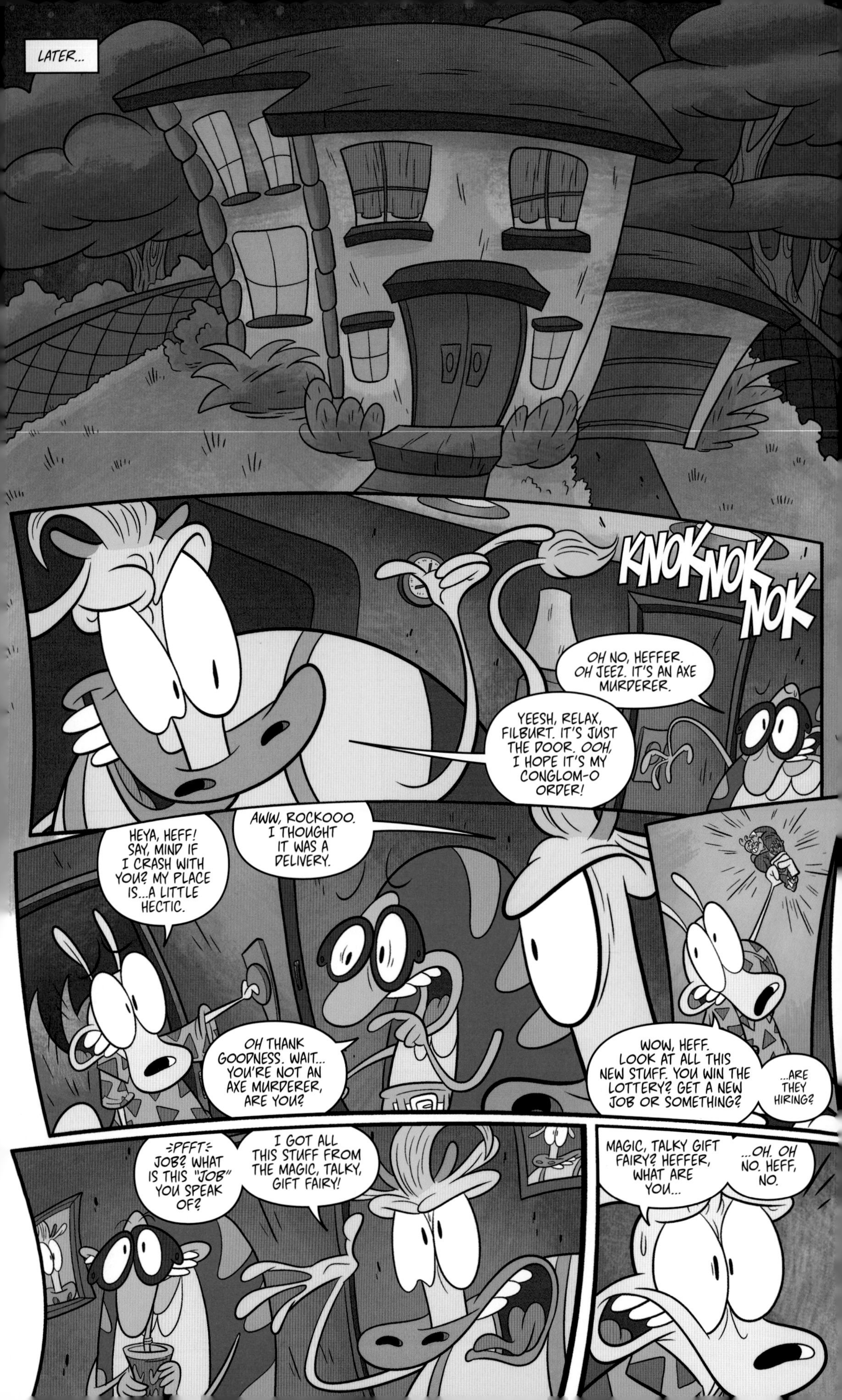
LATER...
KNOK NOK NOK
OH NO, HEFFER. OH JEEZ. IT'S AN AXE MURDERER.
YEESH, RELAX, FILBURT. IT'S JUST THE DOOR. OOH, I HOPE IT'S MY CONGLOM-O ORDER!
HEYA, HEFF! SAY, MIND IF I CRASH WITH YOU? MY PLACE IS...A LITTLE HECTIC.
AWW, ROCKOOO. I THOUGHT IT WAS A DELIVERY.
OH THANK GOODNESS. WAIT... YOU'RE NOT AN AXE MURDERER, ARE YOU?
WOW, HEFF. LOOK AT ALL THIS NEW STUFF. YOU WIN THE LOTTERY? GET A NEW JOB OR SOMETHING?
...ARE THEY HIRING?
=PFFT= JOB? WHAT IS THIS "JOB" YOU SPEAK OF?
I GOT ALL THIS STUFF FROM THE MAGIC, TALKY, GIFT FAIRY!
MAGIC, TALKY GIFT FAIRY? HEFFER, WHAT ARE YOU...
...OH. OH NO. HEFF, NO.

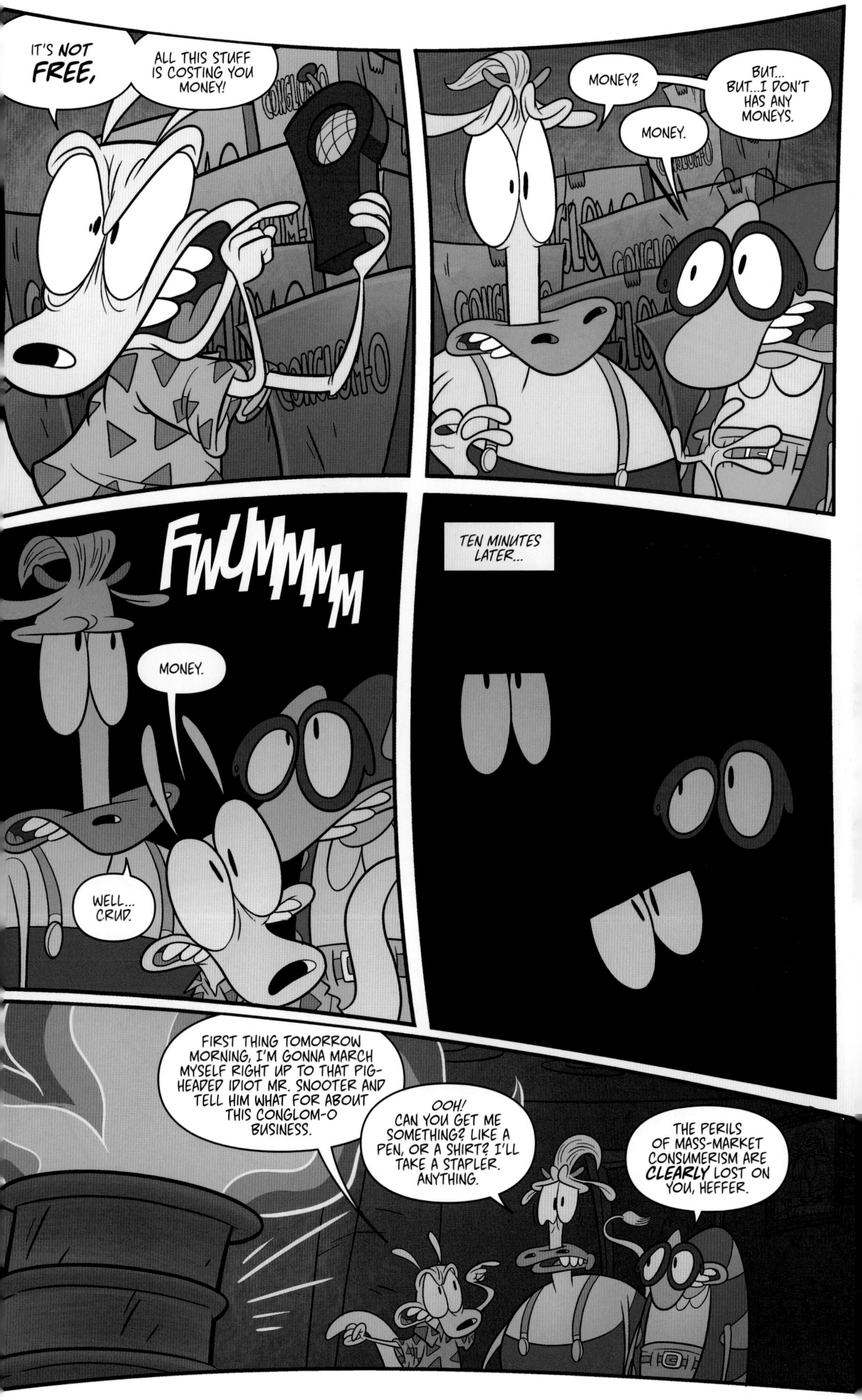
IT'S NOT FREE,
ALL THIS STUFF IS COSTING YOU MONEY!
MONEY?
BUT... BUT...I DON'T HAS ANY MONEYS.
MONEY.
FWUMMMMM
MONEY.
WELL... CRUD.
TEN MINUTES LATER...
FIRST THING TOMORROW MORNING, I'M GONNA MARCH MYSELF RIGHT UP TO THAT PIG-HEADED IDIOT MR. SNOOTER AND TELL HIM WHAT FOR ABOUT THIS CONGLOM-O BUSINESS.
OOH! CAN YOU GET ME SOMETHING? LIKE A PEN, OR A SHIRT? I'LL TAKE A STAPLER. ANYTHING.
THE PERILS OF MASS-MARKET CONSUMERISM ARE CLEARLY LOST ON YOU, HEFFER.

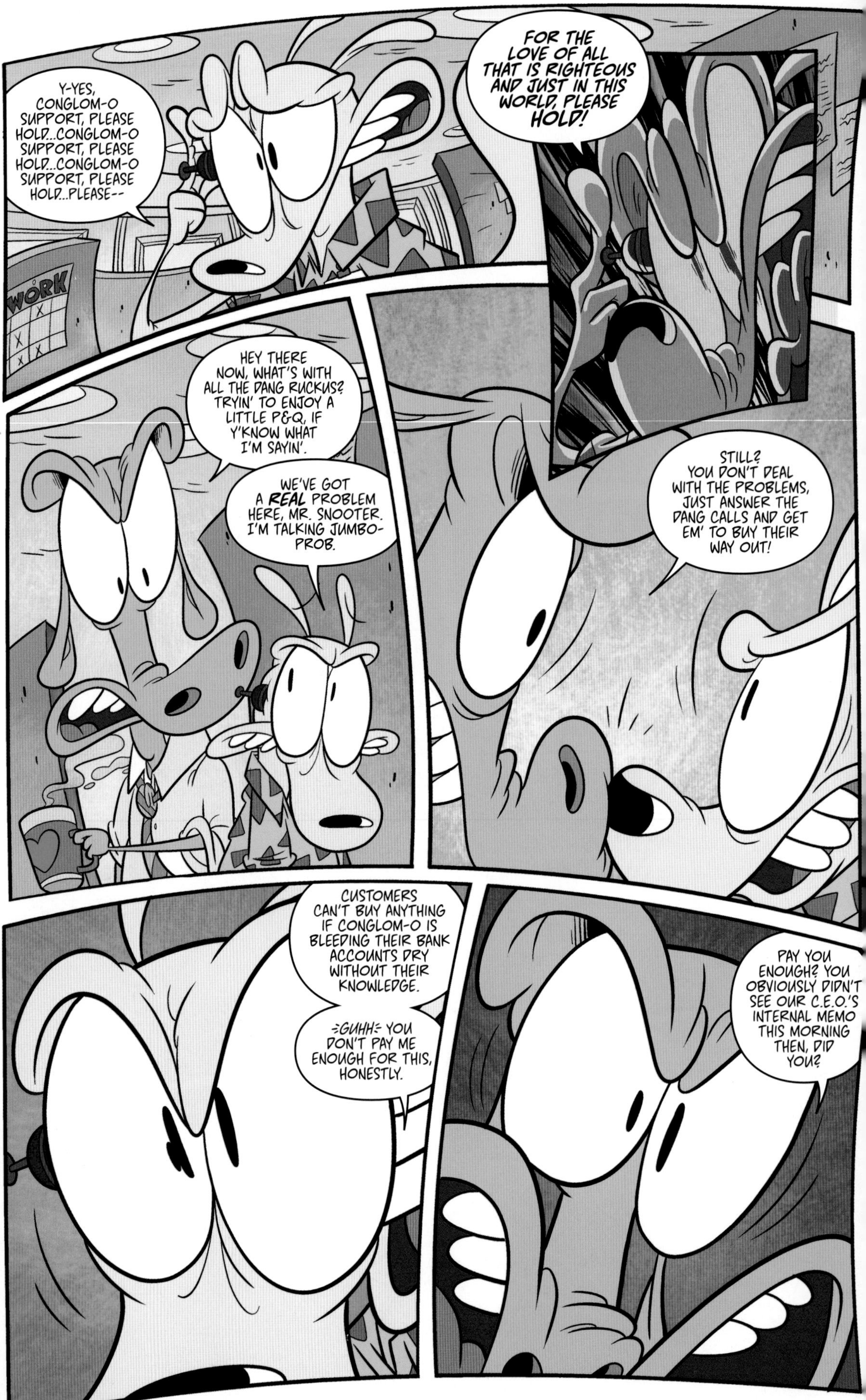

Y-YES, CONGLOM-O SUPPORT, PLEASE HOLD...CONGLOM-O SUPPORT, PLEASE HOLD...CONGLOM-O SUPPORT, PLEASE HOLD...PLEASE--
WORK
FOR THE LOVE OF ALL THAT IS RIGHTEOUS AND JUST IN THIS WORLD, PLEASE HOLD!
HEY THERE NOW, WHAT'S WITH ALL THE DANG RUCKUS? TRYIN' TO ENJOY A LITTLE P&Q, IF Y'KNOW WHAT I'M SAYIN'.
WE'VE GOT A REAL PROBLEM HERE, MR. SNOOTER. I'M TALKING JUMBO-PROB.
STILL? YOU DON'T DEAL WITH THE PROBLEMS, JUST ANSWER THE DANG CALLS AND GET EM' TO BUY THEIR WAY OUT!
CUSTOMERS CAN'T BUY ANYTHING IF CONGLOM-O IS BLEEDING THEIR BANK ACCOUNTS DRY WITHOUT THEIR KNOWLEDGE.
=GUHH= YOU DON'T PAY ME ENOUGH FOR THIS, HONESTLY.
PAY YOU ENOUGH? YOU OBVIOUSLY DIDN'T SEE OUR C.E.O.'S INTERNAL MEMO THIS MORNING THEN, DID YOU?

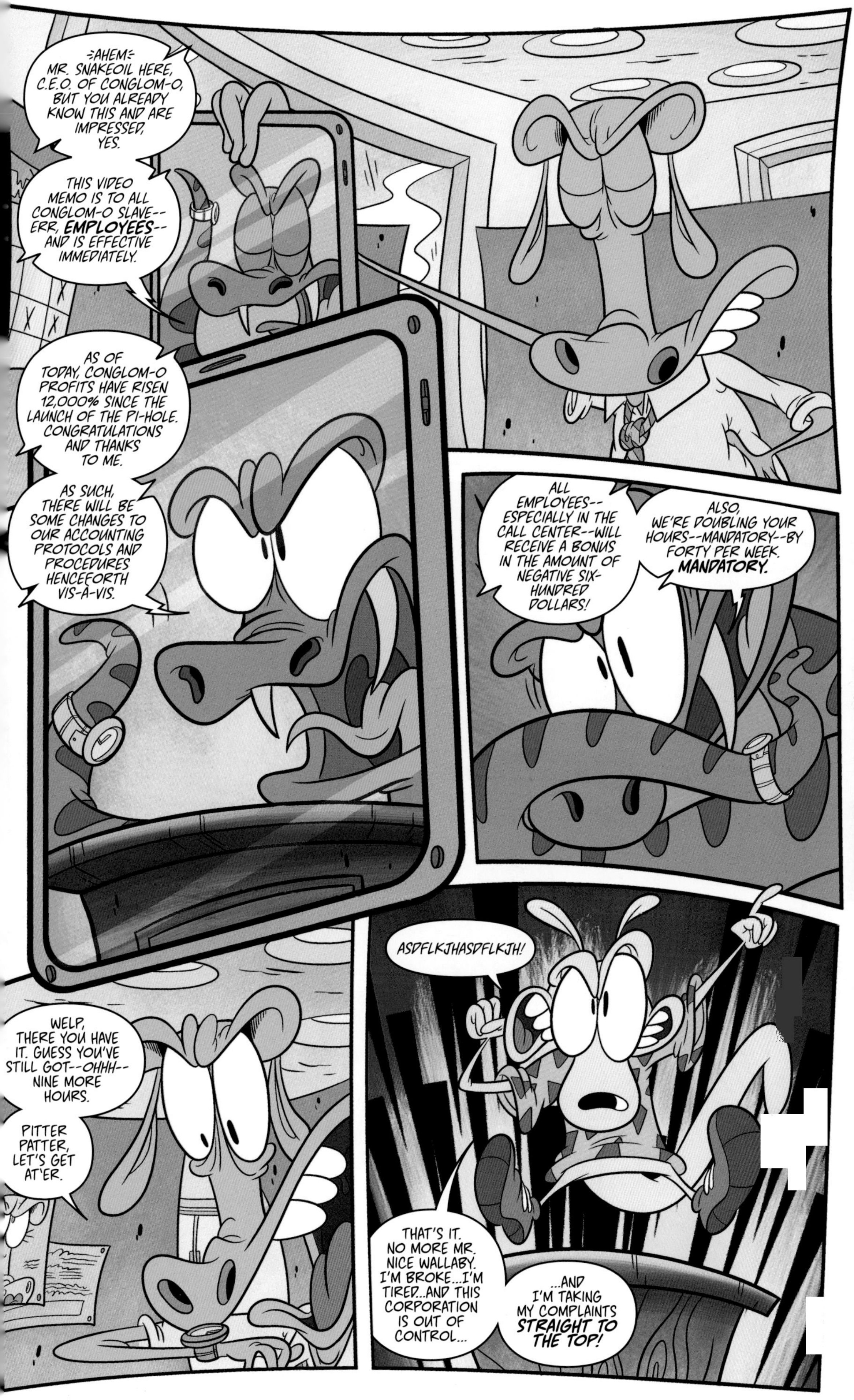
=AHEM= MR. SNAKEOIL HERE, C.E.O. OF CONGLOM-O, BUT YOU ALREADY KNOW THIS AND ARE IMPRESSED, YES.
THIS VIDEO MEMO IS TO ALL CONGLOM-O SLAVE--ERR, EMPLOYEES--AND IS EFFECTIVE IMMEDIATELY.
AS OF TODAY, CONGLOM-O PROFITS HAVE RISEN 12,000% SINCE THE LAUNCH OF THE PI-HOLE. CONGRATULATIONS AND THANKS TO ME.
AS SUCH, THERE WILL BE SOME CHANGES TO OUR ACCOUNTING PROTOCOLS AND PROCEDURES HENCEFORTH VIS-À-VIS.
ALL EMPLOYEES--ESPECIALLY IN THE CALL CENTER--WILL RECEIVE A BONUS IN THE AMOUNT OF NEGATIVE SIX-HUNDRED DOLLARS!
ALSO, WE'RE DOUBLING YOUR HOURS--MANDATORY--BY FORTY PER WEEK. MANDATORY.
WELP, THERE YOU HAVE IT. GUESS YOU'VE STILL GOT--OHHH--NINE MORE HOURS.
PITTER PATTER, LET'S GET AT'ER.
ASDFLKJHASDFLKJH!
THAT'S IT. NO MORE MR. NICE WALLABY. I'M BROKE...I'M TIRED...AND THIS CORPORATION IS OUT OF CONTROL...
...AND I'M TAKING MY COMPLAINTS STRAIGHT TO THE TOP!

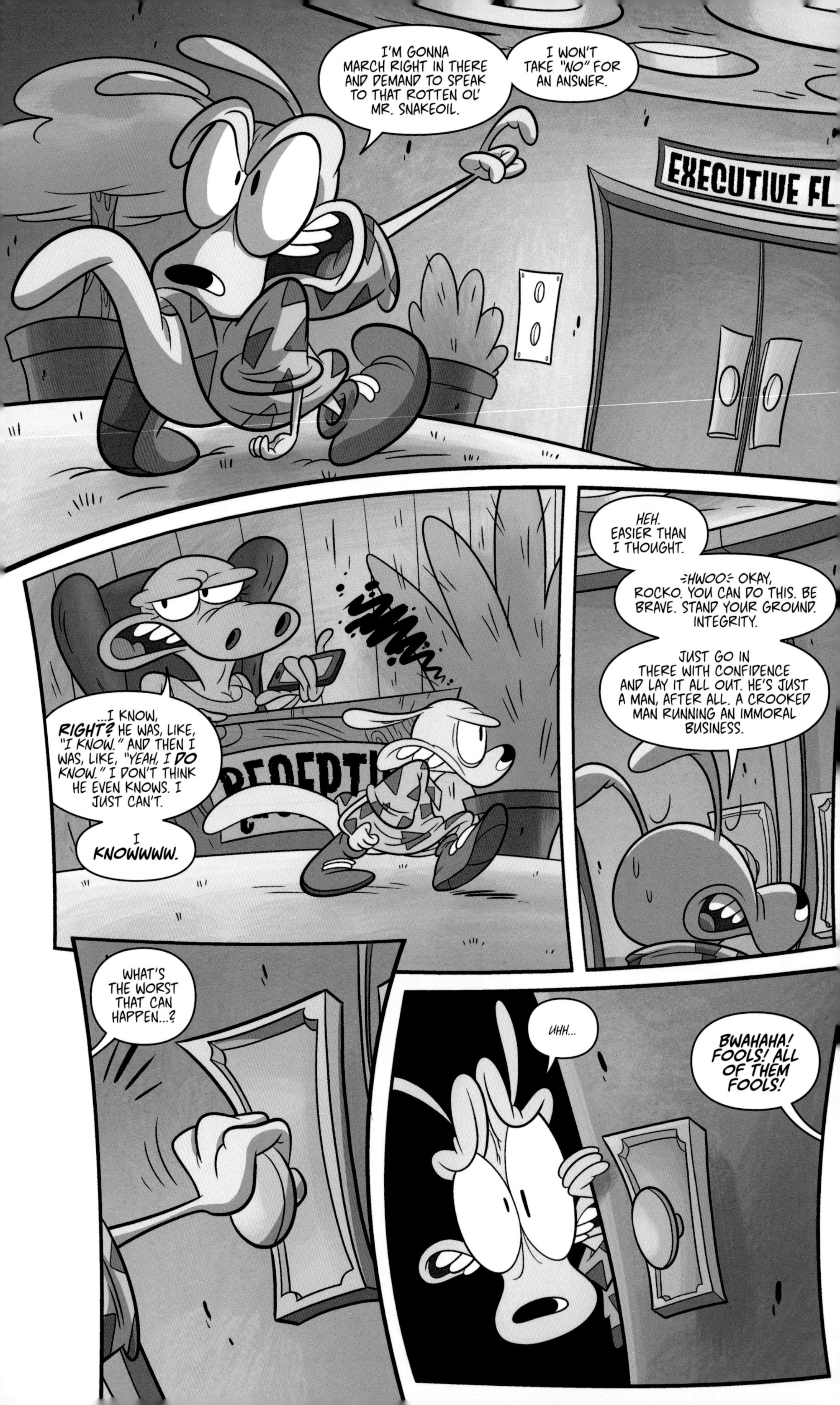

I'M GONNA MARCH RIGHT IN THERE AND DEMAND TO SPEAK TO THAT ROTTEN OL' MR. SNAKEOIL.
I WON'T TAKE "NO" FOR AN ANSWER.
EXECUTIVE FL
...I KNOW, RIGHT? HE WAS, LIKE, "I KNOW." AND THEN I WAS, LIKE, "YEAH, I DO KNOW." I DON'T THINK HE EVEN KNOWS. I JUST CAN'T.
I KNOWWWW.
HEH. EASIER THAN I THOUGHT.
=HWOO= OKAY, ROCKO. YOU CAN DO THIS. BE BRAVE. STAND YOUR GROUND. INTEGRITY.
JUST GO IN THERE WITH CONFIDENCE AND LAY IT ALL OUT. HE'S JUST A MAN, AFTER ALL. A CROOKED MAN RUNNING AN IMMORAL BUSINESS.
WHAT'S THE WORST THAT CAN HAPPEN...?
UHH...
BWAHAHA! FOOLS! ALL OF THEM FOOLS!

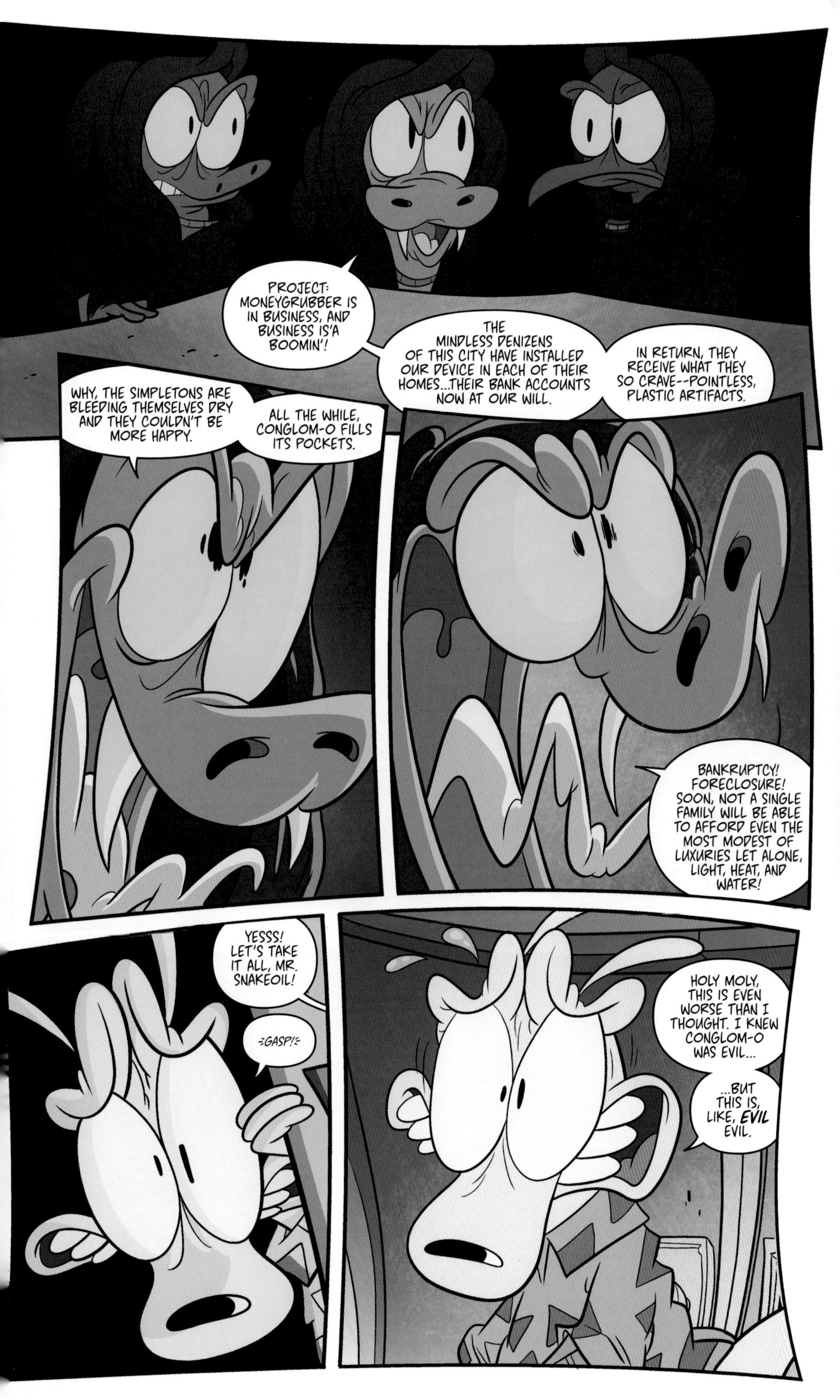
PROJECT: MONEYGRUBBER IS IN BUSINESS, AND BUSINESS IS'A BOOMIN'!
THE MINDLESS DENIZENS OF THIS CITY HAVE INSTALLED OUR DEVICE IN EACH OF THEIR HOMES...THEIR BANK ACCOUNTS NOW AT OUR WILL.
IN RETURN, THEY RECEIVE WHAT THEY SO CRAVE--POINTLESS, PLASTIC ARTIFACTS.
WHY, THE SIMPLETONS ARE BLEEDING THEMSELVES DRY AND THEY COULDN'T BE MORE HAPPY.
ALL THE WHILE, CONGLOM-O FILLS ITS POCKETS.
BANKRUPTCY! FORECLOSURE! SOON, NOT A SINGLE FAMILY WILL BE ABLE TO AFFORD EVEN THE MOST MODEST OF LUXURIES LET ALONE, LIGHT, HEAT, AND WATER!
YESSS! LET'S TAKE IT ALL, MR. SNAKEOIL!
GASP!
HOLY MOLY, THIS IS EVEN WORSE THAN I THOUGHT. I KNEW CONGLOM-O WAS EVIL...
...BUT THIS IS, LIKE, **EVIL** EVIL.

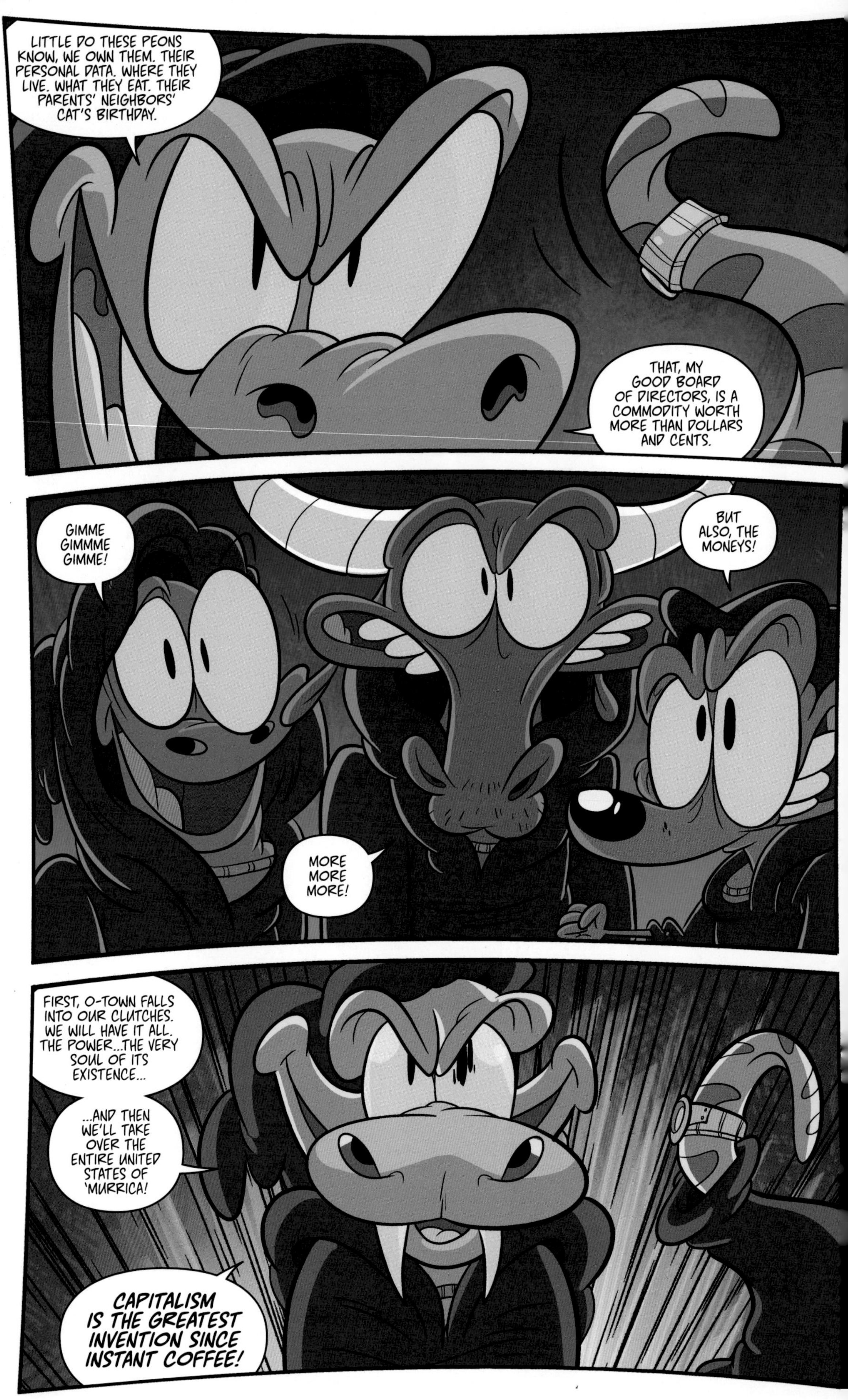
LITTLE DO THESE PEONS KNOW, WE OWN THEM. THEIR PERSONAL DATA. WHERE THEY LIVE. WHAT THEY EAT. THEIR PARENTS' NEIGHBORS' CAT'S BIRTHDAY.
THAT, MY GOOD BOARD OF DIRECTORS, IS A COMMODITY WORTH MORE THAN DOLLARS AND CENTS.
GIMME GIMMME GIMME!
BUT ALSO, THE MONEYS!
MORE MORE MORE!
FIRST, O-TOWN FALLS INTO OUR CLUTCHES. WE WILL HAVE IT ALL. THE POWER...THE VERY SOUL OF ITS EXISTENCE...
...AND THEN WE'LL TAKE OVER THE ENTIRE UNITED STATES OF 'MURRICA!
CAPITALISM IS THE GREATEST INVENTION SINCE INSTANT COFFEE!

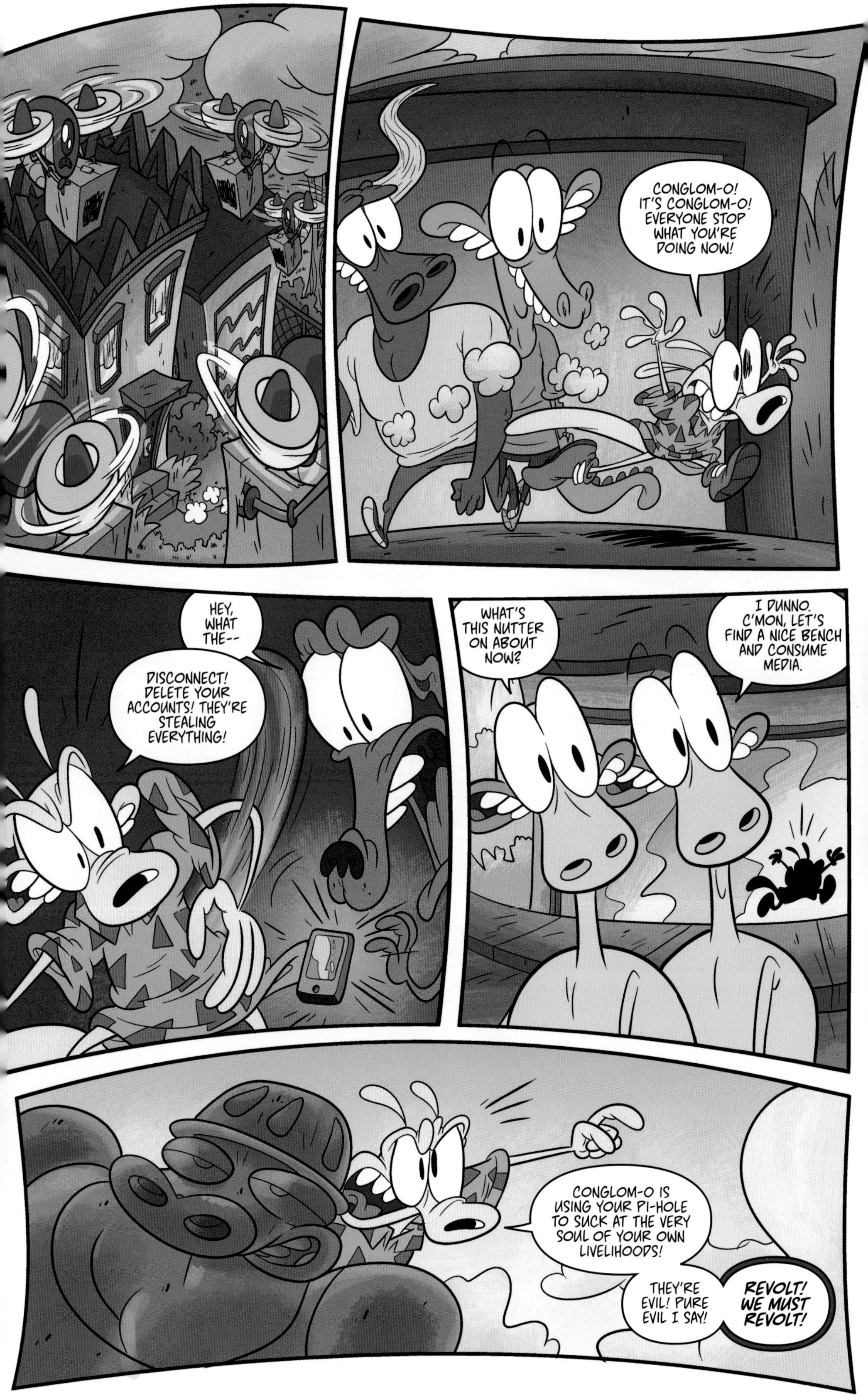
CONGLOM-O! IT'S CONGLOM-O! EVERYONE STOP WHAT YOU'RE DOING NOW!
HEY, WHAT THE--
DISCONNECT! DELETE YOUR ACCOUNTS! THEY'RE STEALING EVERYTHING!
WHAT'S THIS NUTTER ON ABOUT NOW?
I DUNNO. C'MON, LET'S FIND A NICE BENCH AND CONSUME MEDIA.
CONGLOM-O IS USING YOUR PI-HOLE TO SUCK AT THE VERY SOUL OF YOUR OWN LIVELIHOODS!
THEY'RE EVIL! PURE EVIL I SAY!
REVOLT! WE MUST REVOLT!

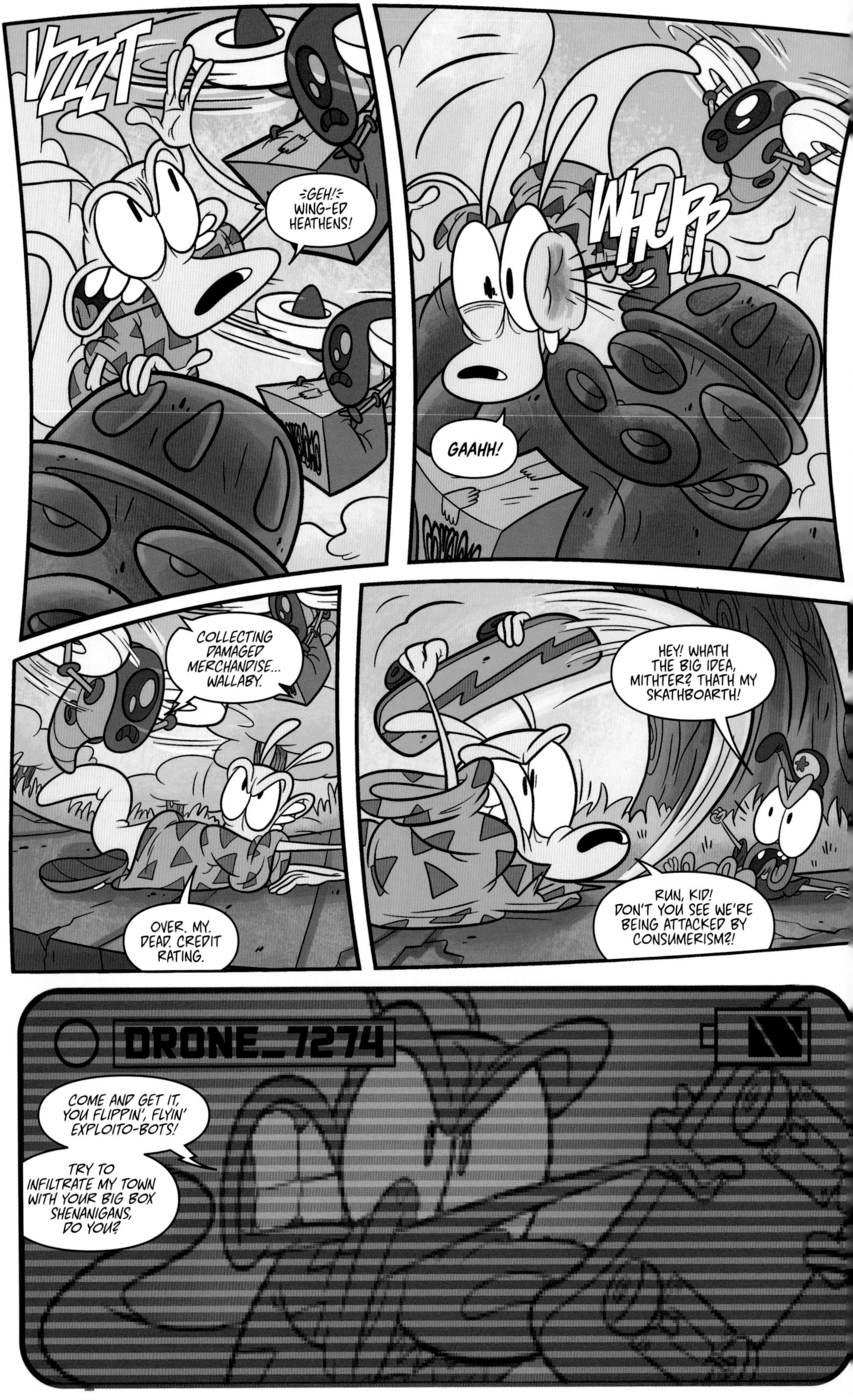
VZZZT
=GEH!= WING-ED HEATHENS!
WHUPP
GAAHH!
COLLECTING DAMAGED MERCHANDISE... WALLABY.
OVER. MY. DEAD. CREDIT RATING.
HEY! WHATH THE BIG IDEA, MITHTER? THATH MY SKATHBOARTH!
RUN, KID! DON'T YOU SEE WE'RE BEING ATTACKED BY CONSUMERISM?!
DRONE_7274
COME AND GET IT, YOU FLIPPIN', FLYIN' EXPLOITO-BOTS!
TRY TO INFILTRATE MY TOWN WITH YOUR BIG BOX SHENANIGANS, DO YOU?

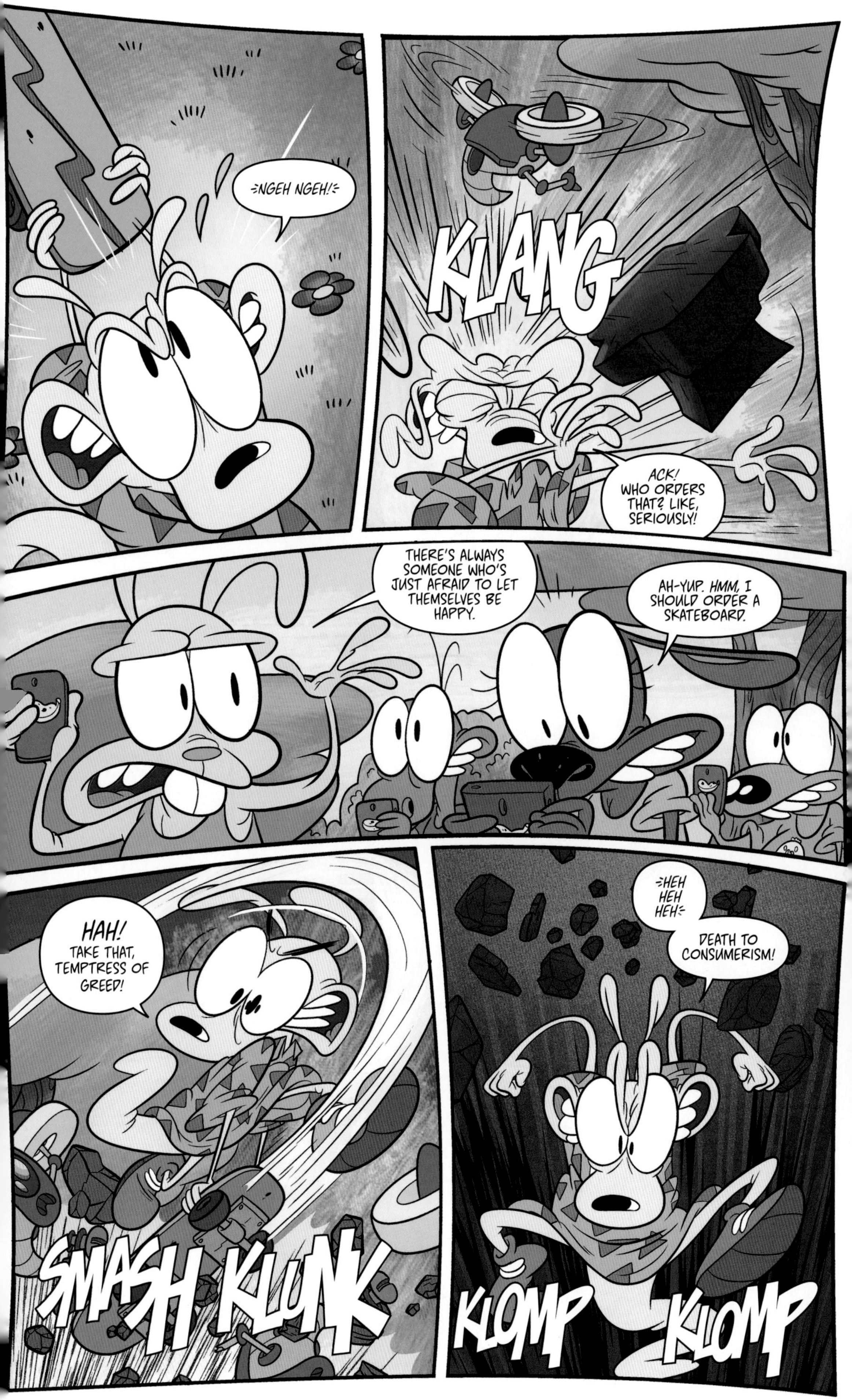

=NGEH NGEH!=
KLANG
ACK! WHO ORDERS THAT? LIKE, SERIOUSLY!
THERE'S ALWAYS SOMEONE WHO'S JUST AFRAID TO LET THEMSELVES BE HAPPY.
AH-YUP. HMM, I SHOULD ORDER A SKATEBOARD.
HAH! TAKE THAT, TEMPTRESS OF GREED!
SMASH KLUNK
=HEH HEH HEH=
DEATH TO CONSUMERISM!
KLOMP KLOMP

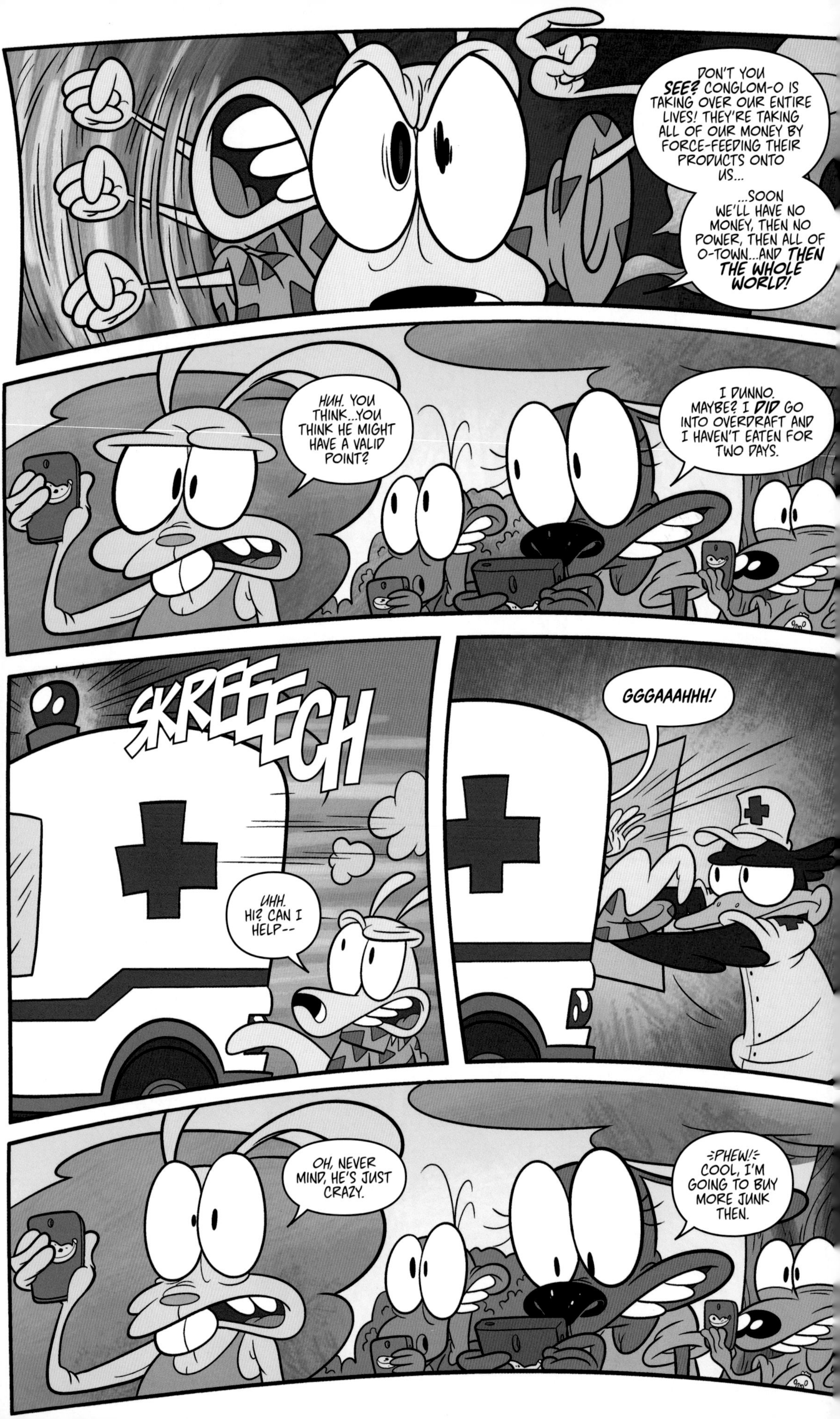
DON'T YOU SEE? CONGLOM-O IS TAKING OVER OUR ENTIRE LIVES! THEY'RE TAKING ALL OF OUR MONEY BY FORCE-FEEDING THEIR PRODUCTS ONTO US...
...SOON WE'LL HAVE NO MONEY, THEN NO POWER, THEN ALL OF O-TOWN...AND THEN THE WHOLE WORLD!
HUH. YOU THINK...YOU THINK HE MIGHT HAVE A VALID POINT?
I DUNNO. MAYBE? I DID GO INTO OVERDRAFT AND I HAVEN'T EATEN FOR TWO DAYS.
SKREEEECH
UHH. HI? CAN I HELP--
GGGAAAHHH!
OH, NEVER MIND, HE'S JUST CRAZY.
PHEW! COOL, I'M GOING TO BUY MORE JUNK THEN.

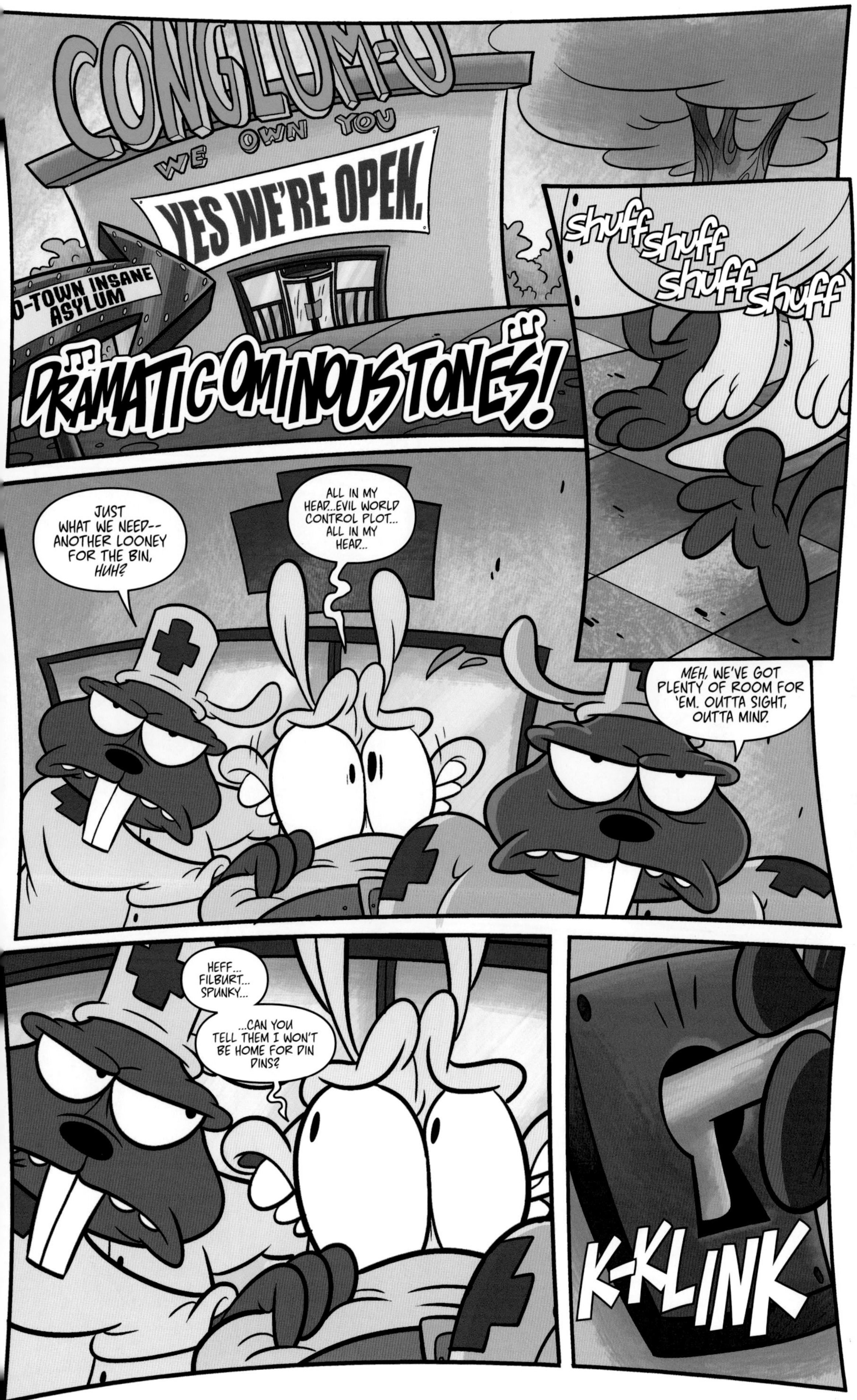
CONGLOM-O
WE OWN YOU
YES WE'RE OPEN.
O-TOWN INSANE ASYLUM
DRAMATIC OMINOUS TONES!
shuff shuff shuff shuff shuff
JUST WHAT WE NEED-- ANOTHER LOONEY FOR THE BIN, HUH?
ALL IN MY HEAD...EVIL WORLD CONTROL PLOT... ALL IN MY HEAD...
MEH, WE'VE GOT PLENTY OF ROOM FOR 'EM. OUTTA SIGHT, OUTTA MIND.
HEFF... FILBURT... SPUNKY...
...CAN YOU TELL THEM I WON'T BE HOME FOR DIN DINS?
K-KLINK

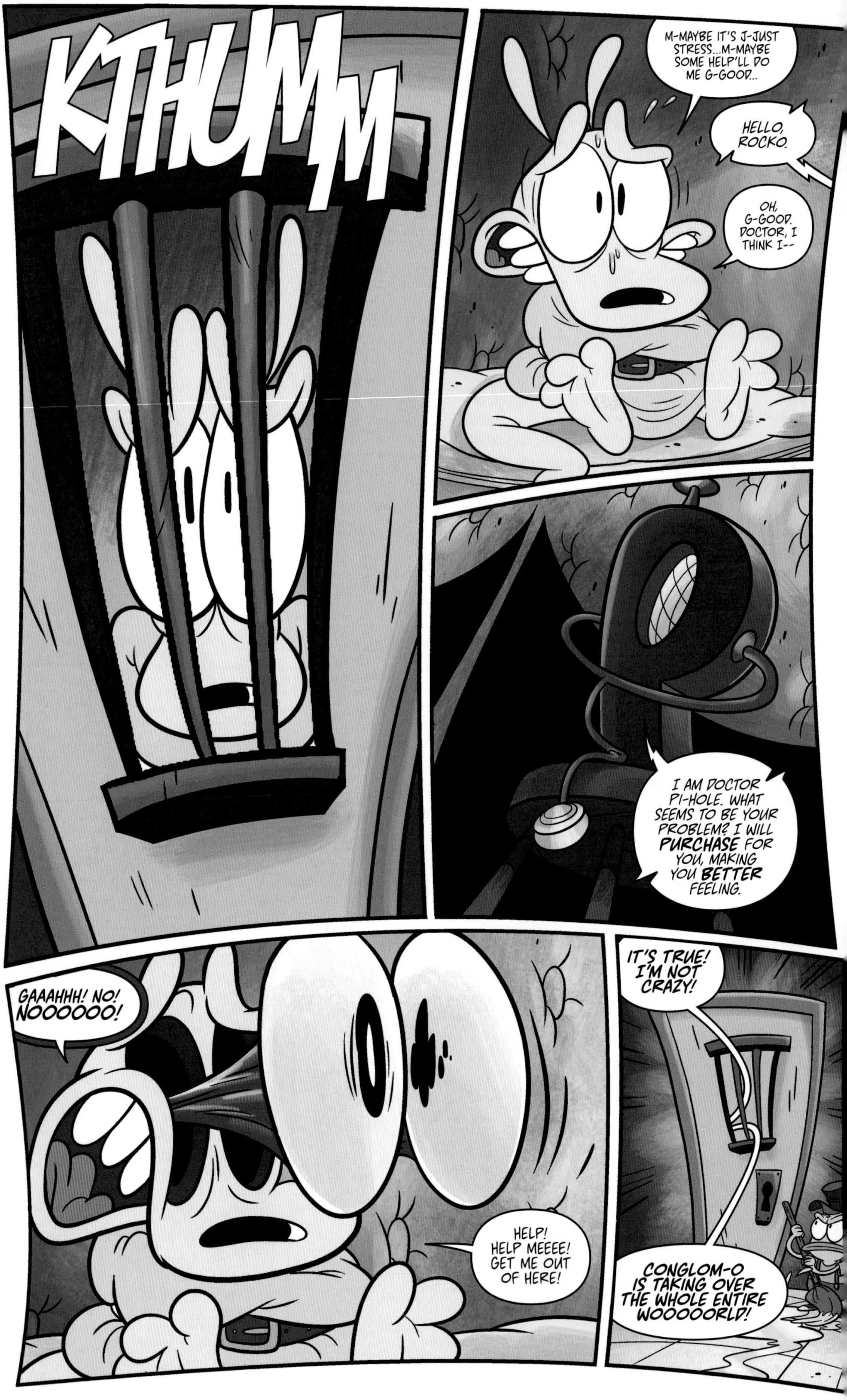
KTHUMMM
M-MAYBE IT'S J-JUST STRESS...M-MAYBE SOME HELP'LL DO ME G-GOOD...
HELLO, ROCKO.
OH, G-GOOD. DOCTOR, I THINK I--
I AM DOCTOR PI-HOLE. WHAT SEEMS TO BE YOUR PROBLEM? I WILL PURCHASE FOR YOU, MAKING YOU BETTER FEELING.
GAAAHHH! NO! NOOOOOO!
HELP! HELP MEEEE! GET ME OUT OF HERE!
IT'S TRUE! I'M NOT CRAZY!
CONGLOM-O IS TAKING OVER THE WHOLE ENTIRE WOOOOORLD!

CHAPTER
EIGHT

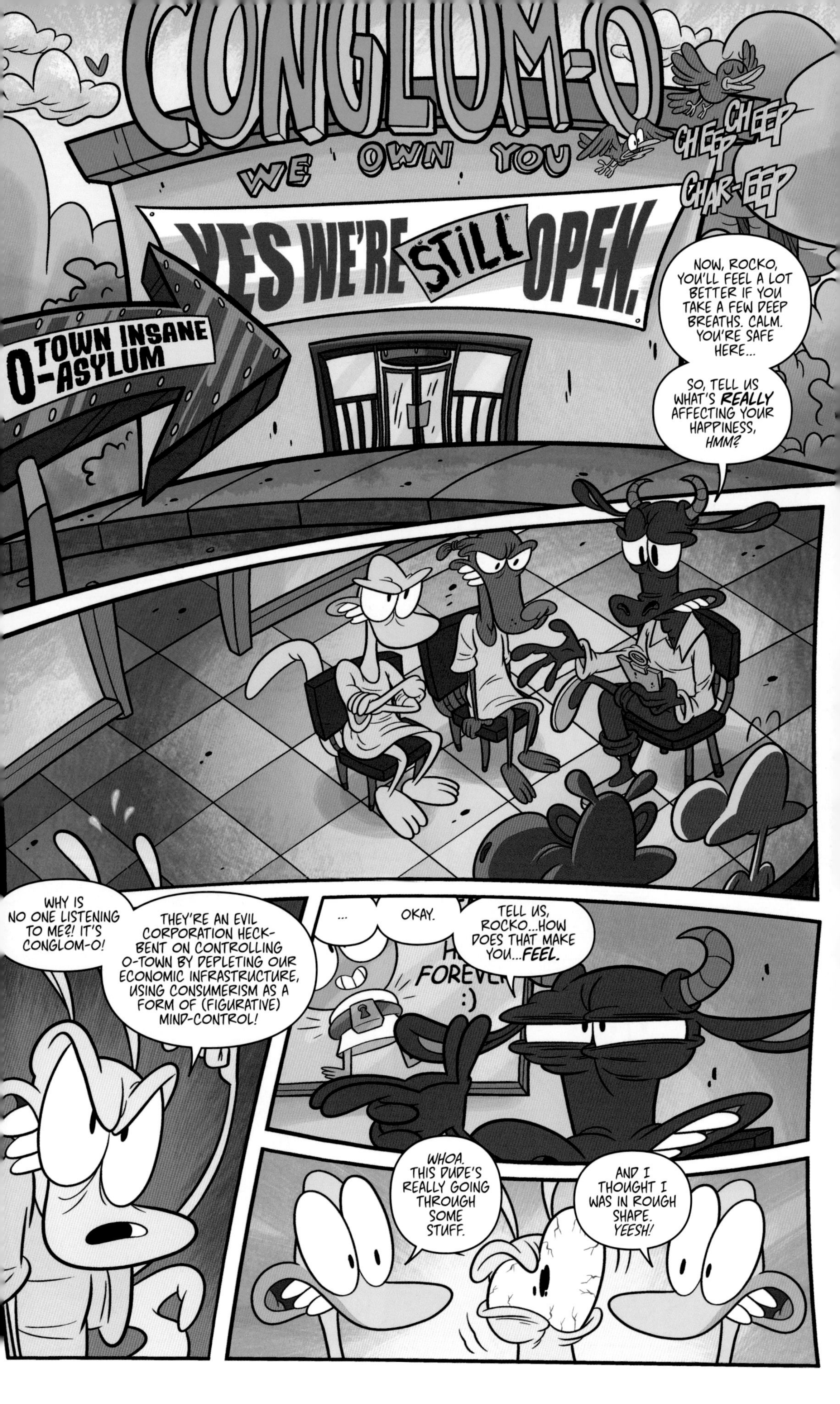
CONGLUM-O
WE OWN YOU
CHEEP CHEEP
CHEEP
CHAR-EEP
YES WE'RE STILL OPEN.
O-TOWN INSANE ASYLUM
NOW, ROCKO, YOU'LL FEEL A LOT BETTER IF YOU TAKE A FEW DEEP BREATHS. CALM. YOU'RE SAFE HERE...
SO, TELL US WHAT'S REALLY AFFECTING YOUR HAPPINESS, HMM?
WHY IS NO ONE LISTENING TO ME?! IT'S CONGLOM-O!
THEY'RE AN EVIL CORPORATION HECK-BENT ON CONTROLLING O-TOWN BY DEPLETING OUR ECONOMIC INFRASTRUCTURE, USING CONSUMERISM AS A FORM OF (FIGURATIVE) MIND-CONTROL!
...
OKAY.
TELL US, ROCKO...HOW DOES THAT MAKE YOU...FEEL.
FOREVE
:)
WHOA. THIS DUDE'S REALLY GOING THROUGH SOME STUFF.
AND I THOUGHT I WAS IN ROUGH SHAPE. YEESH!

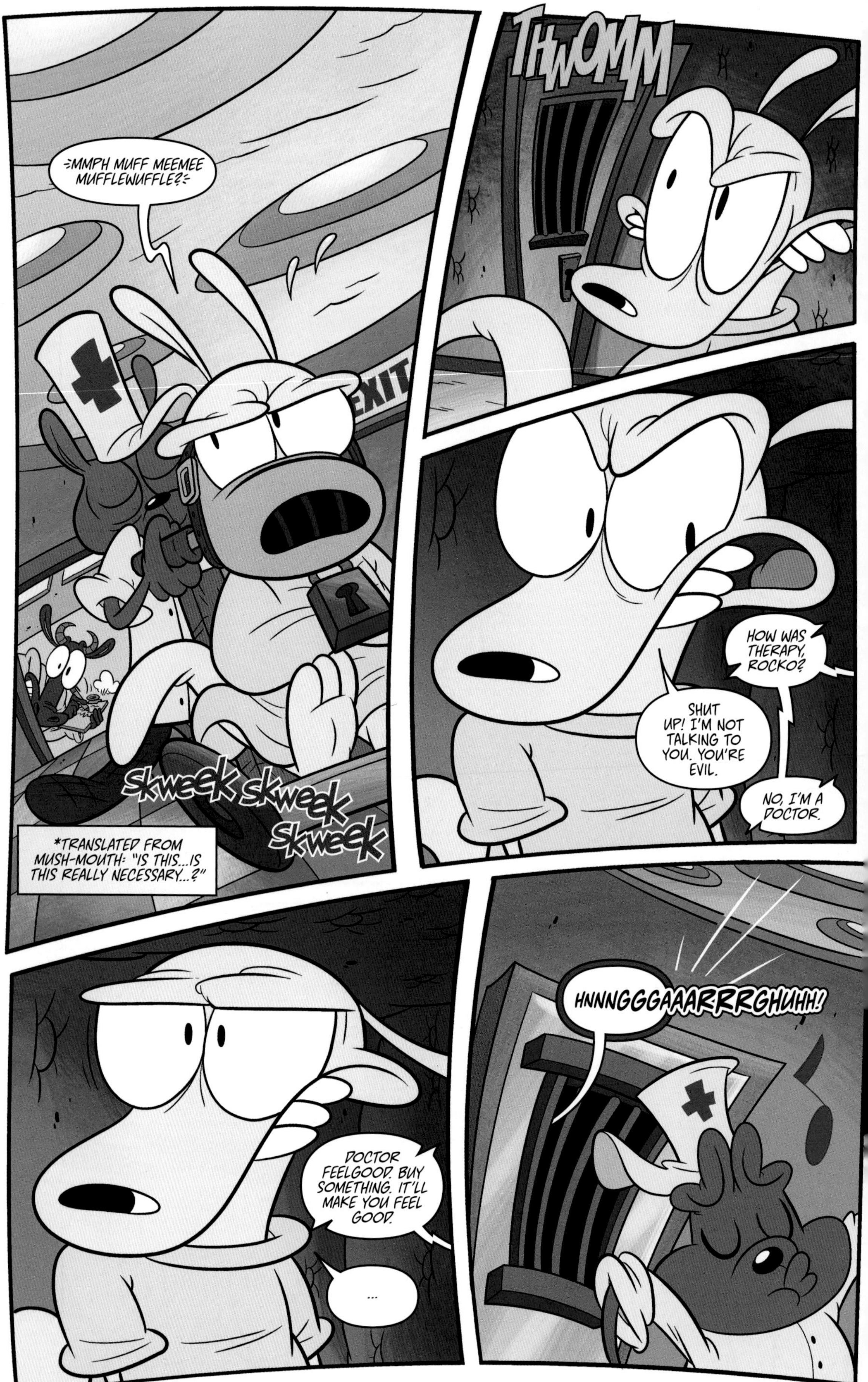

=MMPH MUFF MEEMEE MUFFLEWUFFLE?=
EXIT
SKWEEK SKWEEK SKWEEK
*TRANSLATED FROM MUSH-MOUTH: "IS THIS...IS THIS REALLY NECESSARY...?"
THWOMM
HOW WAS THERAPY, ROCKO?
SHUT UP! I'M NOT TALKING TO YOU. YOU'RE EVIL.
NO, I'M A DOCTOR.
DOCTOR FEELGOOD. BUY SOMETHING. IT'LL MAKE YOU FEEL GOOD.
...
HNNNGGGAAARRRGHUHH!

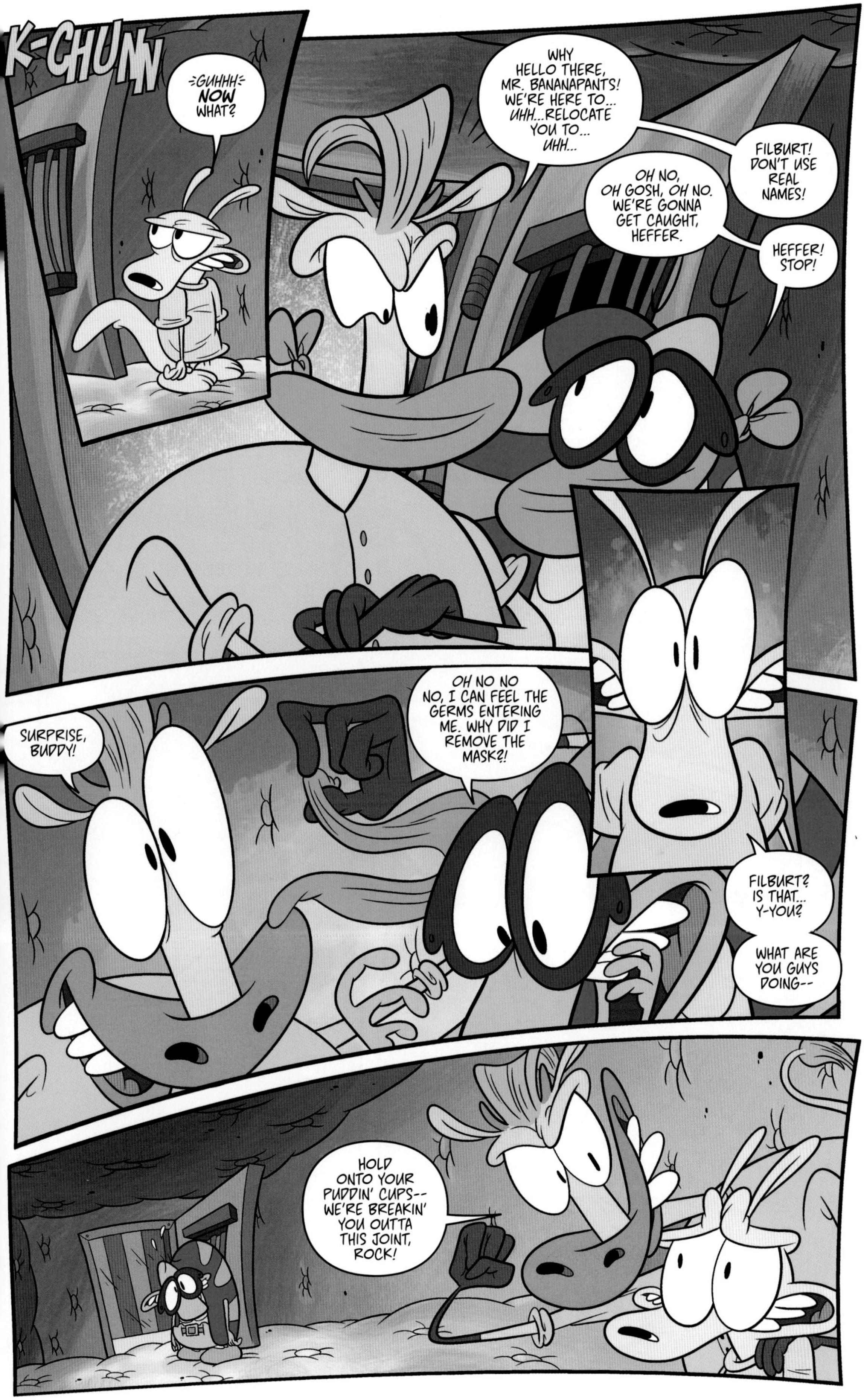
K-CHUNN
-GUHHH- NOW WHAT?
WHY HELLO THERE, MR. BANANAPANTS! WE'RE HERE TO... UHH...RELOCATE YOU TO... UHH...
FILBURT! DON'T USE REAL NAMES!
OH NO, OH GOSH, OH NO. WE'RE GONNA GET CAUGHT, HEFFER.
HEFFER! STOP!
SURPRISE, BUDDY!
OH NO NO NO, I CAN FEEL THE GERMS ENTERING ME. WHY DID I REMOVE THE MASK?!
FILBURT? IS THAT... Y-YOU?
WHAT ARE YOU GUYS DOING--
HOLD ONTO YOUR PUDDIN' CUPS-- WE'RE BREAKIN' YOU OUTTA THIS JOINT, ROCK!

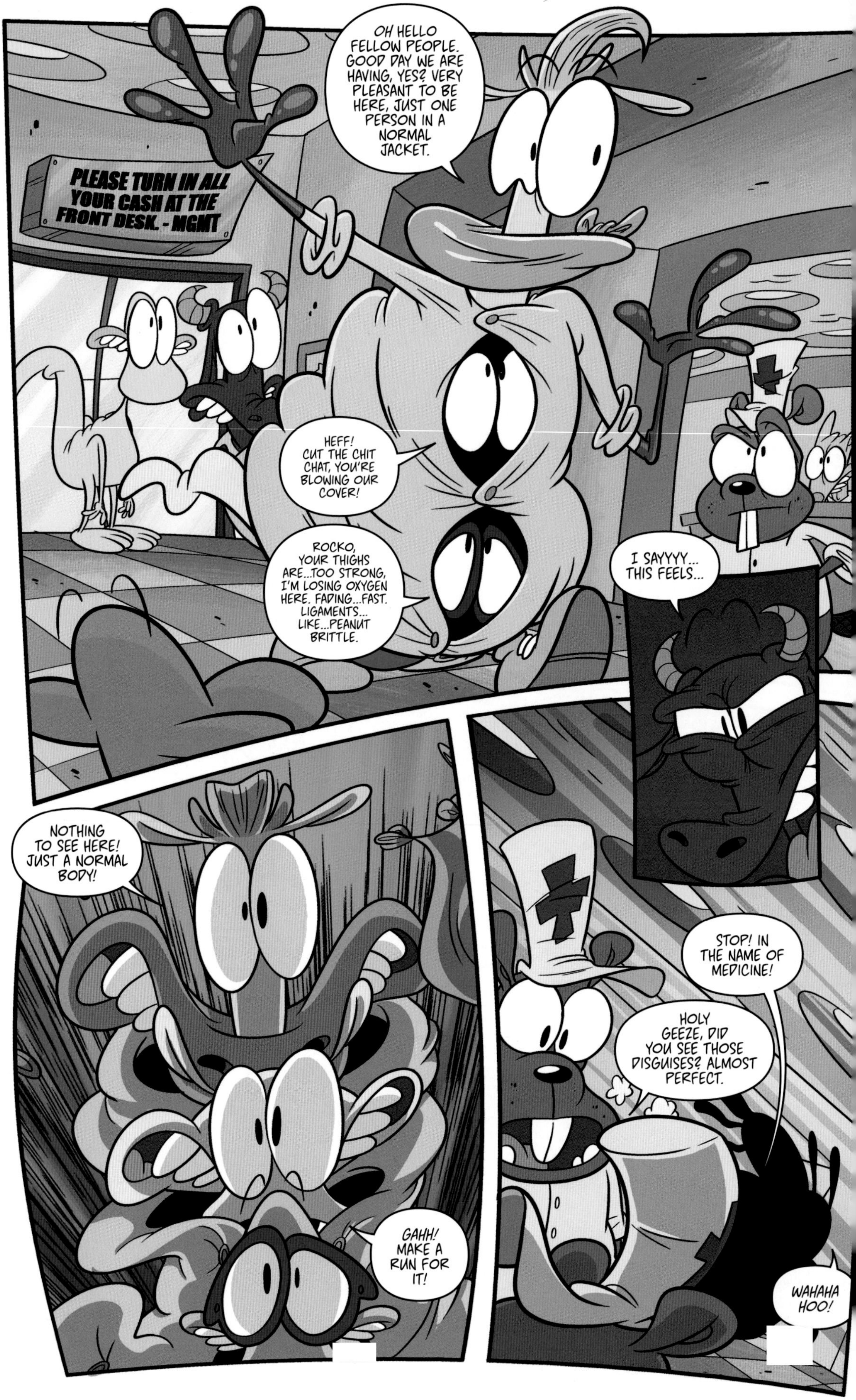
OH HELLO FELLOW PEOPLE. GOOD DAY WE ARE HAVING, YES? VERY PLEASANT TO BE HERE, JUST ONE PERSON IN A NORMAL JACKET.
PLEASE TURN IN ALL YOUR CASH AT THE FRONT DESK. - MGMT
HEFF! CUT THE CHIT CHAT, YOU'RE BLOWING OUR COVER!
ROCKO, YOUR THIGHS ARE...TOO STRONG, I'M LOSING OXYGEN HERE. FADING...FAST. LIGAMENTS... LIKE...PEANUT BRITTLE.
I SAYYYY... THIS FEELS...
NOTHING TO SEE HERE! JUST A NORMAL BODY!
GAHH! MAKE A RUN FOR IT!
STOP! IN THE NAME OF MEDICINE!
HOLY GEEZE, DID YOU SEE THOSE DISGUISES? ALMOST PERFECT.
WAHAHA HOO!

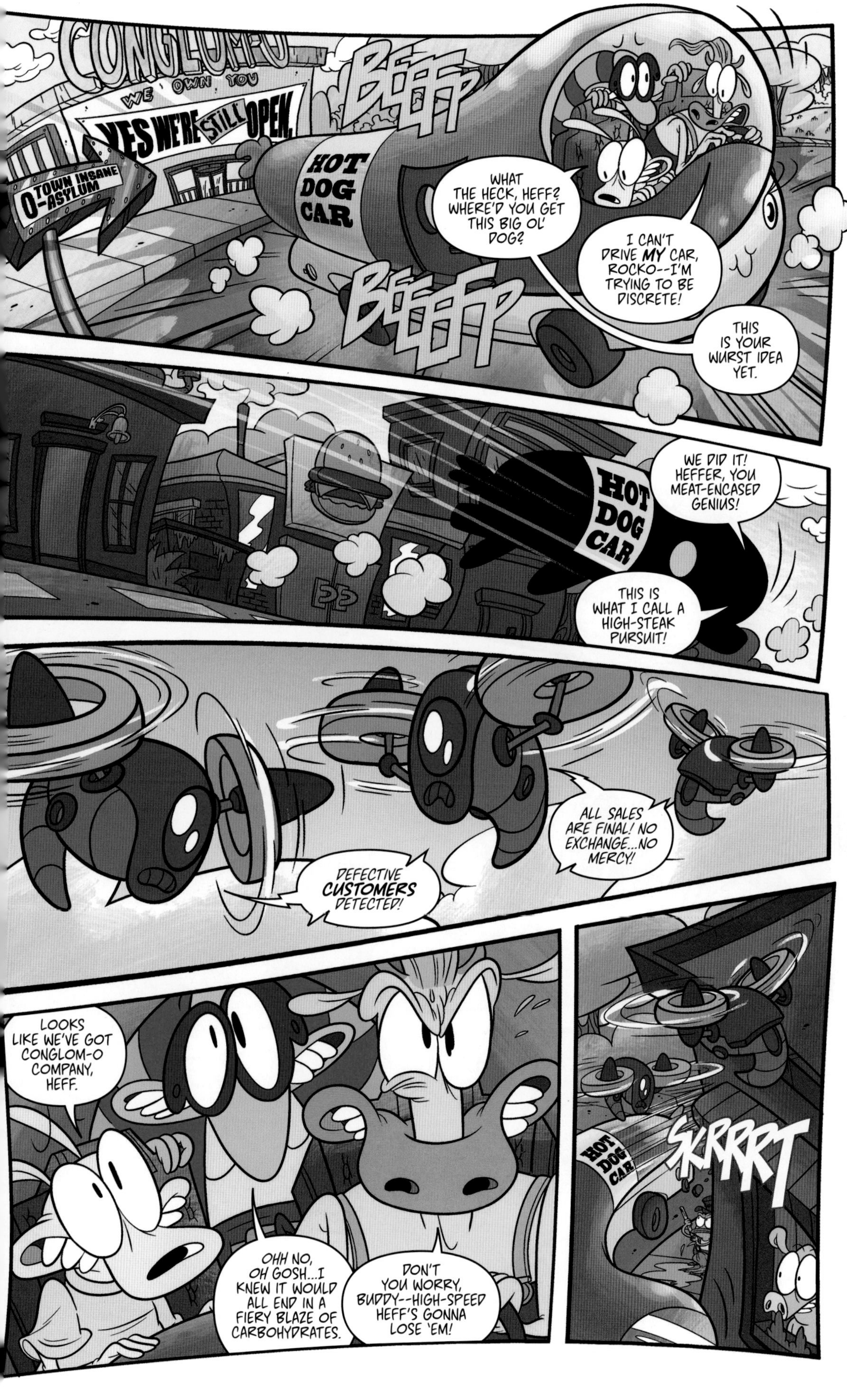
CONGLOM-O
WE OWN YOU
YES WE'RE STILL OPEN.
O-TOWN INSANE O-ASYLUM
BEEEP
HOT DOG CAR
WHAT THE HECK, HEFF? WHERE'D YOU GET THIS BIG OL' DOG?
I CAN'T DRIVE MY CAR, ROCKO--I'M TRYING TO BE DISCRETE!
BEEEP
THIS IS YOUR WURST IDEA YET.
HOT DOG CAR
WE DID IT! HEFFER, YOU MEAT-ENCASED GENIUS!
THIS IS WHAT I CALL A HIGH-STEAK PURSUIT!
ALL SALES ARE FINAL! NO EXCHANGE...NO MERCY!
DEFECTIVE CUSTOMERS DETECTED!
LOOKS LIKE WE'VE GOT CONGLOM-O COMPANY, HEFF.
OHH NO, OH GOSH...I KNEW IT WOULD ALL END IN A FIERY BLAZE OF CARBOHYDRATES.
DON'T YOU WORRY, BUDDY--HIGH-SPEED HEFF'S GONNA LOSE 'EM!
HOT DOG CAR
SKRRRT

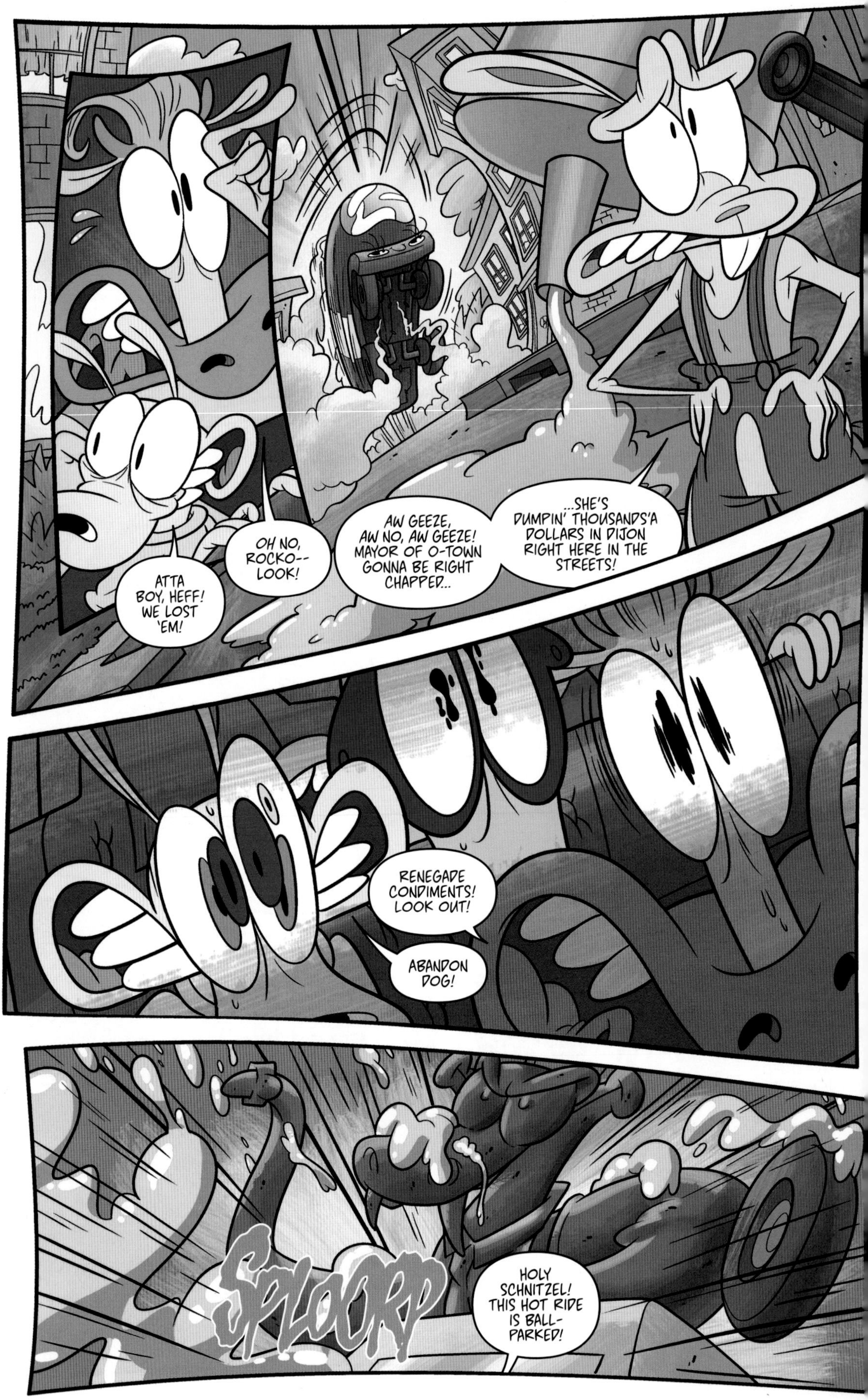
ATTA BOY, HEFF! WE LOST 'EM!
OH NO, ROCKO-- LOOK!
AW GEEZE, AW NO, AW GEEZE! MAYOR OF O-TOWN GONNA BE RIGHT CHAPPED...
...SHE'S DUMPIN' THOUSANDS'A DOLLARS IN DIJON RIGHT HERE IN THE STREETS!
RENEGADE CONDIMENTS! LOOK OUT!
ABANDON DOG!
SPLOORP
HOLY SCHNITZEL! THIS HOT RIDE IS BALL-PARKED!

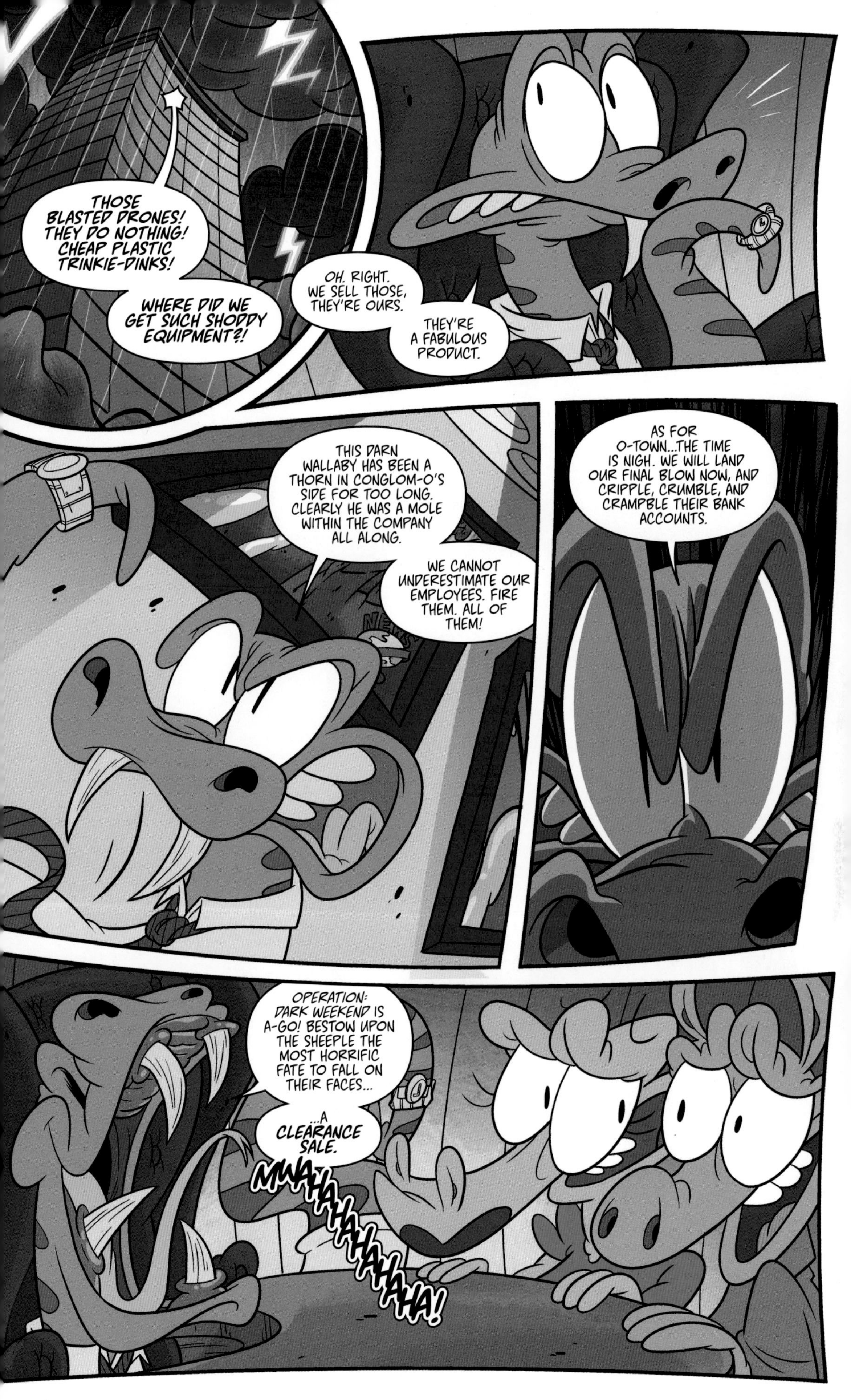
THOSE BLASTED DRONES! THEY DO NOTHING! CHEAP PLASTIC TRINKIE-DINKS!
WHERE DID WE GET SUCH SHODDY EQUIPMENT?!
OH. RIGHT. WE SELL THOSE, THEY'RE OURS.
THEY'RE A FABULOUS PRODUCT.
THIS DARN WALLABY HAS BEEN A THORN IN CONGLOM-O'S SIDE FOR TOO LONG. CLEARLY HE WAS A MOLE WITHIN THE COMPANY ALL ALONG.
WE CANNOT UNDERESTIMATE OUR EMPLOYEES. FIRE THEM. ALL OF THEM!
NEWS
AS FOR O-TOWN...THE TIME IS NIGH. WE WILL LAND OUR FINAL BLOW NOW, AND CRIPPLE, CRUMBLE, AND CRAMPBLE THEIR BANK ACCOUNTS.
OPERATION: DARK WEEKEND IS A-GO! BESTOW UPON THE SHEEPLE THE MOST HORRIFIC FATE TO FALL ON THEIR FACES...
...A CLEARANCE SALE.
MWAHAHAHAHAHAHA!

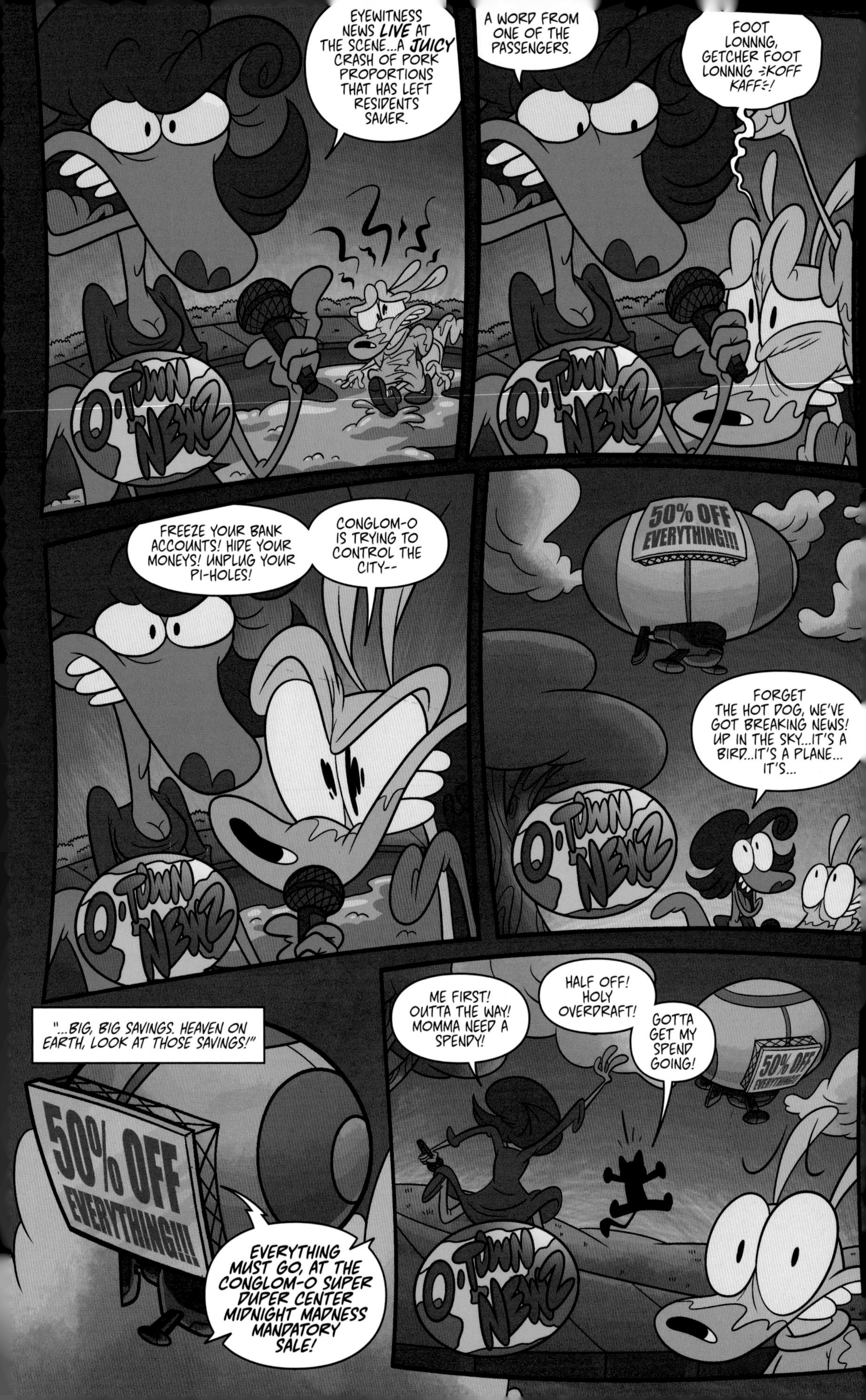
EYEWITNESS NEWS LIVE AT THE SCENE...A JUICY CRASH OF PORK PROPORTIONS THAT HAS LEFT RESIDENTS SAUER.
A WORD FROM ONE OF THE PASSENGERS.
FOOT LONNNG, GETCHER FOOT LONNNG =KOFF KAFF=!
FREEZE YOUR BANK ACCOUNTS! HIDE YOUR MONEYS! UNPLUG YOUR PI-HOLES!
CONGLOM-O IS TRYING TO CONTROL THE CITY--
50% OFF EVERYTHING!!!
FORGET THE HOT DOG, WE'VE GOT BREAKING NEWS! UP IN THE SKY...IT'S A BIRD...IT'S A PLANE... IT'S...
"...BIG, BIG SAVINGS. HEAVEN ON EARTH, LOOK AT THOSE SAVINGS!"
50% OFF EVERYTHING!!!
EVERYTHING MUST GO, AT THE CONGLOM-O SUPER DUPER CENTER MIDNIGHT MADNESS MANDATORY SALE!
ME FIRST! OUTTA THE WAY! MOMMA NEED A SPENDY!
HALF OFF! HOLY OVERDRAFT!
GOTTA GET MY SPEND GOING!

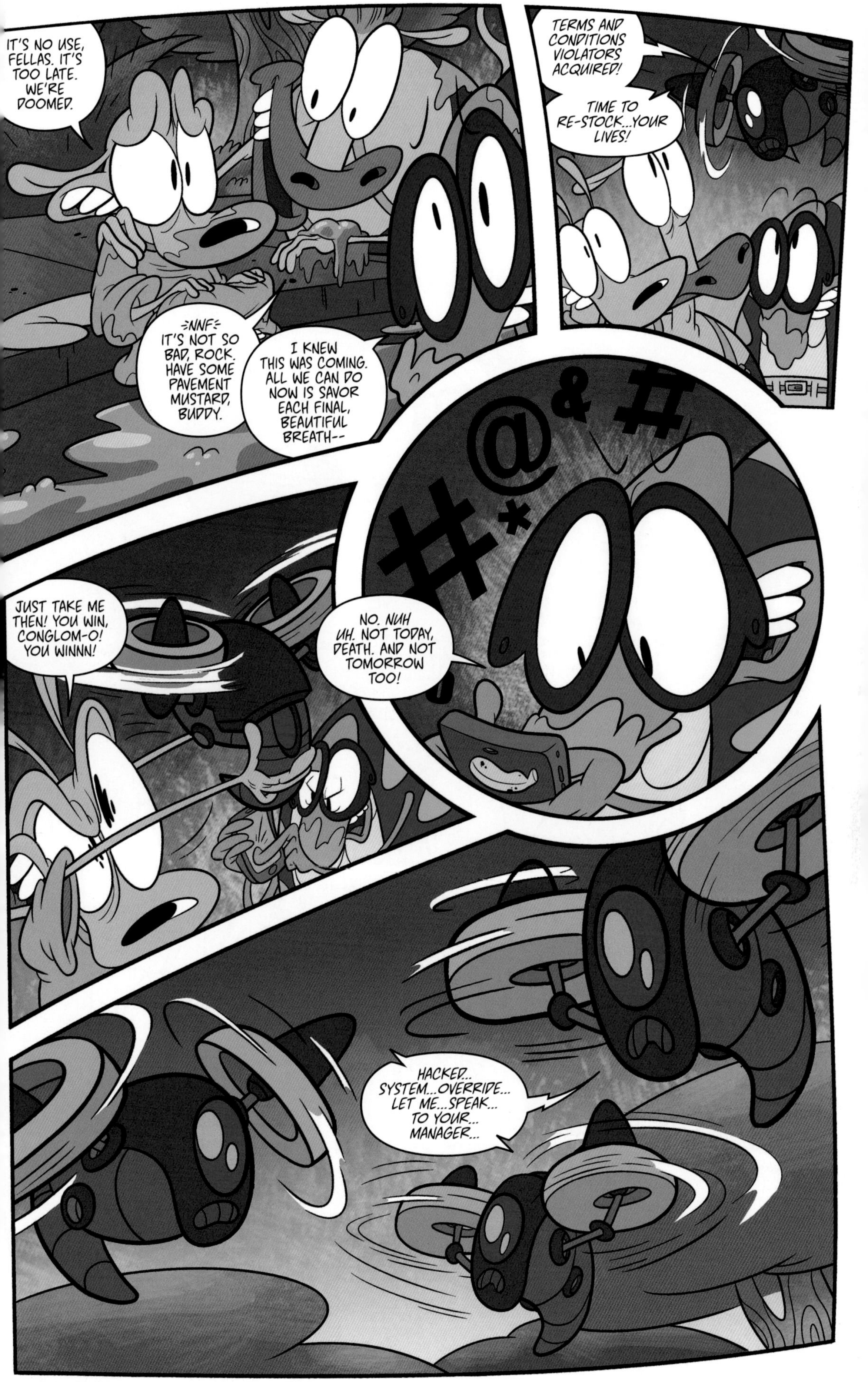

IT'S NO USE, FELLAS. IT'S TOO LATE. WE'RE DOOMED.
=NNF= IT'S NOT SO BAD, ROCK. HAVE SOME PAVEMENT MUSTARD, BUDDY.
I KNEW THIS WAS COMING. ALL WE CAN DO NOW IS SAVOR EACH FINAL, BEAUTIFUL BREATH--
TERMS AND CONDITIONS VIOLATORS ACQUIRED!
TIME TO RE-STOCK...YOUR LIVES!
JUST TAKE ME THEN! YOU WIN, CONGLOM-O! YOU WINNN!
#@&#*
NO. NUH UH. NOT TODAY, DEATH. AND NOT TOMORROW TOO!
HACKED... SYSTEM...OVERRIDE... LET ME...SPEAK... TO YOUR... MANAGER...

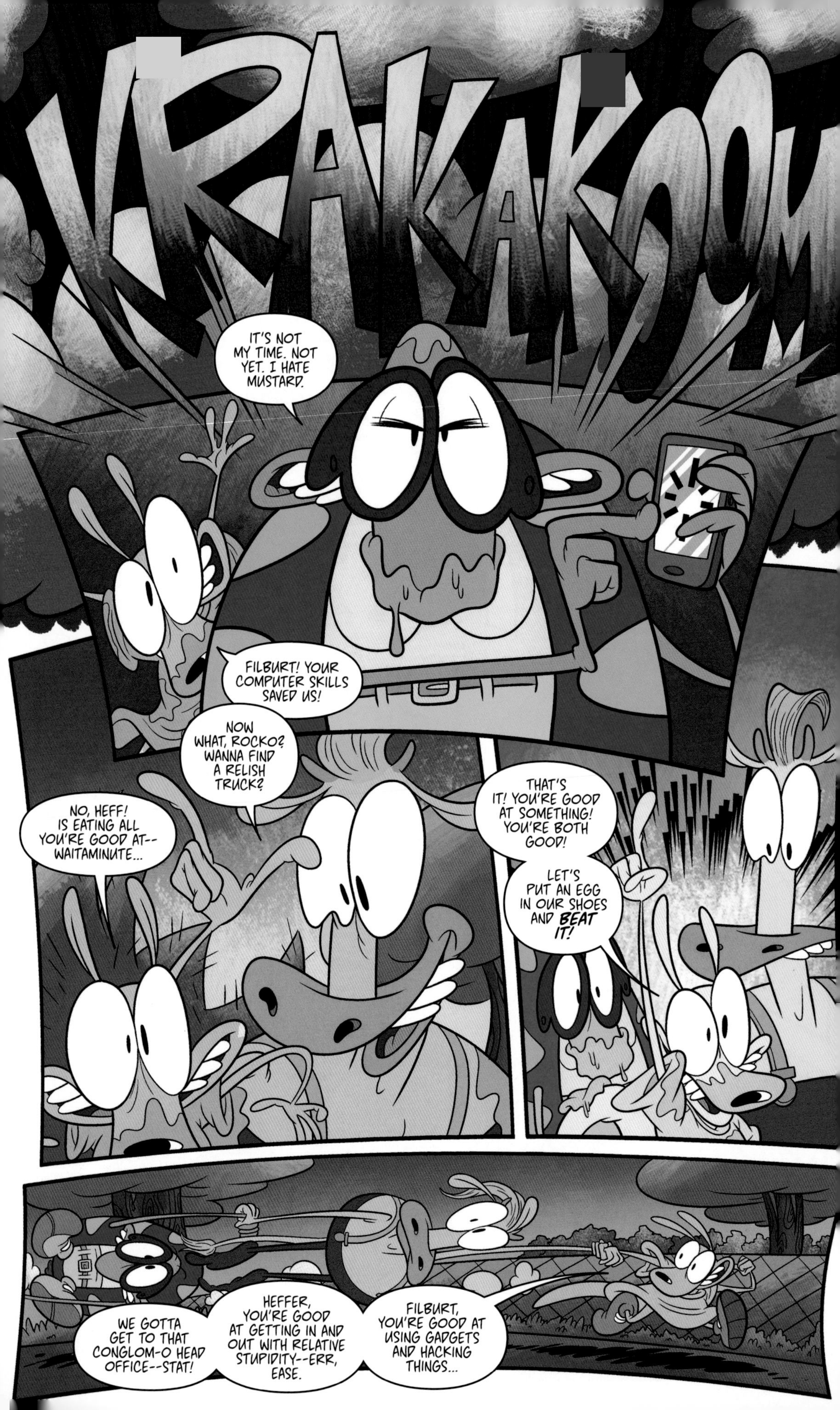

KRAKAKOOM
IT'S NOT MY TIME. NOT YET. I HATE MUSTARD.
FILBURT! YOUR COMPUTER SKILLS SAVED US!
NOW WHAT, ROCKO? WANNA FIND A RELISH TRUCK?
NO, HEFF! IS EATING ALL YOU'RE GOOD AT--WAITAMINUTE...
THAT'S IT! YOU'RE GOOD AT SOMETHING! YOU'RE BOTH GOOD!
LET'S PUT AN EGG IN OUR SHOES AND BEAT IT!
WE GOTTA GET TO THAT CONGLOM-O HEAD OFFICE--STAT!
HEFFER, YOU'RE GOOD AT GETTING IN AND OUT WITH RELATIVE STUPIDITY--ERR, EASE.
FILBURT, YOU'RE GOOD AT USING GADGETS AND HACKING THINGS...

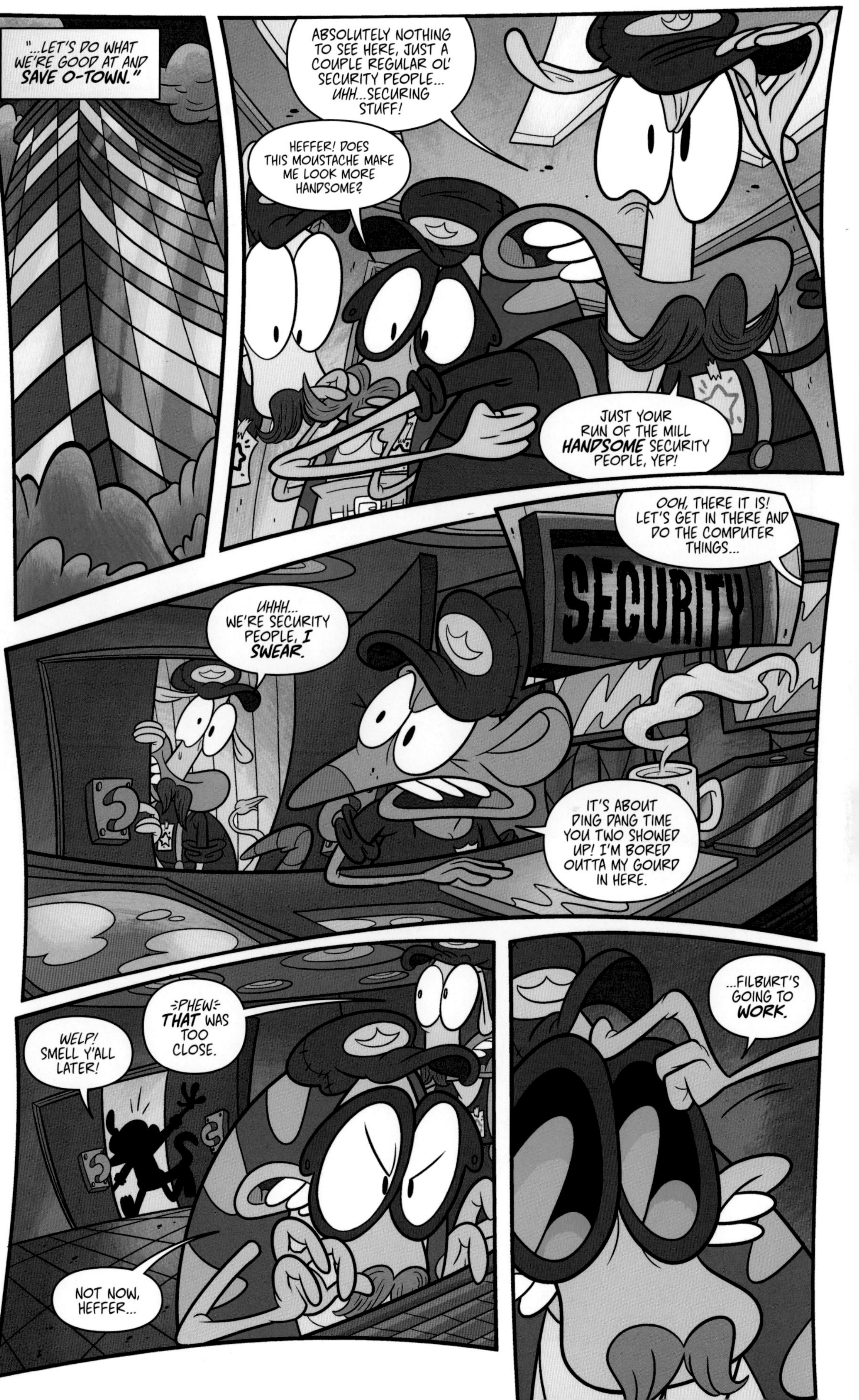

"...LET'S DO WHAT WE'RE GOOD AT AND SAVE O-TOWN."
ABSOLUTELY NOTHING TO SEE HERE, JUST A COUPLE REGULAR OL' SECURITY PEOPLE... UHH...SECURING STUFF!
HEFFER! DOES THIS MOUSTACHE MAKE ME LOOK MORE HANDSOME?
JUST YOUR RUN OF THE MILL HANDSOME SECURITY PEOPLE, YEP!
OOH, THERE IT IS! LET'S GET IN THERE AND DO THE COMPUTER THINGS...
SECURITY
UHHH... WE'RE SECURITY PEOPLE, I SWEAR.
IT'S ABOUT DING DANG TIME YOU TWO SHOWED UP! I'M BORED OUTTA MY GOURD IN HERE.
WELP! SMELL Y'ALL LATER!
PHEW THAT WAS TOO CLOSE.
NOT NOW, HEFFER...
...FILBURT'S GOING TO WORK.

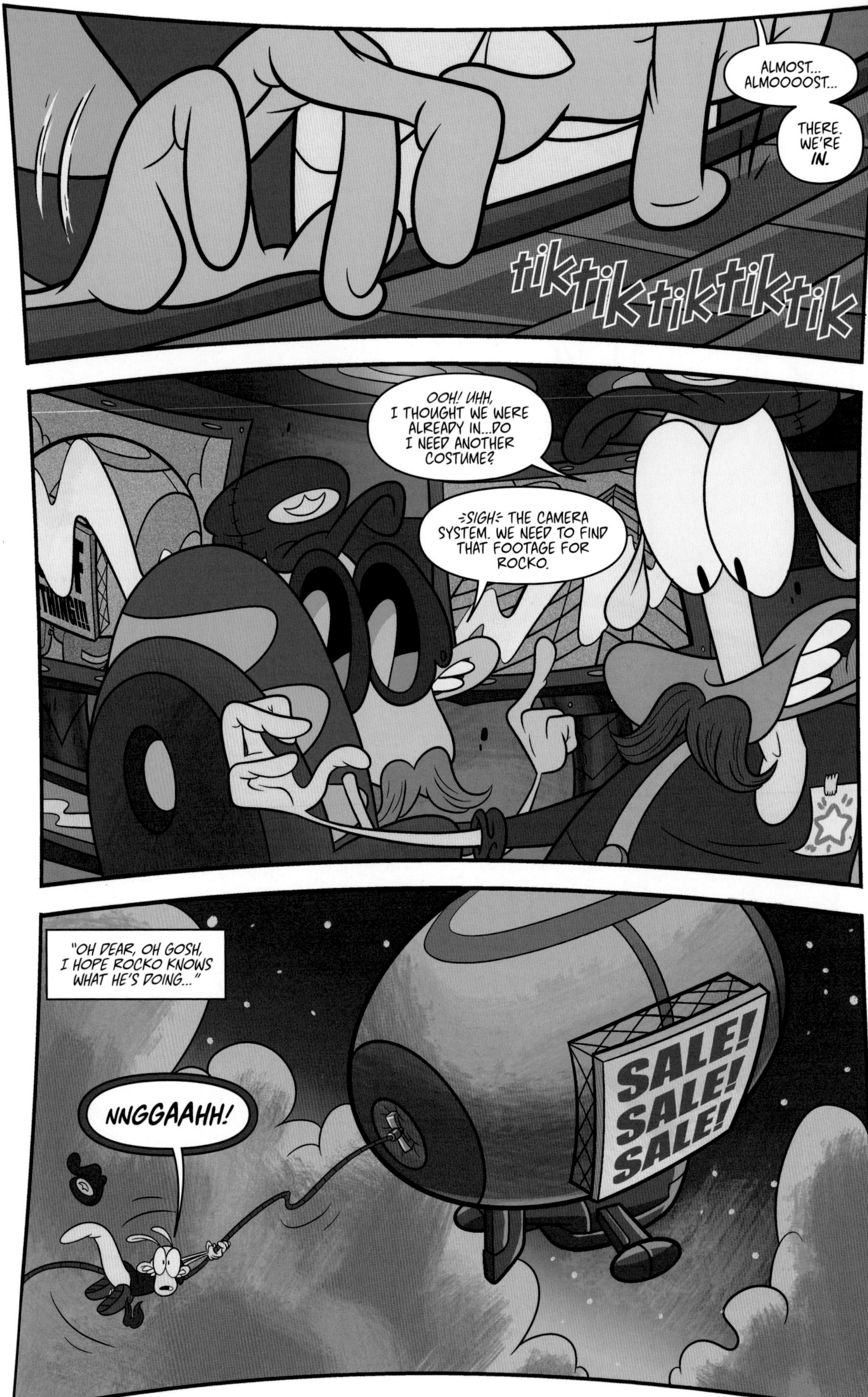
ALMOST... ALMOOOOST...
THERE. WE'RE IN.
tiktiktiktiktiktik
OOH! UHH, I THOUGHT WE WERE ALREADY IN...DO I NEED ANOTHER COSTUME?
=SIGH= THE CAMERA SYSTEM. WE NEED TO FIND THAT FOOTAGE FOR ROCKO.
"OH DEAR, OH GOSH, I HOPE ROCKO KNOWS WHAT HE'S DOING..."
NNGGAAHH!
SALE! SALE! SALE!

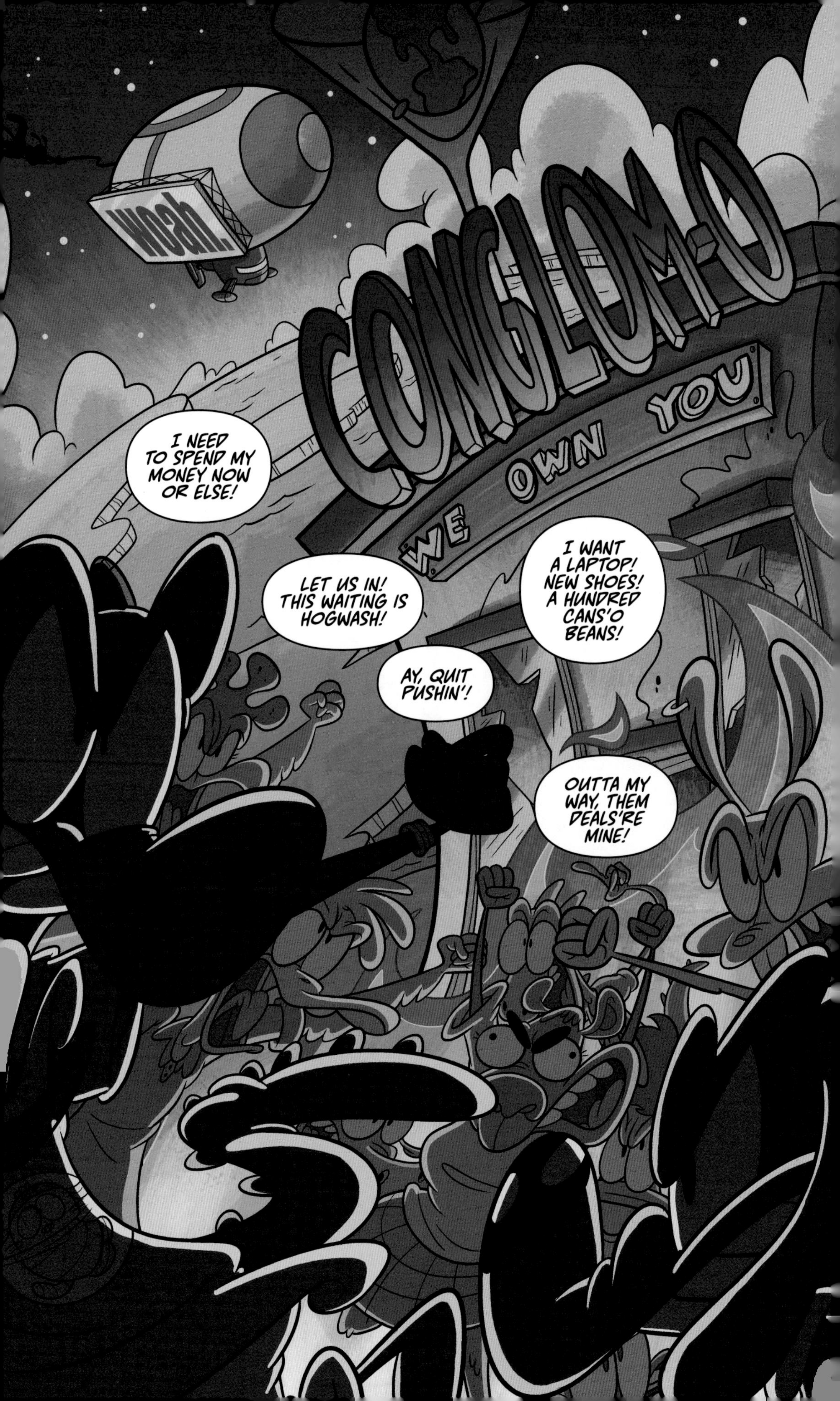
woah.
CONGLOM-O
WE OWN YOU
I NEED TO SPEND MY MONEY NOW OR ELSE!
LET US IN! THIS WAITING IS HOGWASH!
I WANT A LAPTOP! NEW SHOES! A HUNDRED CANS'O BEANS!
AY, QUIT PUSHIN'!
OUTTA MY WAY, THEM DEALS'RE MINE!

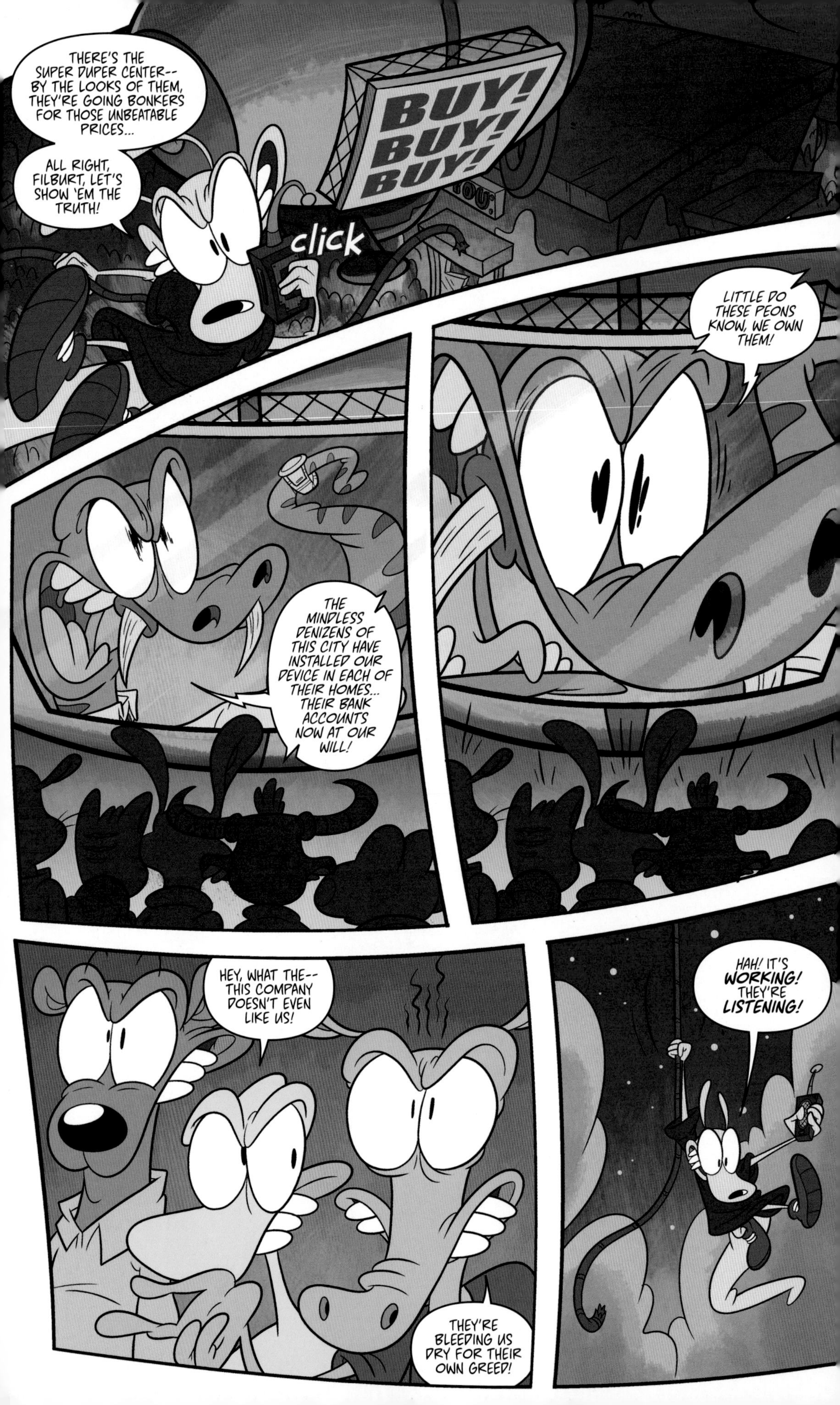
THERE'S THE SUPER DUPER CENTER-- BY THE LOOKS OF THEM, THEY'RE GOING BONKERS FOR THOSE UNBEATABLE PRICES...
ALL RIGHT, FILBURT, LET'S SHOW 'EM THE TRUTH!
BUY! BUY! BUY!
click
THE MINDLESS DENIZENS OF THIS CITY HAVE INSTALLED OUR DEVICE IN EACH OF THEIR HOMES... THEIR BANK ACCOUNTS NOW AT OUR WILL!
LITTLE DO THESE PEONS KNOW, WE OWN THEM!
HEY, WHAT THE-- THIS COMPANY DOESN'T EVEN LIKE US!
THEY'RE BLEEDING US DRY FOR THEIR OWN GREED!
HAH! IT'S WORKING! THEY'RE LISTENING!

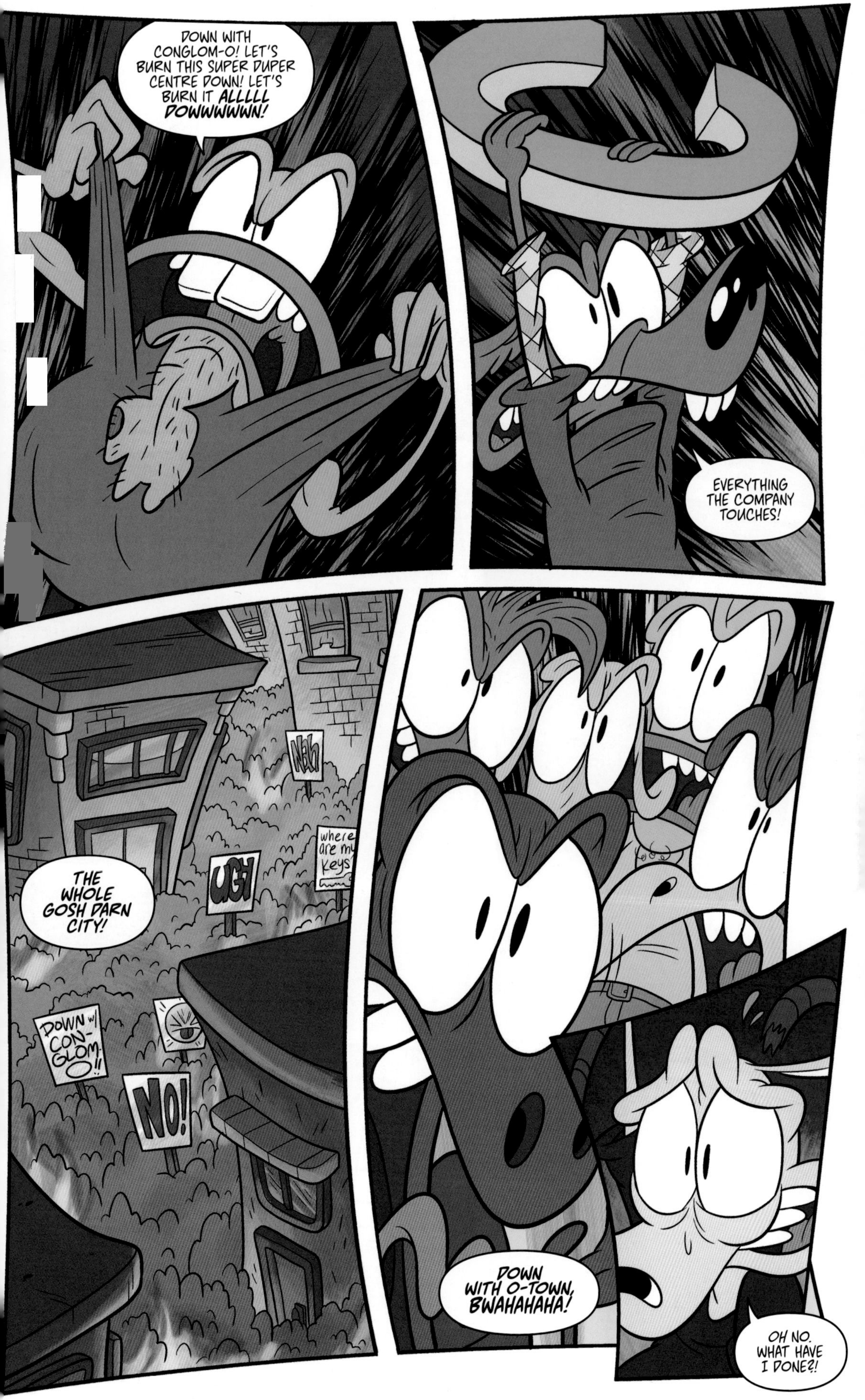
DOWN WITH CONGLOM-O! LET'S BURN THIS SUPER DUPER CENTRE DOWN! LET'S BURN IT ALLLLL DOWWWWWN!
EVERYTHING THE COMPANY TOUCHES!
THE WHOLE GOSH DARN CITY!
Nah
where are my keys
UGH
DOWN w/ CON-GLOM-O!!
NO!
DOWN WITH O-TOWN, BWAHAHAHA!
OH NO. WHAT HAVE I DONE?!

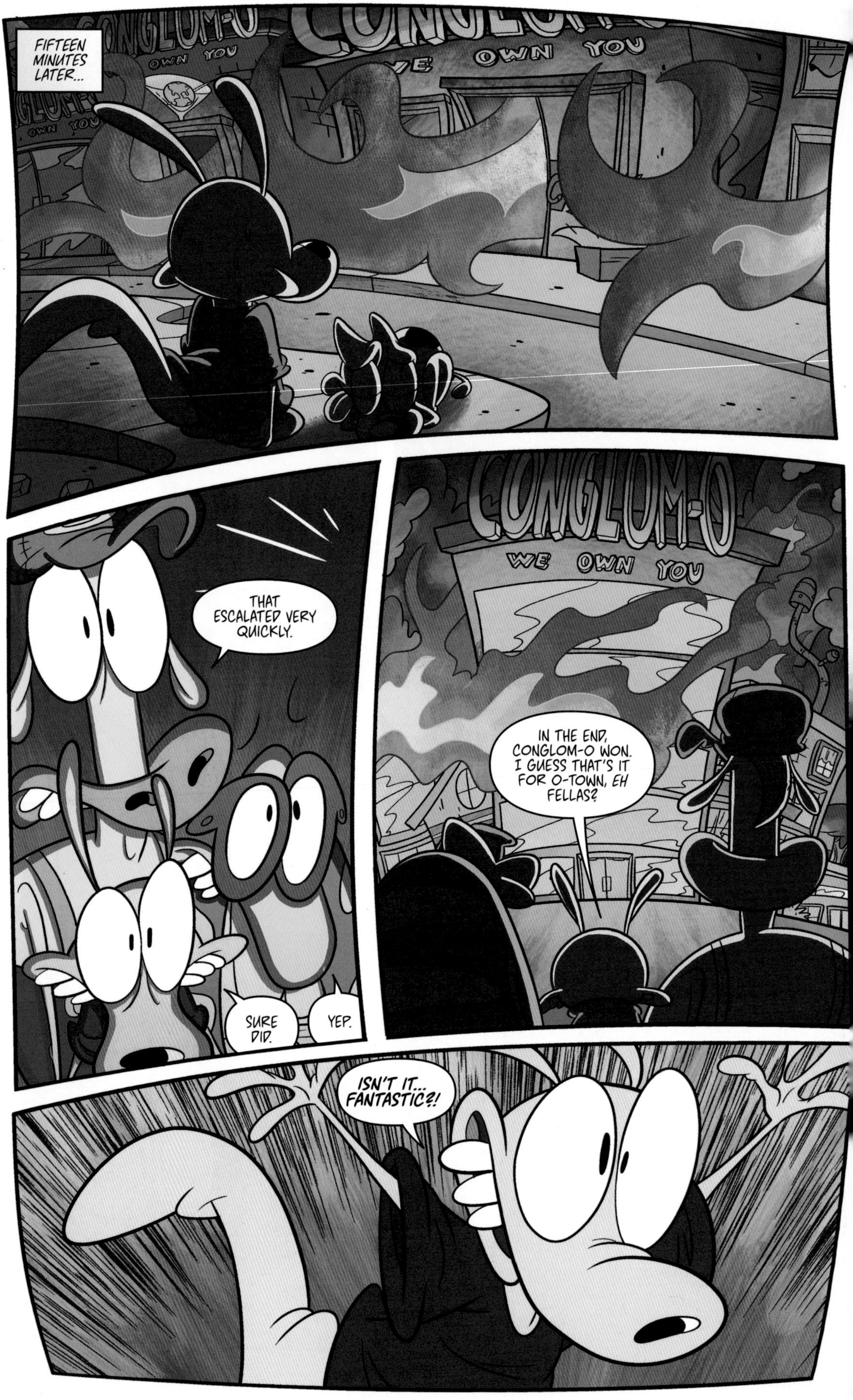
FIFTEEN MINUTES LATER...
CONGLOM-O
WE OWN YOU
THAT ESCALATED VERY QUICKLY.
SURE DID.
YEP.
CONGLOM-O
WE OWN YOU
IN THE END, CONGLOM-O WON. I GUESS THAT'S IT FOR O-TOWN, EH FELLAS?
ISN'T IT... FANTASTIC?!

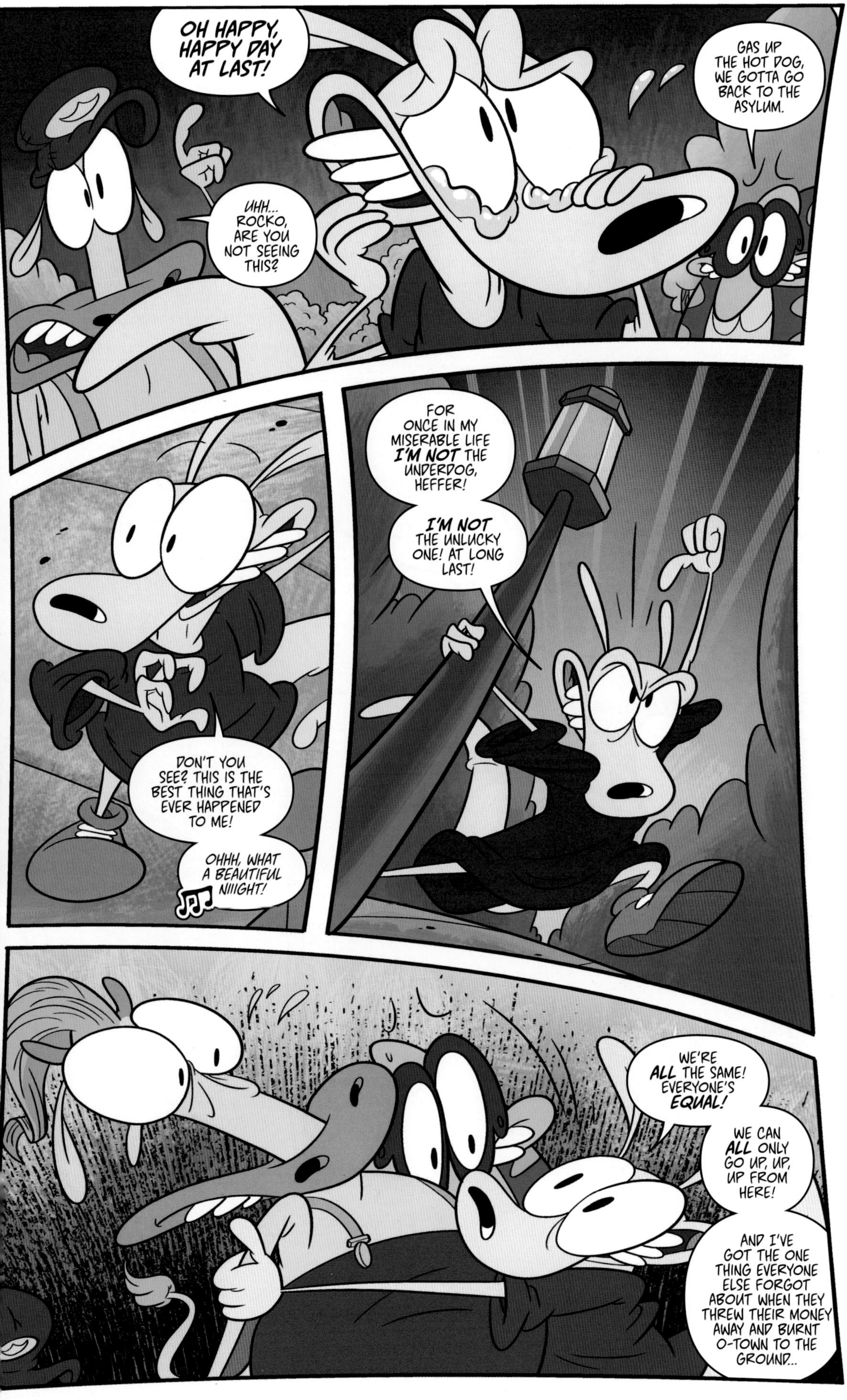
OH HAPPY, HAPPY DAY AT LAST!
GAS UP THE HOT DOG, WE GOTTA GO BACK TO THE ASYLUM.
UHH... ROCKO, ARE YOU NOT SEEING THIS?
DON'T YOU SEE? THIS IS THE BEST THING THAT'S EVER HAPPENED TO ME!
OHHH, WHAT A BEAUTIFUL NIIIGHT!
FOR ONCE IN MY MISERABLE LIFE I'M NOT THE UNDERDOG, HEFFER!
I'M NOT THE UNLUCKY ONE! AT LONG LAST!
WE'RE ALL THE SAME! EVERYONE'S EQUAL!
WE CAN ALL ONLY GO UP, UP, UP FROM HERE!
AND I'VE GOT THE ONE THING EVERYONE ELSE FORGOT ABOUT WHEN THEY THREW THEIR MONEY AWAY AND BURNT O-TOWN TO THE GROUND...

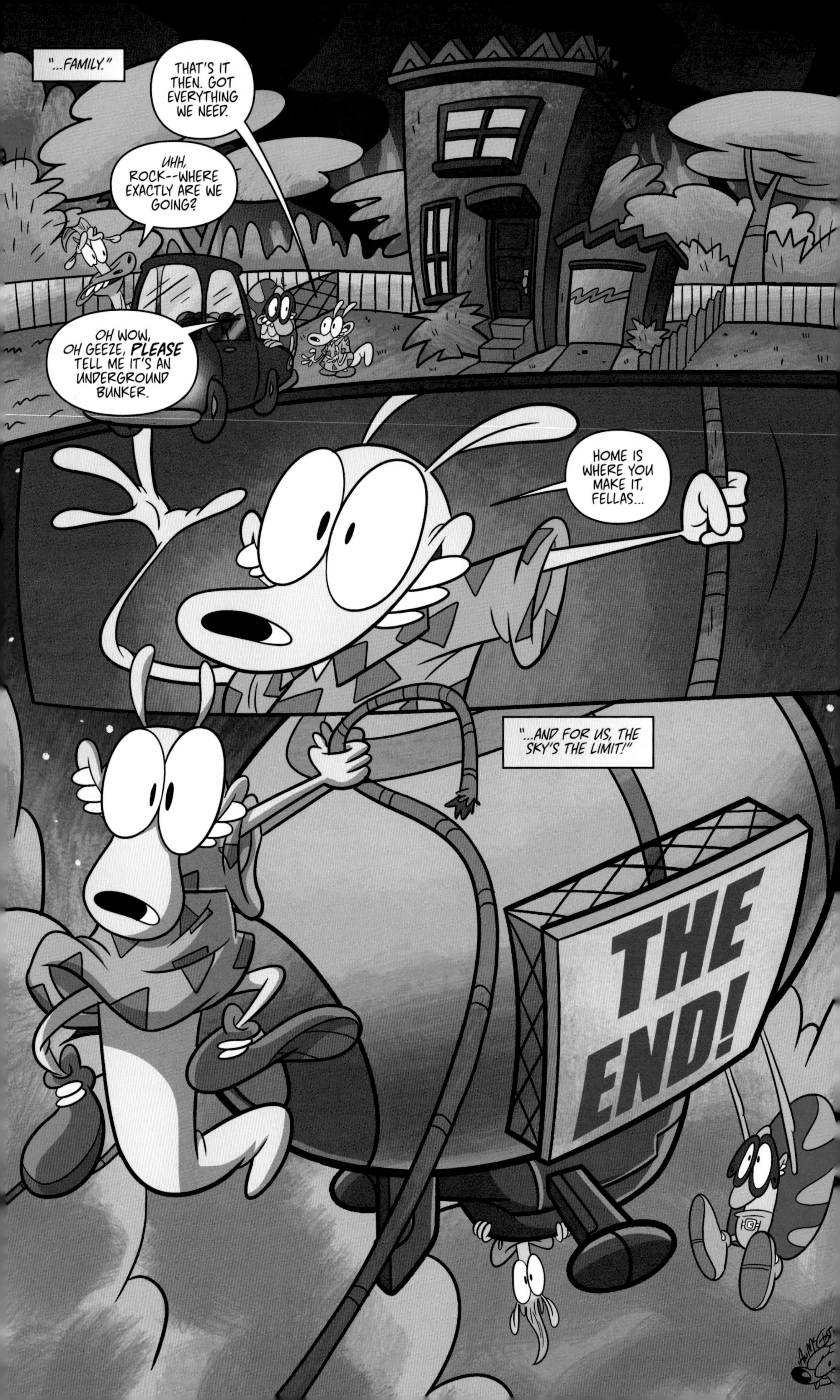

"...FAMILY."
THAT'S IT THEN. GOT EVERYTHING WE NEED.
UHH, ROCK--WHERE EXACTLY ARE WE GOING?
OH WOW, OH GEEZE, **PLEASE** TELL ME IT'S AN UNDERGROUND BUNKER.
HOME IS WHERE YOU MAKE IT, FELLAS...
"...AND FOR US, THE SKY'S THE LIMIT!"
THE END!

SHORTS

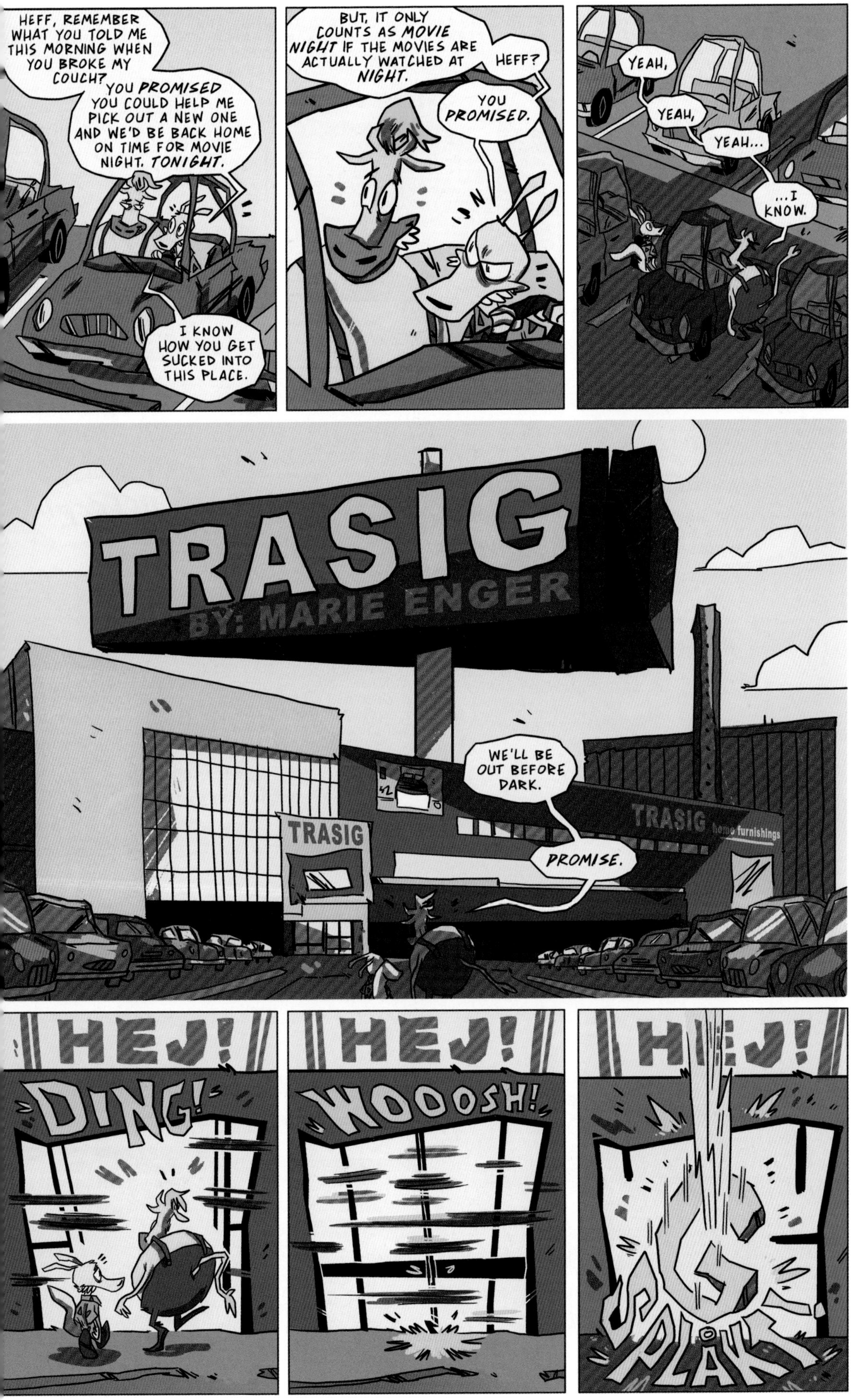
HEFF, REMEMBER WHAT YOU TOLD ME THIS MORNING WHEN YOU BROKE MY COUCH?
YOU PROMISED YOU COULD HELP ME PICK OUT A NEW ONE AND WE'D BE BACK HOME ON TIME FOR MOVIE NIGHT. TONIGHT.
I KNOW HOW YOU GET SUCKED INTO THIS PLACE.
BUT, IT ONLY COUNTS AS MOVIE NIGHT IF THE MOVIES ARE ACTUALLY WATCHED AT NIGHT.
HEFF?
YOU PROMISED.
YEAH,
YEAH,
YEAH...
...I KNOW.
TRASIG
BY: MARIE ENGER
TRASIG
TRASIG home furnishings
WE'LL BE OUT BEFORE DARK.
PROMISE.
HEJ!
DING!
HEJ!
WOOOSH!
HEJ!
SPLÅK!

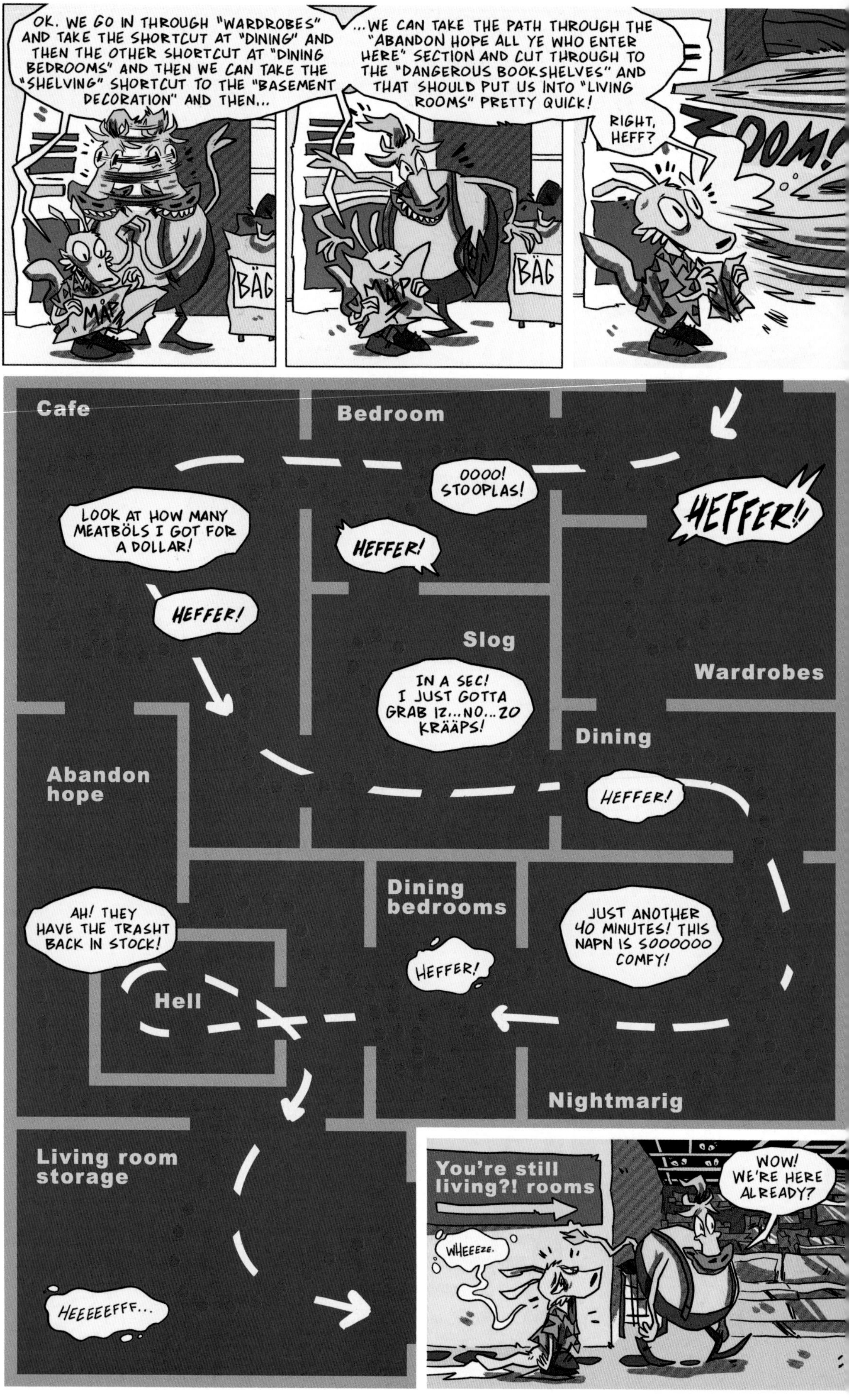

OK. WE GO IN THROUGH "WARDROBES" AND TAKE THE SHORTCUT AT "DINING" AND THEN THE OTHER SHORTCUT AT "DINING BEDROOMS" AND THEN WE CAN TAKE THE "SHELVING" SHORTCUT TO THE "BASEMENT DECORATION" AND THEN...
MÅP
BÄG
...WE CAN TAKE THE PATH THROUGH THE "ABANDON HOPE ALL YE WHO ENTER HERE" SECTION AND CUT THROUGH TO THE "DANGEROUS BOOKSHELVES" AND THAT SHOULD PUT US INTO "LIVING ROOMS" PRETTY QUICK!
MÅP
BÄG
RIGHT, HEFF?
ZOOM!
Cafe
Bedroom
OOOO! STOOPLAS!
HEFFER!!
LOOK AT HOW MANY MEATBÖLS I GOT FOR A DOLLAR!
HEFFER!
HEFFER!
Slog
Wardrobes
IN A SEC! I JUST GOTTA GRAB IZ...NO...ZO KRÄÄPS!
Dining
Abandon hope
HEFFER!
Dining bedrooms
AH! THEY HAVE THE TRASHT BACK IN STOCK!
JUST ANOTHER 40 MINUTES! THIS NAPN IS SOOOOOO COMFY!
HEFFER!
Hell
Nightmarig
Living room storage
HEEEEEFFF...
You're still living?! rooms
WOW! WE'RE HERE ALREADY?
WHEEEZE.

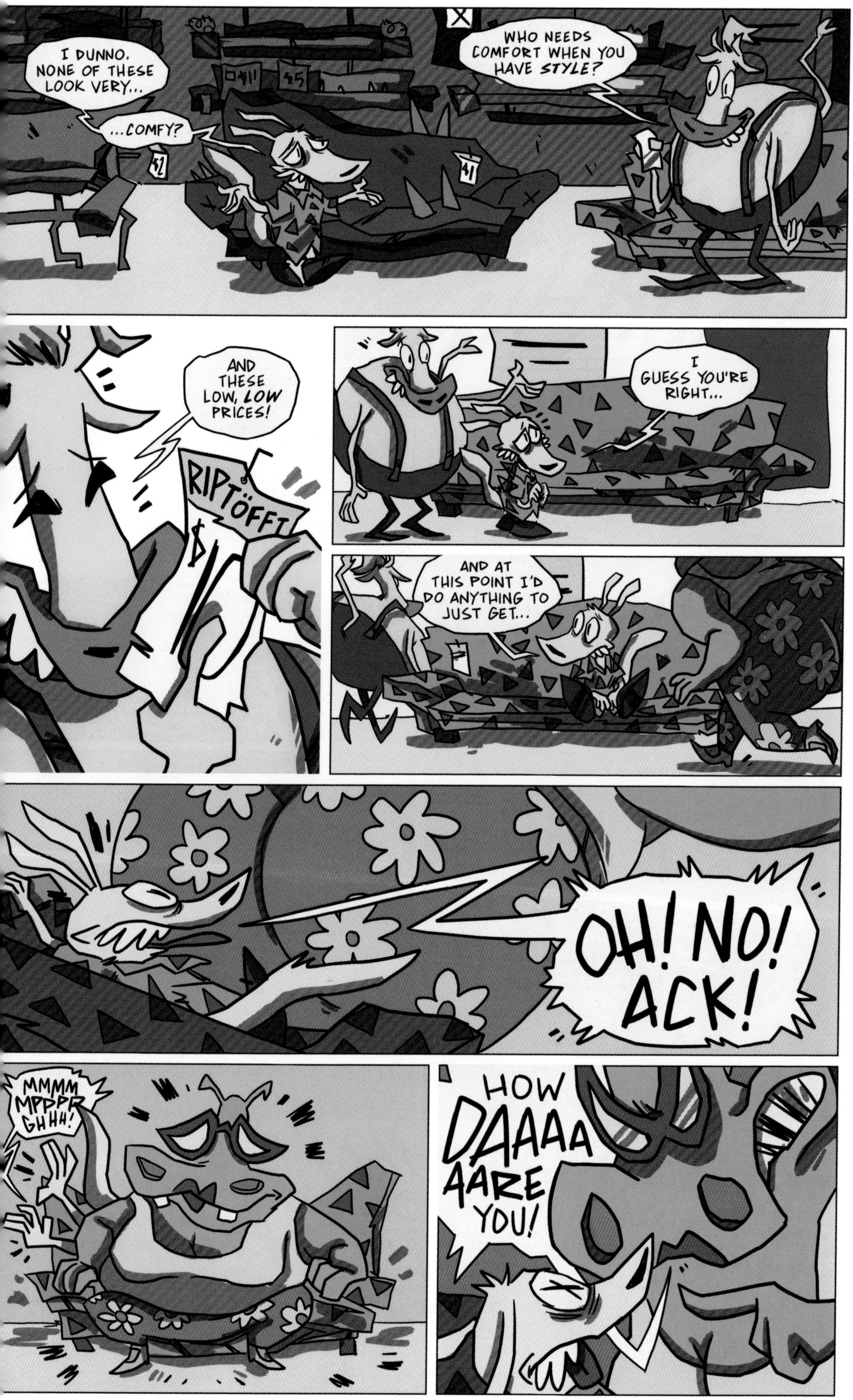
I DUNNO. NONE OF THESE LOOK VERY...
...COMFY?
WHO NEEDS COMFORT WHEN YOU HAVE STYLE?
AND THESE LOW, LOW PRICES!
RIPTÖFFT
I GUESS YOU'RE RIGHT...
AND AT THIS POINT I'D DO ANYTHING TO JUST GET...
OH! NO! ACK!
MMMM MPPPR GHHH!
HOW DAAAA AARE YOU!

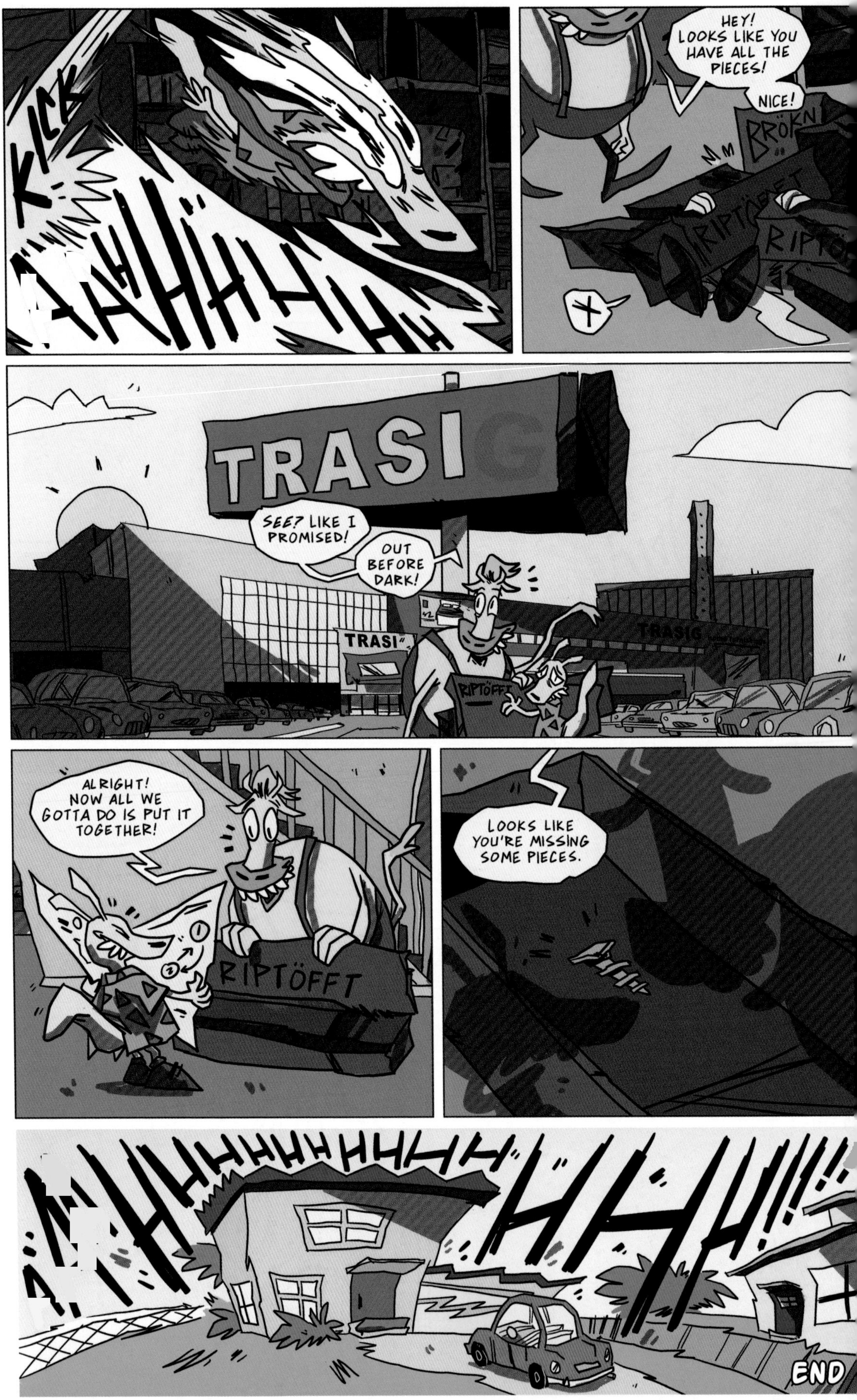
KICK
HEY! LOOKS LIKE YOU HAVE ALL THE PIECES!
NICE!
BRÖKN
TRASI
SEE? LIKE I PROMISED!
OUT BEFORE DARK!
TRASI
TRASIG
RIPTÖFFT
ALRIGHT! NOW ALL WE GOTTA DO IS PUT IT TOGETHER!
RIPTÖFFT
LOOKS LIKE YOU'RE MISSING SOME PIECES.
END

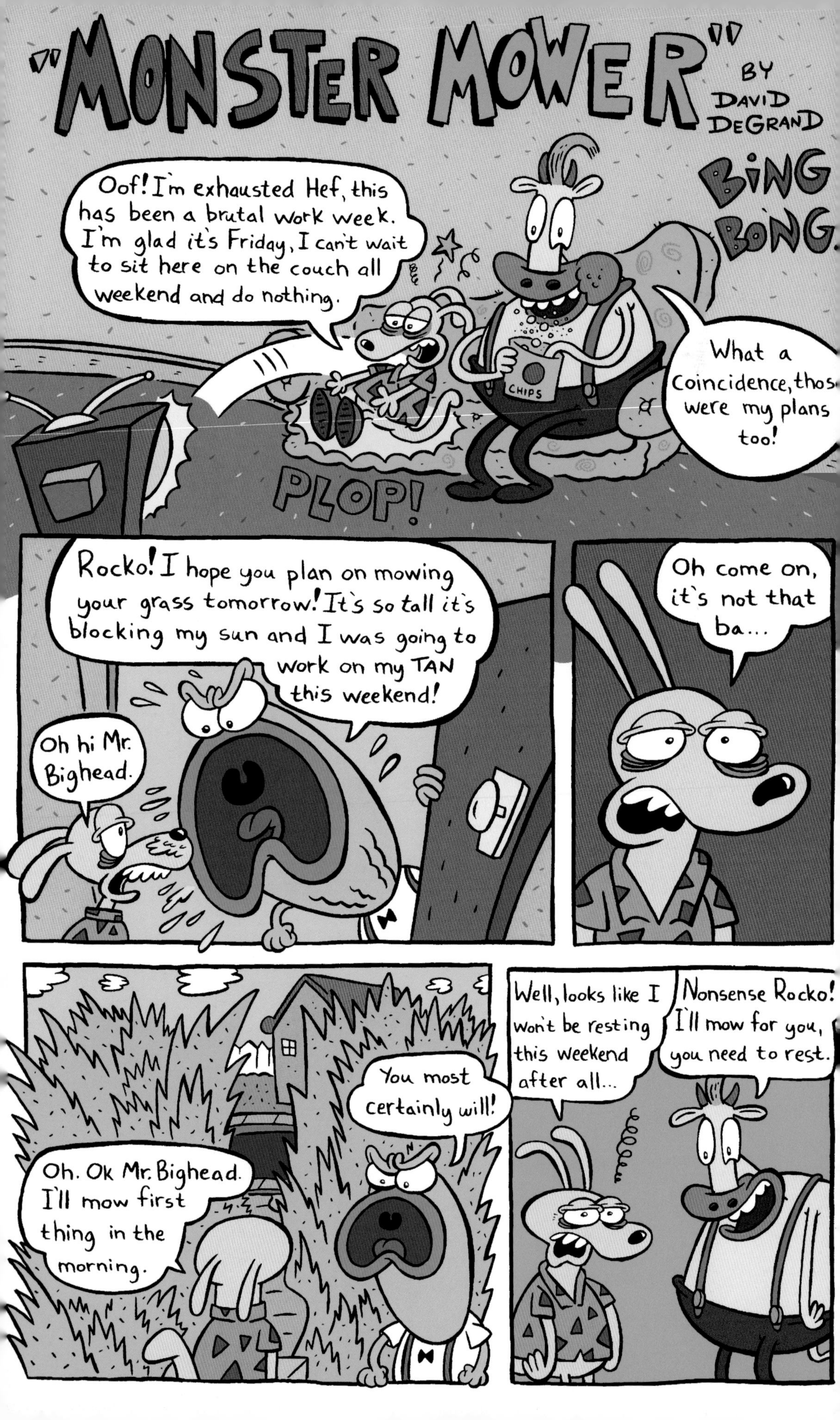
"MONSTER MOWER"
BY DAVID DEGRAND
Oof! I'm exhausted Hef, this has been a brutal work week. I'm glad it's Friday, I can't wait to sit here on the couch all weekend and do nothing.
BING BONG
What a coincidence, thos were my plans too!
PLOP!
CHIPS
Rocko! I hope you plan on mowing your grass tomorrow! It's so tall it's blocking my sun and I was going to work on my TAN this weekend!
Oh hi Mr. Bighead.
Oh come on, it's not that ba...
You most certainly will!
Oh. Ok Mr. Bighead. I'll mow first thing in the morning.
Well, looks like I won't be resting this weekend after all...
Nonsense Rocko! I'll mow for you, you need to rest.

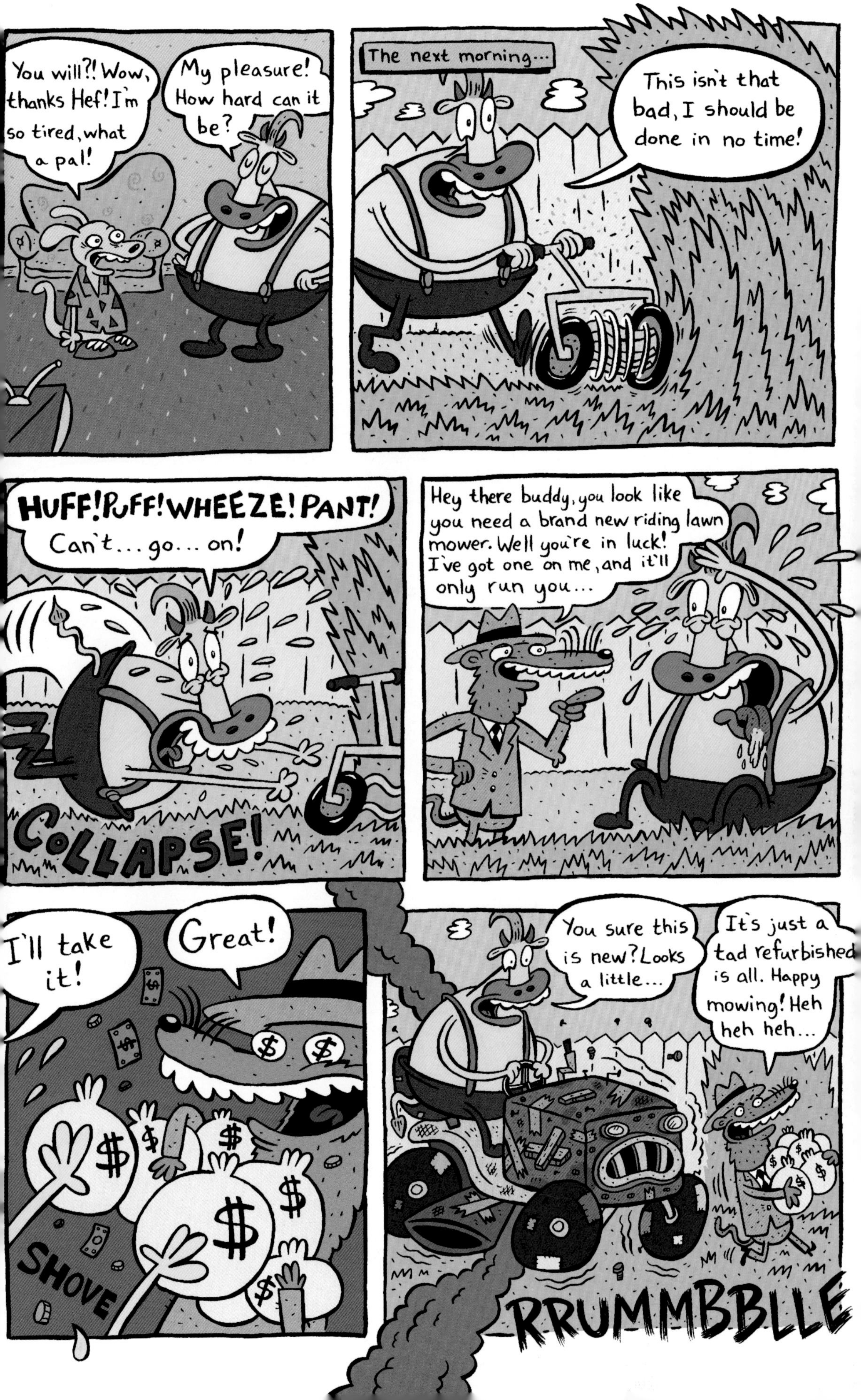

You will?! Wow, thanks Hef! I'm so tired, what a pal!
My pleasure! How hard can it be?
The next morning...
This isn't that bad, I should be done in no time!
HUFF! PUFF! WHEEZE! PANT! Can't... go... on!
COLLAPSE!
Hey there buddy, you look like you need a brand new riding lawn mower. Well you're in luck! I've got one on me, and it'll only run you...
I'll take it!
Great!
SHOVE
You sure this is new? Looks a little...
It's just a tad refurbished is all. Happy mowing! Heh heh heh...
RRUMMBBLLE

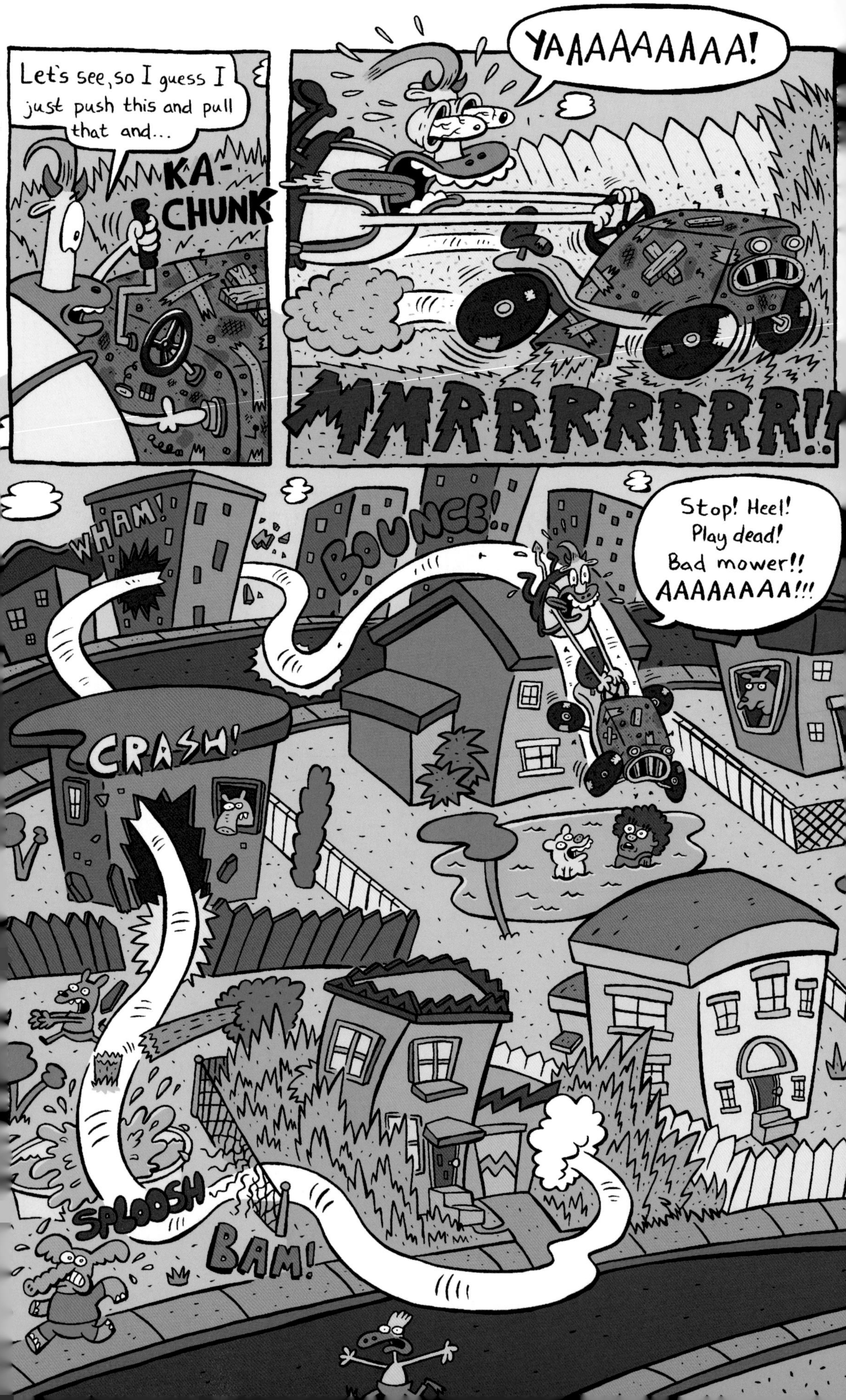

Let's see, so I guess I just push this and pull that and...
KA-CHUNK
YAAAAAAAAA!
MMRRRRRRR!!
WHAM!
BOUNCE!
Stop! Heel! Play dead! Bad mower!! AAAAAAAA!!!
CRASH!
SPLOOSH
BAM!

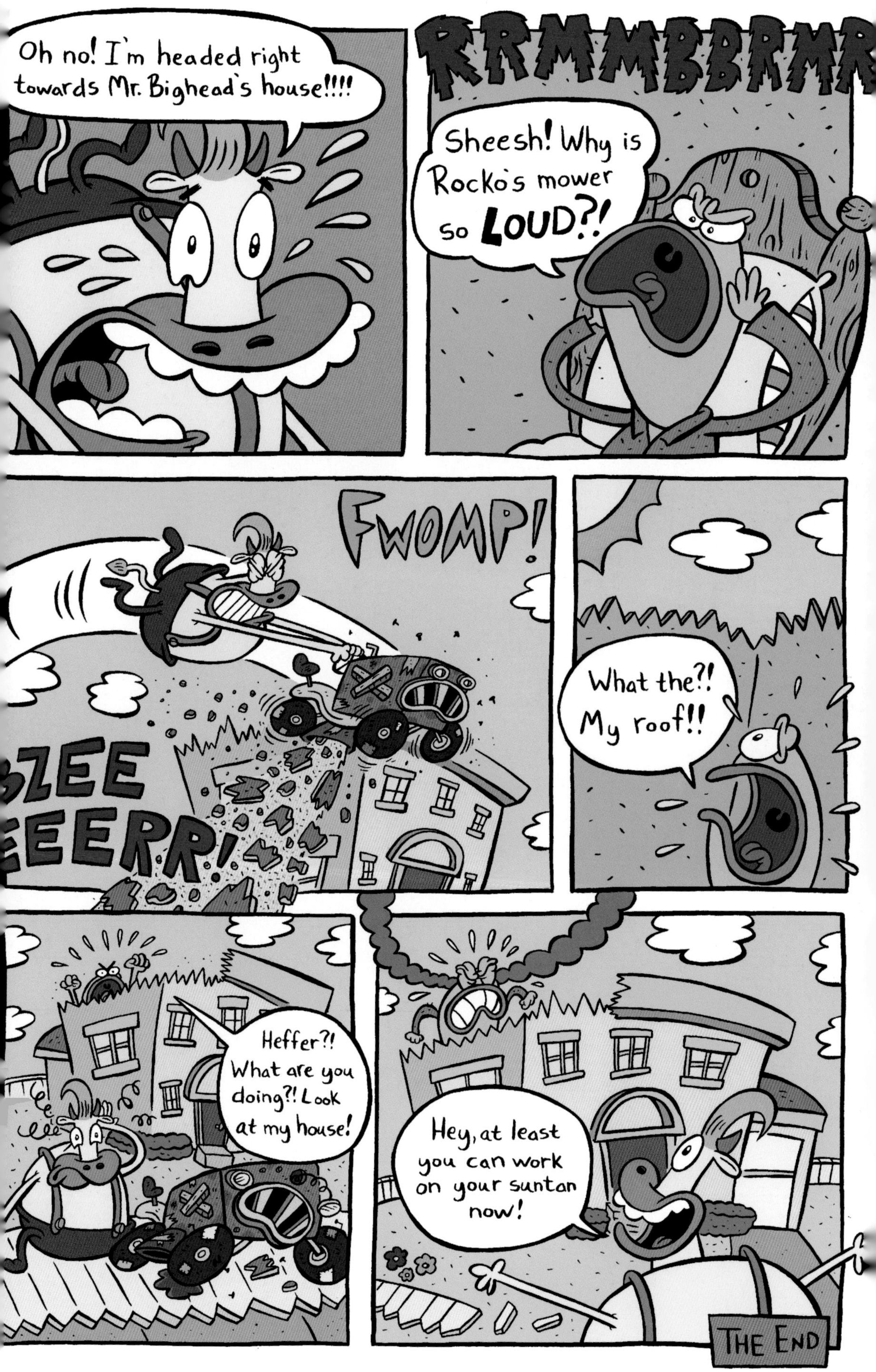
Oh no! I'm headed right towards Mr. Bighead's house!!!!
RRMMBBRMR
Sheesh! Why is Rocko's mower so LOUD?!
FWOMP!
ZEE EEERR!
What the?! My roof!!
Heffer?! What are you doing?! Look at my house!
Hey, at least you can work on your suntan now!
THE END

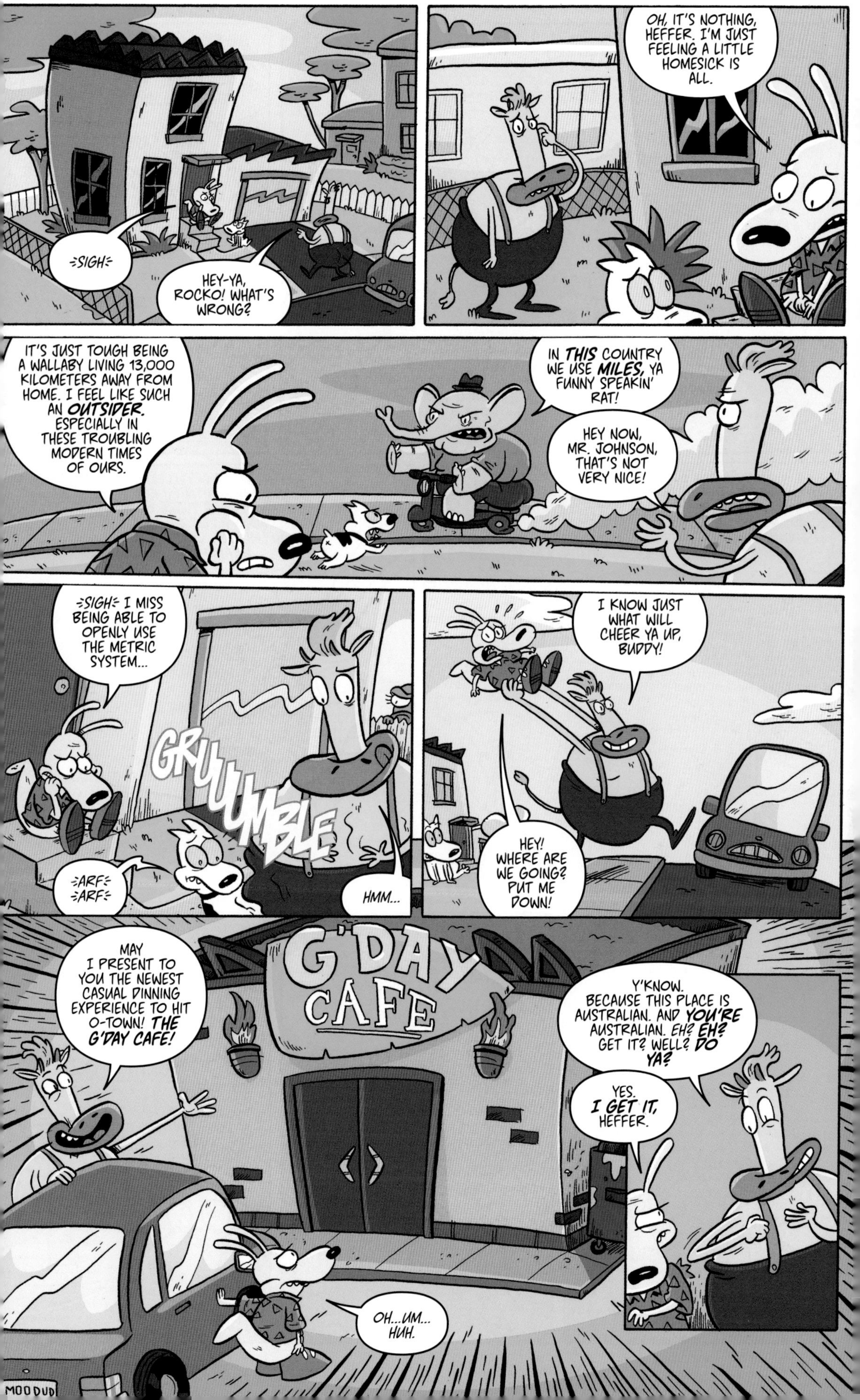

=SIGH=
HEY-YA, ROCKO! WHAT'S WRONG?
OH, IT'S NOTHING, HEFFER. I'M JUST FEELING A LITTLE HOMESICK IS ALL.
IT'S JUST TOUGH BEING A WALLABY LIVING 13,000 KILOMETERS AWAY FROM HOME. I FEEL LIKE SUCH AN OUTSIDER. ESPECIALLY IN THESE TROUBLING MODERN TIMES OF OURS.
IN THIS COUNTRY WE USE MILES, YA FUNNY SPEAKIN' RAT!
HEY NOW, MR. JOHNSON, THAT'S NOT VERY NICE!
=SIGH= I MISS BEING ABLE TO OPENLY USE THE METRIC SYSTEM...
GRUUUMBLE
=ARF= =ARF=
HMM...
I KNOW JUST WHAT WILL CHEER YA UP, BUDDY!
HEY! WHERE ARE WE GOING? PUT ME DOWN!
G'DAY CAFE
MAY I PRESENT TO YOU THE NEWEST CASUAL DINNING EXPERIENCE TO HIT O-TOWN! THE G'DAY CAFE!
Y'KNOW. BECAUSE THIS PLACE IS AUSTRALIAN. AND YOU'RE AUSTRALIAN. EH? EH? GET IT? WELL? DO YA?
YES. I GET IT, HEFFER.
OH...UM... HUH.
MOODUD

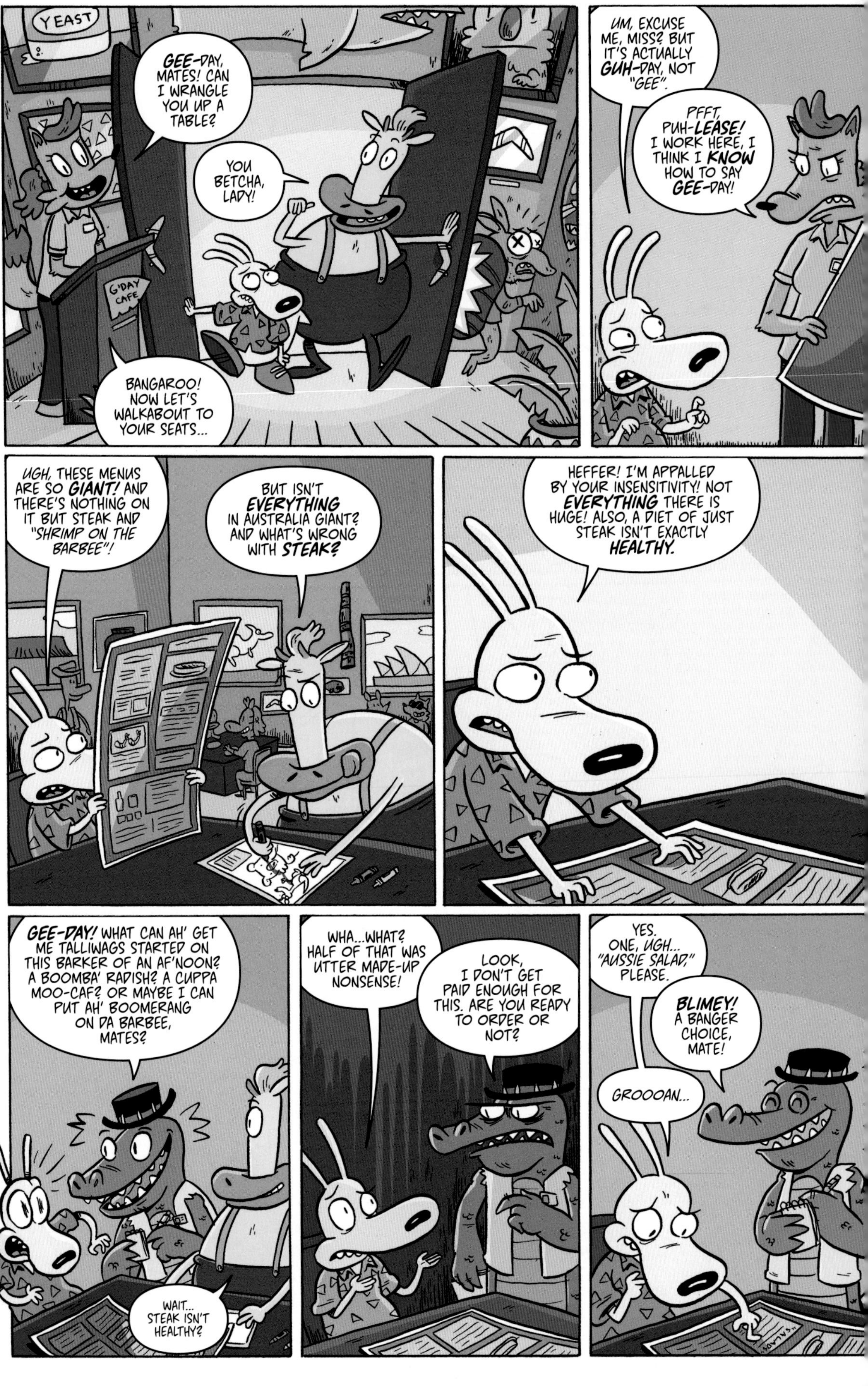
YEAST
GEE-DAY, MATES! CAN I WRANGLE YOU UP A TABLE?
YOU BETCHA, LADY!
G'DAY CAFE
BANGAROO! NOW LET'S WALKABOUT TO YOUR SEATS...
UM, EXCUSE ME, MISS? BUT IT'S ACTUALLY GUH-DAY, NOT "GEE".
PFFT, PUH-LEASE! I WORK HERE, I THINK I KNOW HOW TO SAY GEE-DAY!
UGH, THESE MENUS ARE SO GIANT! AND THERE'S NOTHING ON IT BUT STEAK AND "SHRIMP ON THE BARBEE"!
BUT ISN'T EVERYTHING IN AUSTRALIA GIANT? AND WHAT'S WRONG WITH STEAK?
HEFFER! I'M APPALLED BY YOUR INSENSITIVITY! NOT EVERYTHING THERE IS HUGE! ALSO, A DIET OF JUST STEAK ISN'T EXACTLY HEALTHY.
GEE-DAY! WHAT CAN AH' GET ME TALLIWAGS STARTED ON THIS BARKER OF AN AF'NOON? A BOOMBA' RADISH? A CUPPA MOO-CAF? OR MAYBE I CAN PUT AH' BOOMERANG ON DA BARBEE, MATES?
WAIT... STEAK ISN'T HEALTHY?
WHA...WHAT? HALF OF THAT WAS UTTER MADE-UP NONSENSE!
LOOK, I DON'T GET PAID ENOUGH FOR THIS. ARE YOU READY TO ORDER OR NOT?
YES. ONE, UGH... "AUSSIE SALAD," PLEASE.
BLIMEY! A BANGER CHOICE, MATE!
GROOOAN...

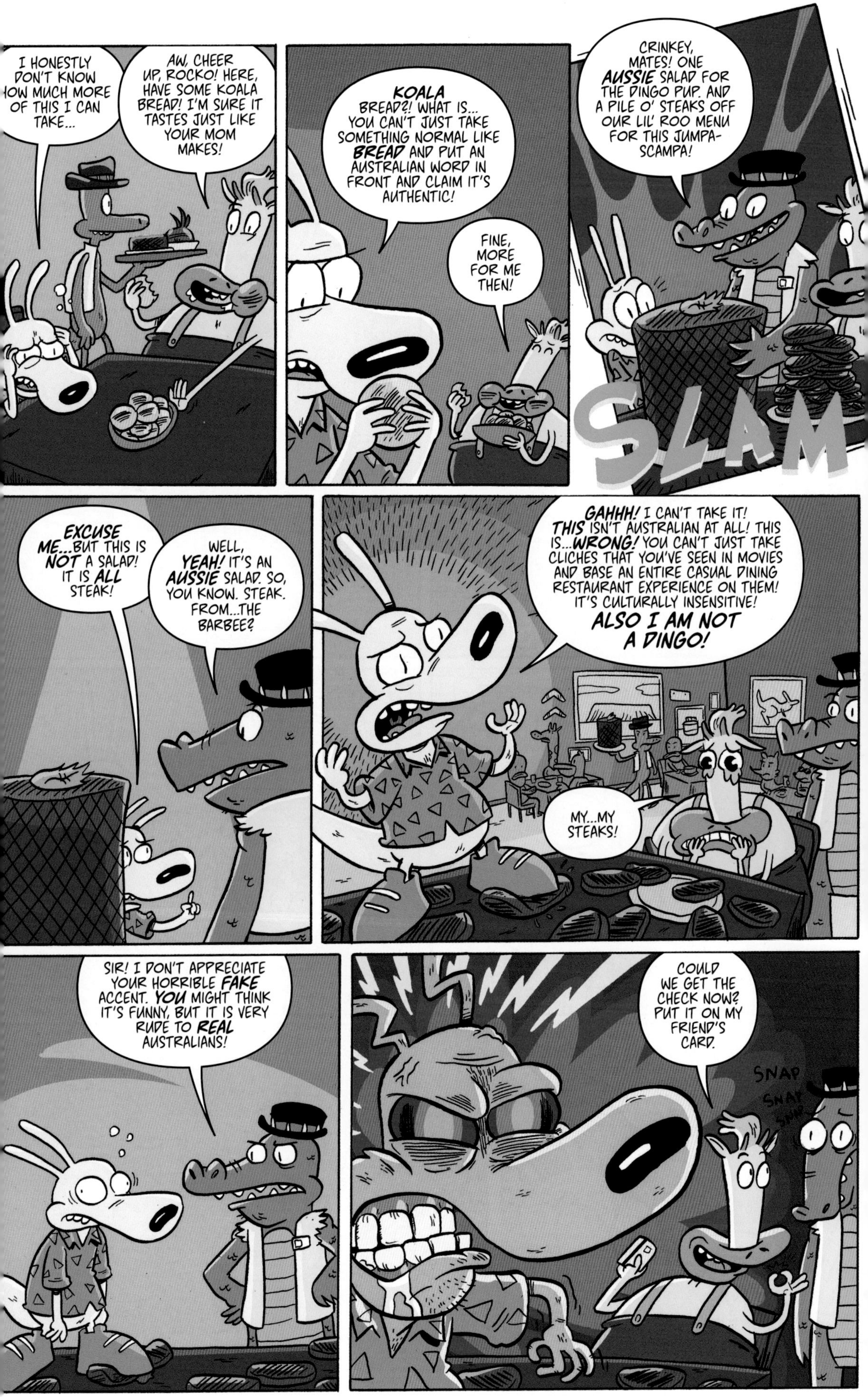

I HONESTLY DON'T KNOW HOW MUCH MORE OF THIS I CAN TAKE...
AW, CHEER UP, ROCKO! HERE, HAVE SOME KOALA BREAD! I'M SURE IT TASTES JUST LIKE YOUR MOM MAKES!
KOALA BREAD?! WHAT IS... YOU CAN'T JUST TAKE SOMETHING NORMAL LIKE BREAD AND PUT AN AUSTRALIAN WORD IN FRONT AND CLAIM IT'S AUTHENTIC!
FINE, MORE FOR ME THEN!
CRINKEY, MATES! ONE AUSSIE SALAD FOR THE DINGO PUP. AND A PILE O' STEAKS OFF OUR LIL' ROO MENU FOR THIS JUMPA-SCAMPA!
SLAM
EXCUSE ME...BUT THIS IS NOT A SALAD! IT IS ALL STEAK!
WELL, YEAH! IT'S AN AUSSIE SALAD. SO, YOU KNOW. STEAK. FROM...THE BARBEE?
GAHHH! I CAN'T TAKE IT! THIS ISN'T AUSTRALIAN AT ALL! THIS IS...WRONG! YOU CAN'T JUST TAKE CLICHES THAT YOU'VE SEEN IN MOVIES AND BASE AN ENTIRE CASUAL DINING RESTAURANT EXPERIENCE ON THEM! IT'S CULTURALLY INSENSITIVE! ALSO I AM NOT A DINGO!
MY...MY STEAKS!
SIR! I DON'T APPRECIATE YOUR HORRIBLE FAKE ACCENT. YOU MIGHT THINK IT'S FUNNY, BUT IT IS VERY RUDE TO REAL AUSTRALIANS!
COULD WE GET THE CHECK NOW? PUT IT ON MY FRIEND'S CARD.
SNAP
SNAP
SNAP

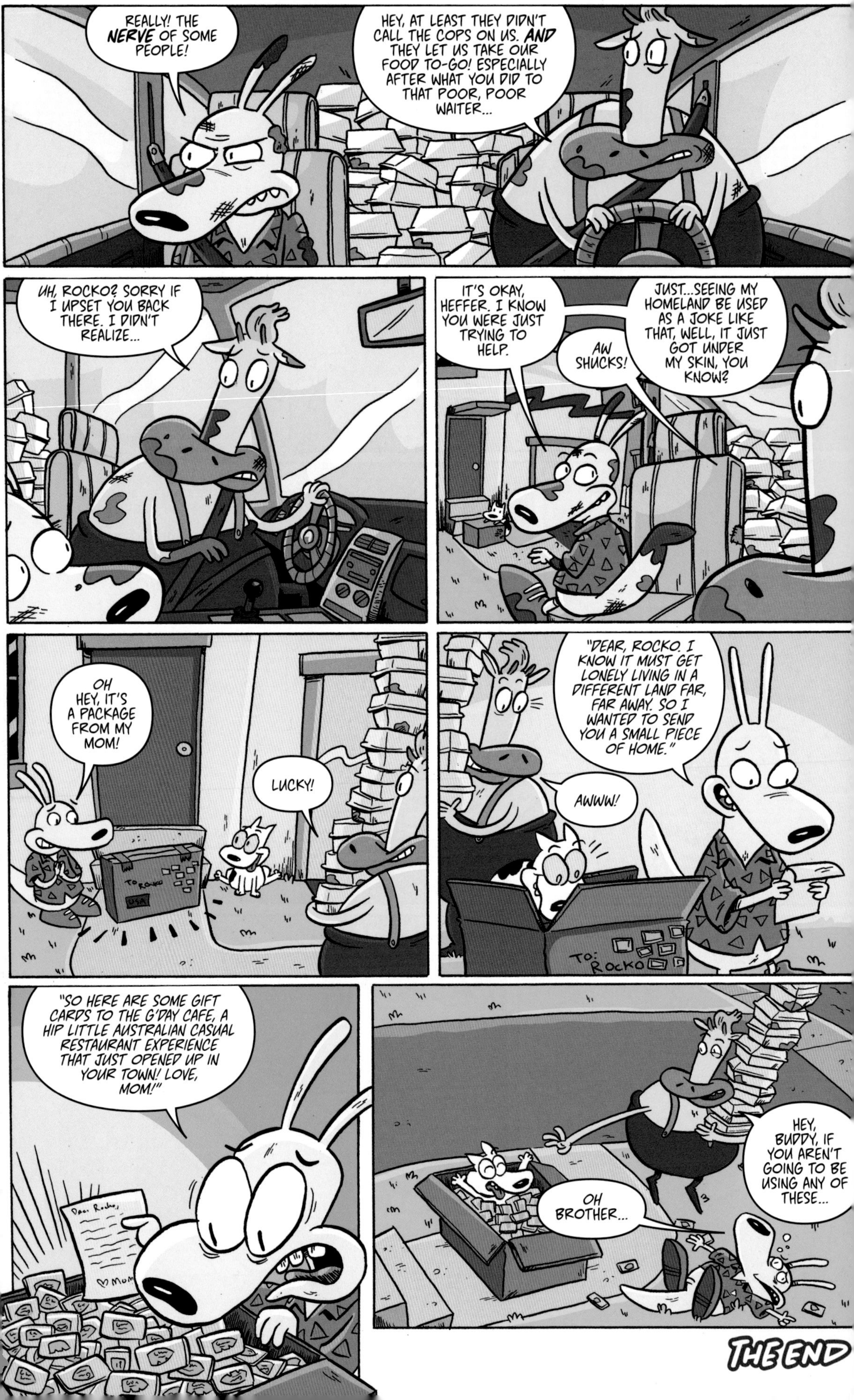
REALLY! THE **NERVE** OF SOME PEOPLE!
HEY, AT LEAST THEY DIDN'T CALL THE COPS ON US. **AND** THEY LET US TAKE OUR FOOD TO-GO! ESPECIALLY AFTER WHAT YOU DID TO THAT POOR, POOR WAITER...
UH, ROCKO? SORRY IF I UPSET YOU BACK THERE. I DIDN'T REALIZE...
IT'S OKAY, HEFFER. I KNOW YOU WERE JUST TRYING TO HELP.
JUST...SEEING MY HOMELAND BE USED AS A JOKE LIKE THAT, WELL, IT JUST GOT UNDER MY SKIN, YOU KNOW?
AW SHUCKS!
OH HEY, IT'S A PACKAGE FROM MY MOM!
LUCKY!
TO ROCKO
USA
"DEAR, ROCKO. I KNOW IT MUST GET LONELY LIVING IN A DIFFERENT LAND FAR, FAR AWAY. SO I WANTED TO SEND YOU A SMALL PIECE OF HOME."
AWWW!
TO: ROCKO
"SO HERE ARE SOME GIFT CARDS TO THE G'DAY CAFE, A HIP LITTLE AUSTRALIAN CASUAL RESTAURANT EXPERIENCE THAT JUST OPENED UP IN YOUR TOWN! LOVE, MOM!"
Dear Rocko,
♡ Mom
HEY, BUDDY, IF YOU AREN'T GOING TO BE USING ANY OF THESE...
OH BROTHER...
THE END

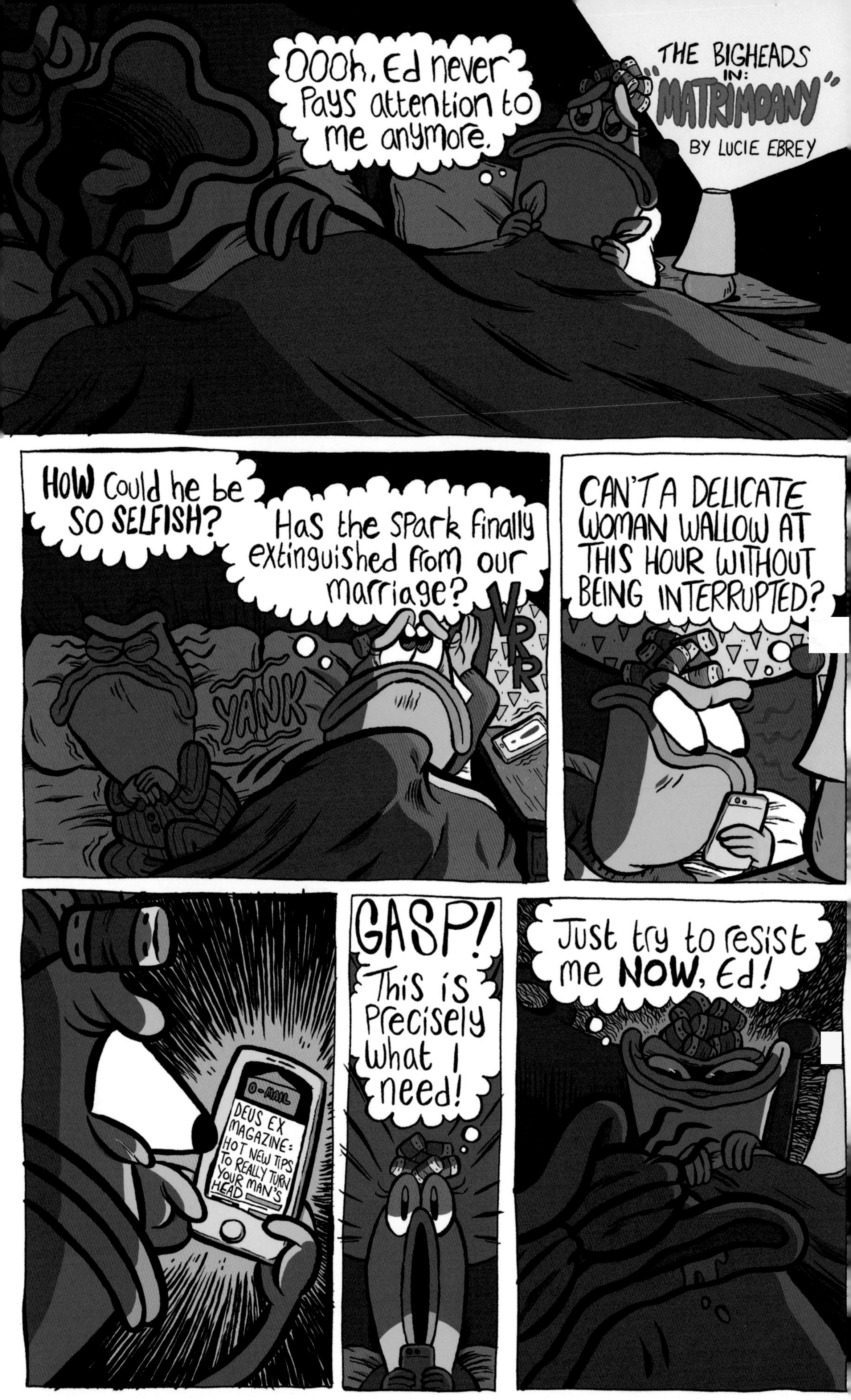
THE BIGHEADS IN: "MATRIMOANY"
BY LUCIE EBREY
Oooh, Ed never pays attention to me anymore.
HOW could he be SO SELFISH?
Has the spark finally extinguished from our marriage?
YANK
VRR
CAN'T A DELICATE WOMAN WALLOW AT THIS HOUR WITHOUT BEING INTERRUPTED?
O-MAIL
DEUS EX MAGAZINE: HOT NEW TIPS TO REALLY TURN YOUR MAN'S HEAD
GASP!
This is precisely what I need!
Just try to resist me NOW, Ed!

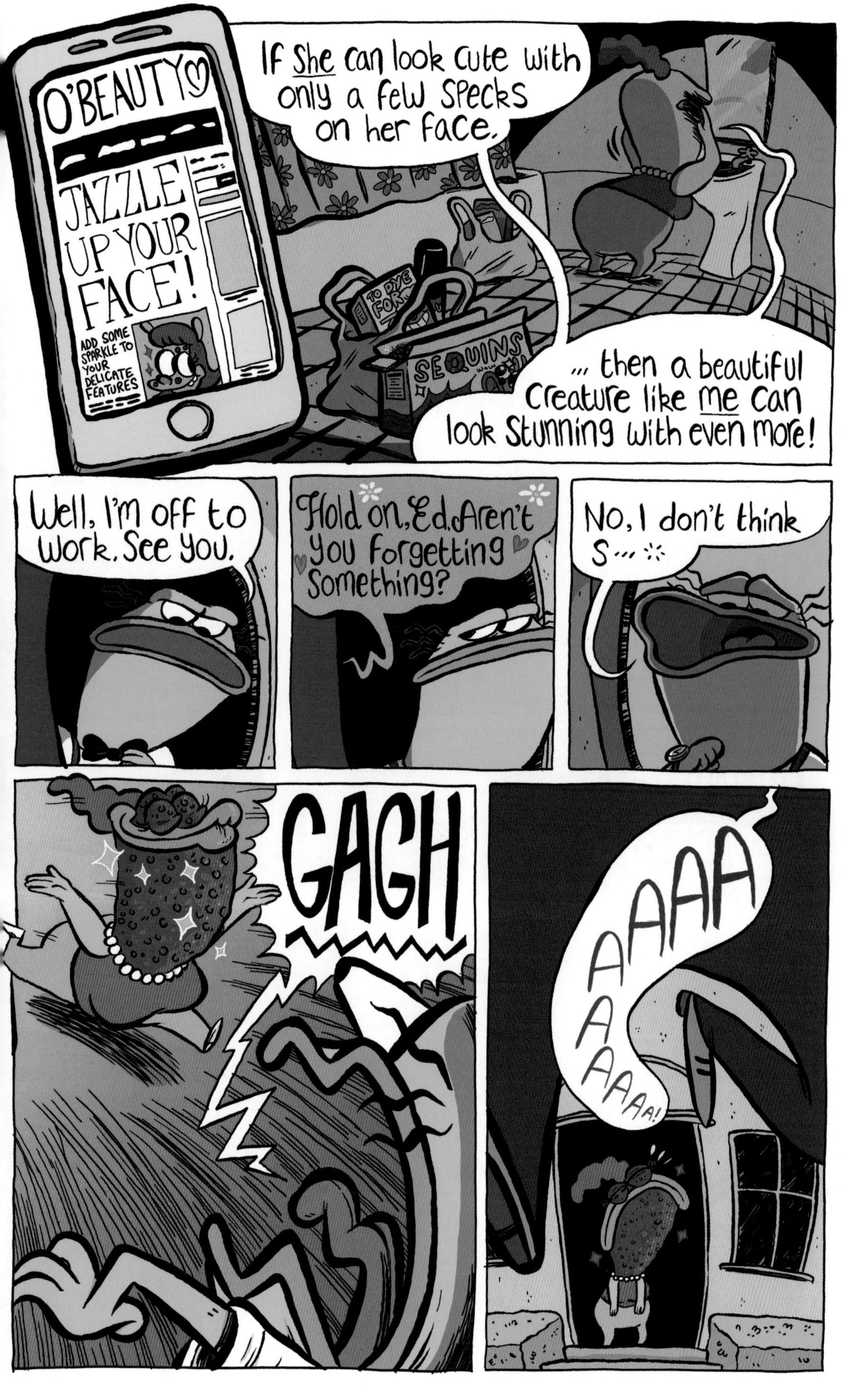
O'BEAUTY
JAZZLE UP YOUR FACE!
ADD SOME SPARKLE TO YOUR DELICATE FEATURES
TO DYE FOR
SEQUINS
If She can look cute with only a few Specks on her face,
... then a beautiful creature like me can look stunning with even more!
Well, I'm off to work. See you.
Hold on, Ed. Aren't you forgetting something?
No, I don't think s...
GAGH
AAAAAAAAA!

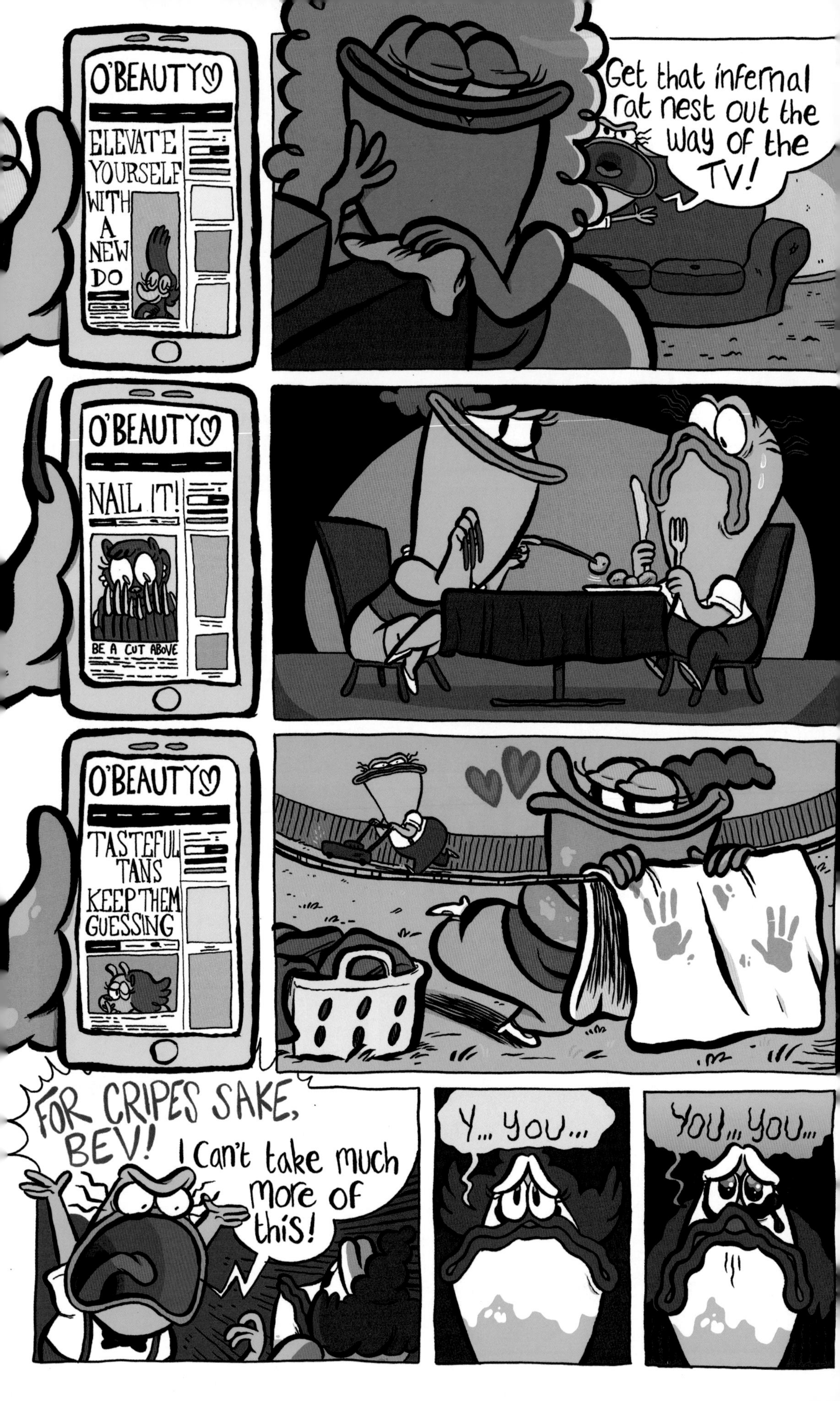

O'BEAUTY
ELEVATE YOURSELF WITH A NEW DO
Get that infernal rat nest out the way of the TV!
O'BEAUTY
NAIL IT!
BE A CUT ABOVE
O'BEAUTY
TASTEFUL TANS KEEP THEM GUESSING
FOR CRIPES SAKE, BEV!
I can't take much more of this!
Y... YOU...
YOU... YOU...

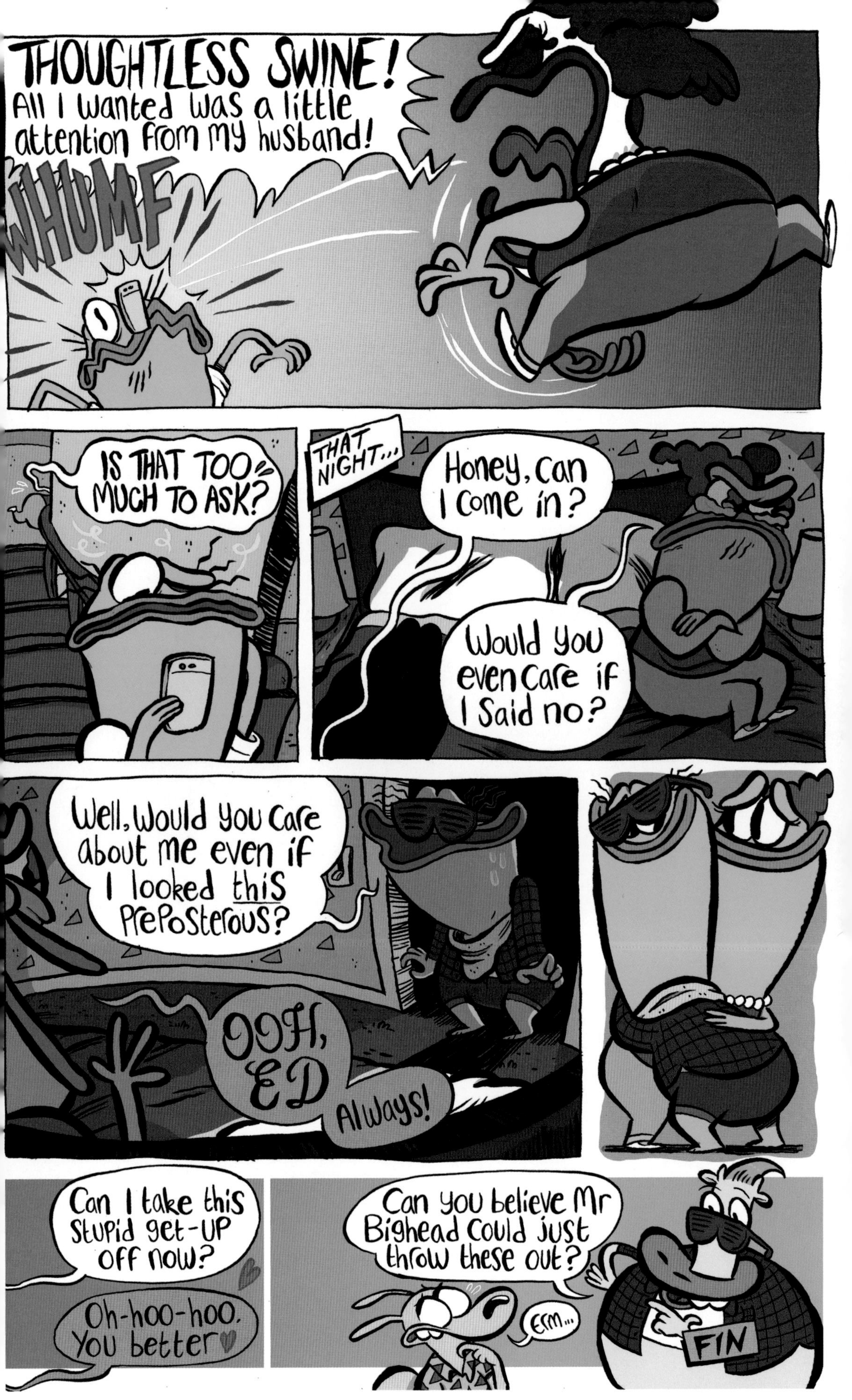
THOUGHTLESS SWINE! All I wanted was a little attention from my husband!
WHUMF
IS THAT TOO MUCH TO ASK?
THAT NIGHT...
Honey, can I come in?
Would you even care if I said no?
Well, would you care about me even if I looked this preposterous?
OOH, ED
Always!
Can I take this stupid get-up off now?
Oh-hoo-hoo. You better
Can you believe Mr Bighead could just throw these out?
Ehm...
FIN

COVER GALLERY

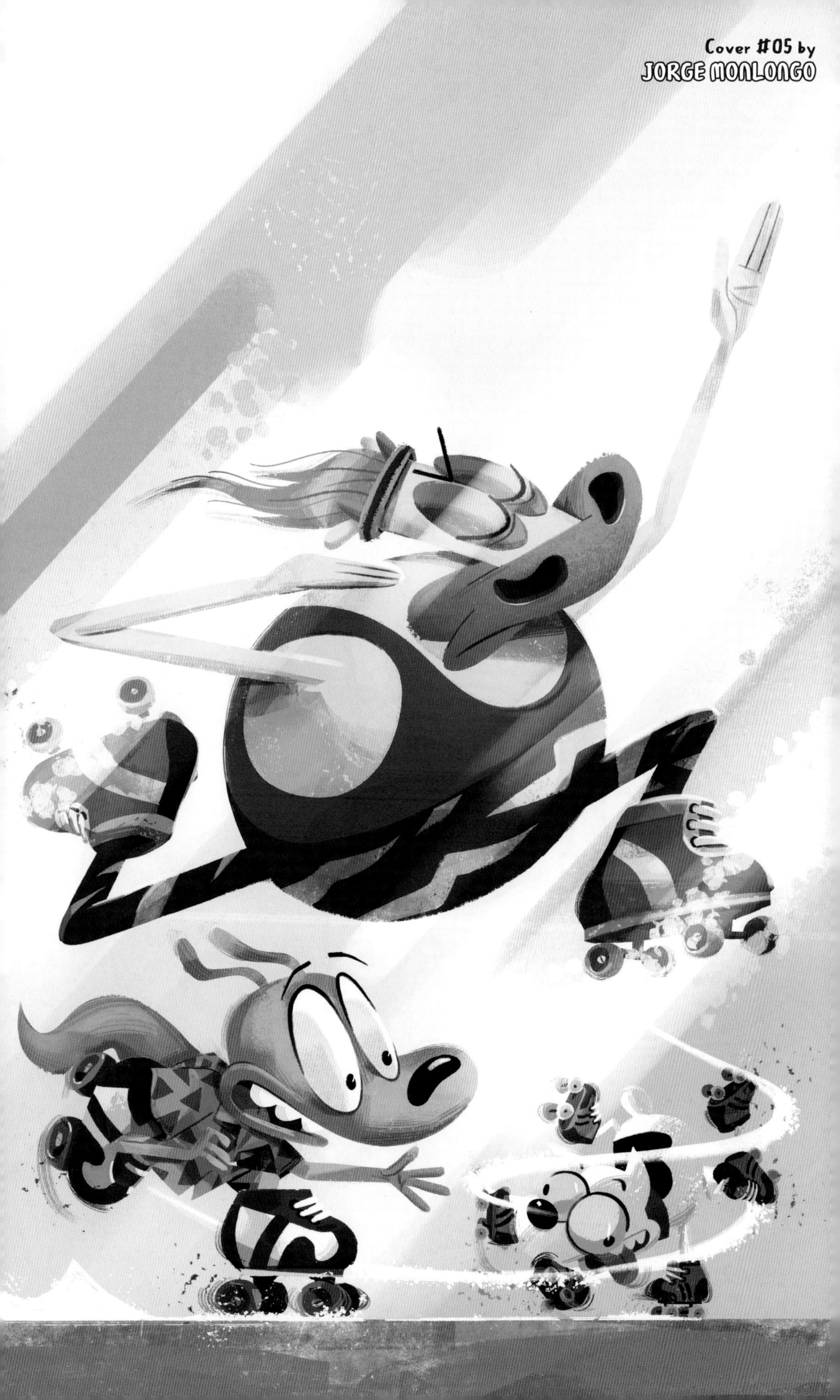

Cover #05 by
JORGE MONLONGO

Subscription Cover #05 by
DEREK CHARM

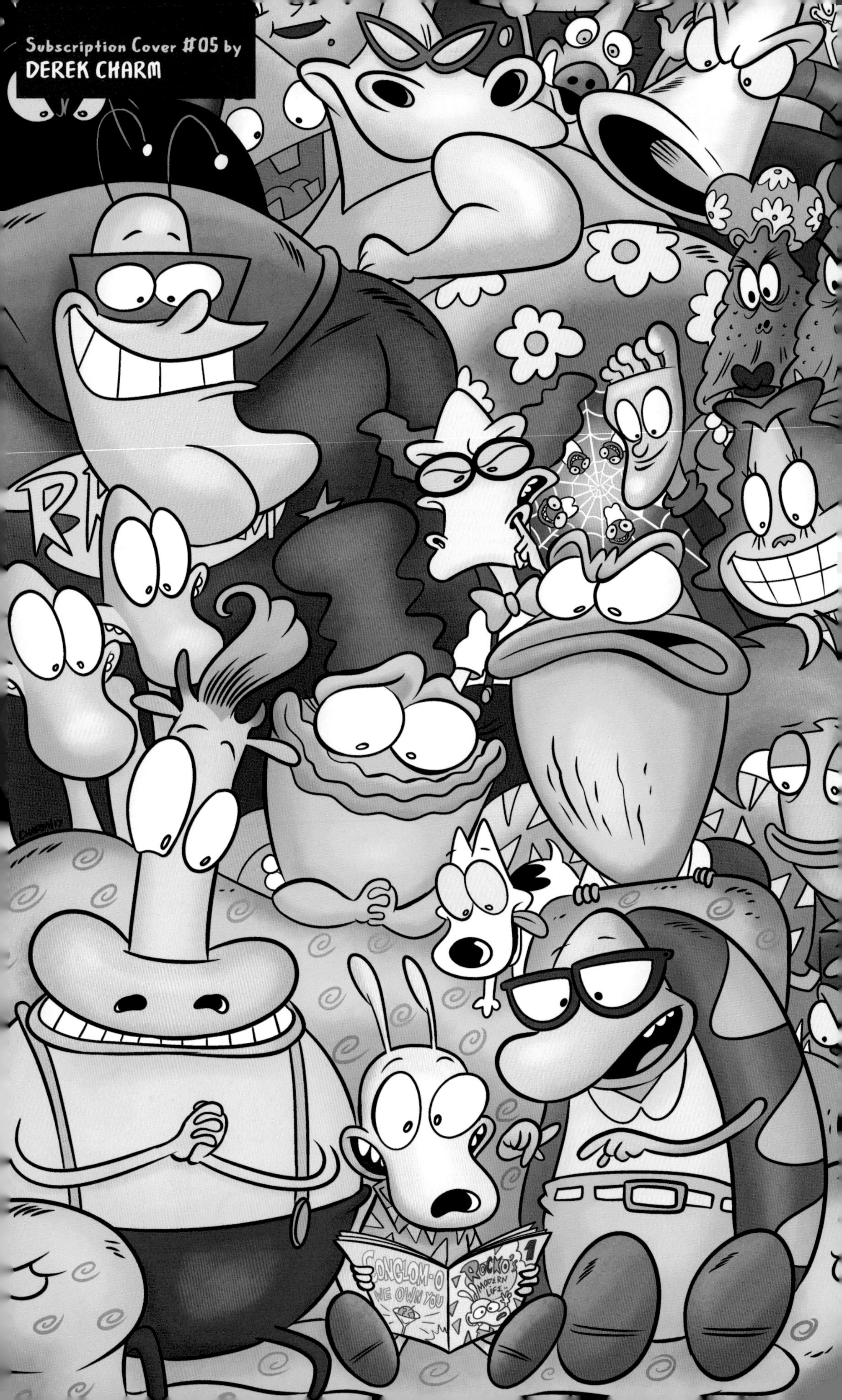
CONGLOM-O
WE OWN YOU
ROCKO'S MODERN LIFE
1

Cover #06 by
JORGE MONLONGO

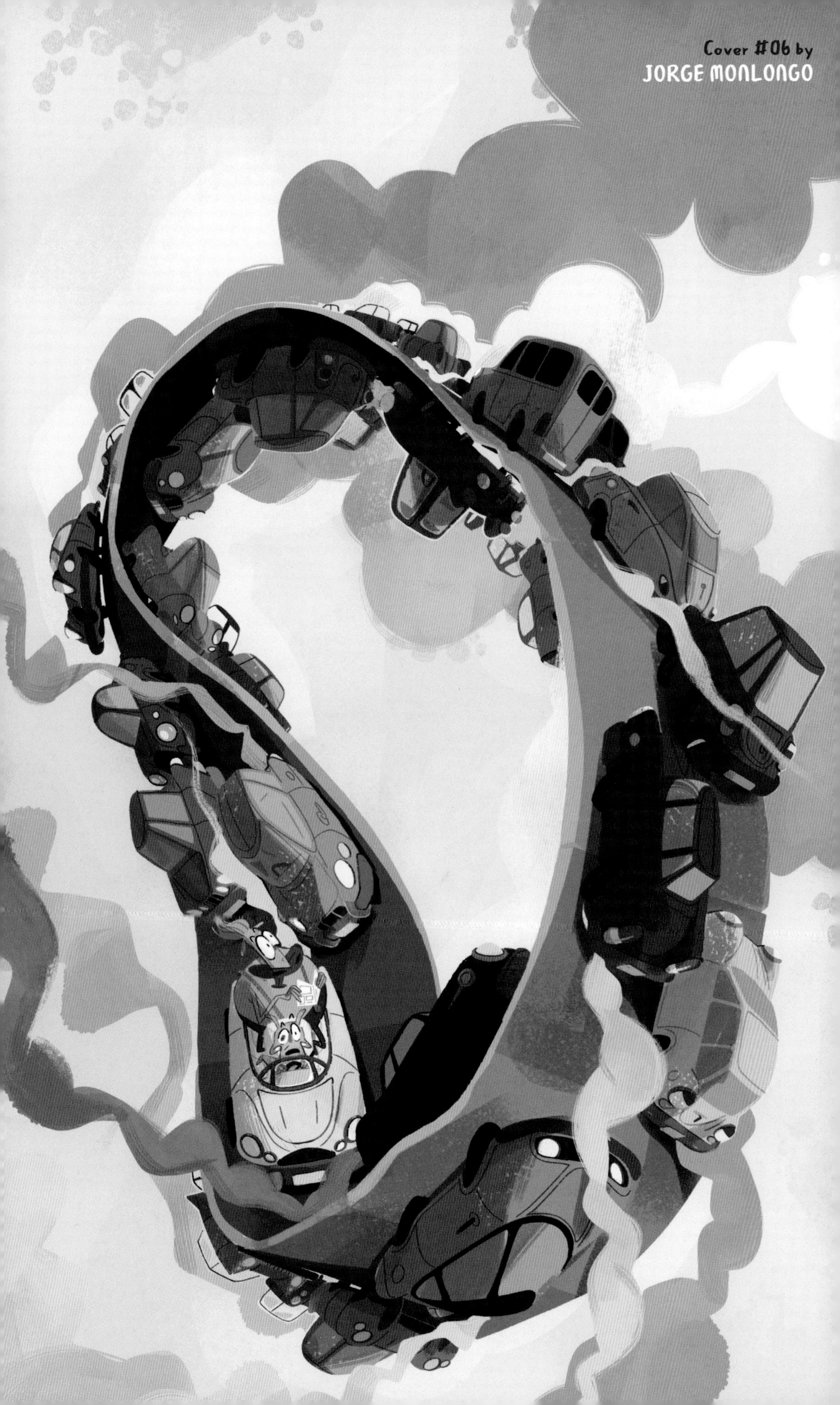

Subscription Cover #06 by
COLE CLOSSER

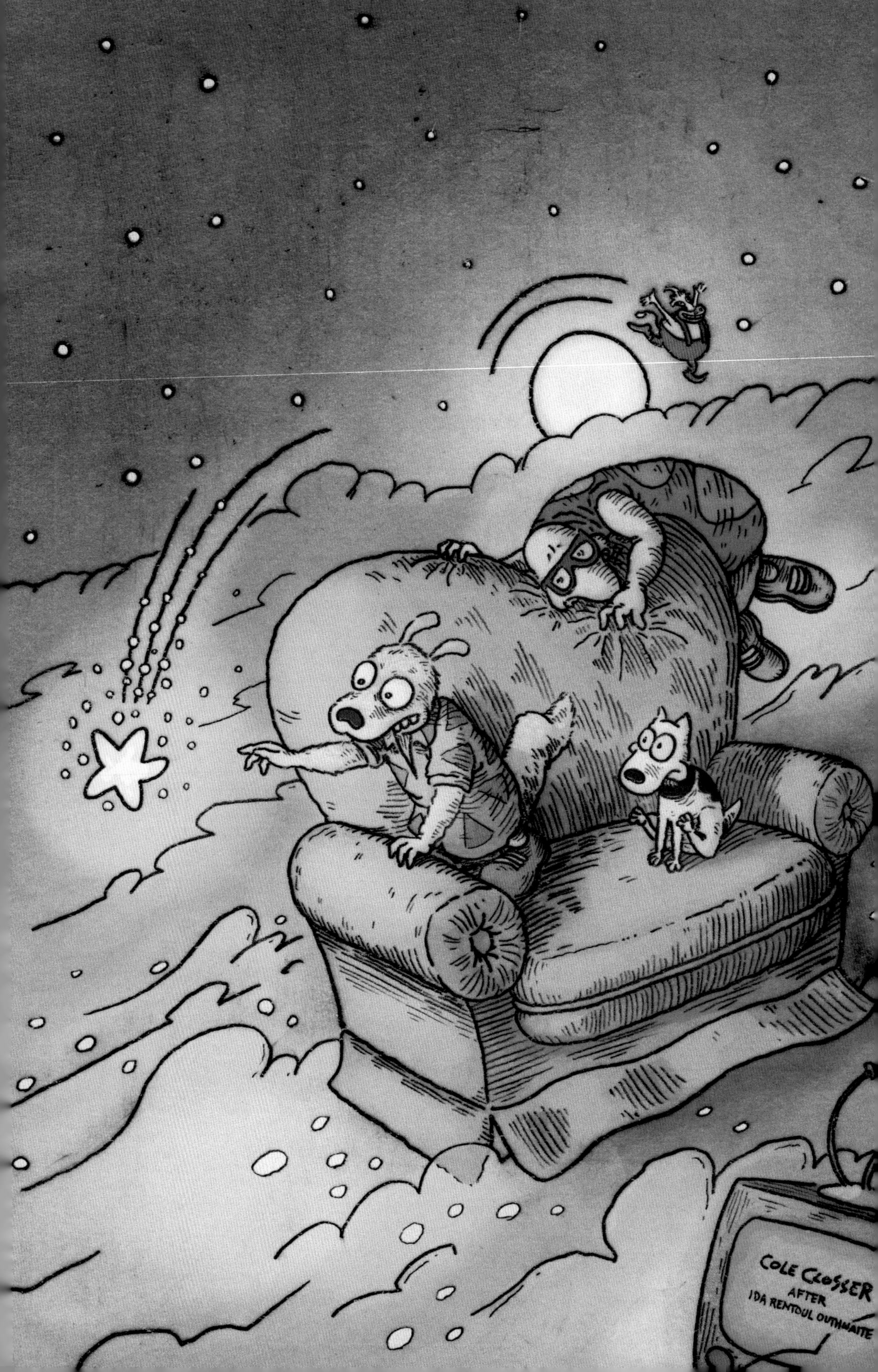
COLE CLOSSER
AFTER
IDA RENTOUL OUTHWAITE

Cover #07 by
JORGE MONLONGO

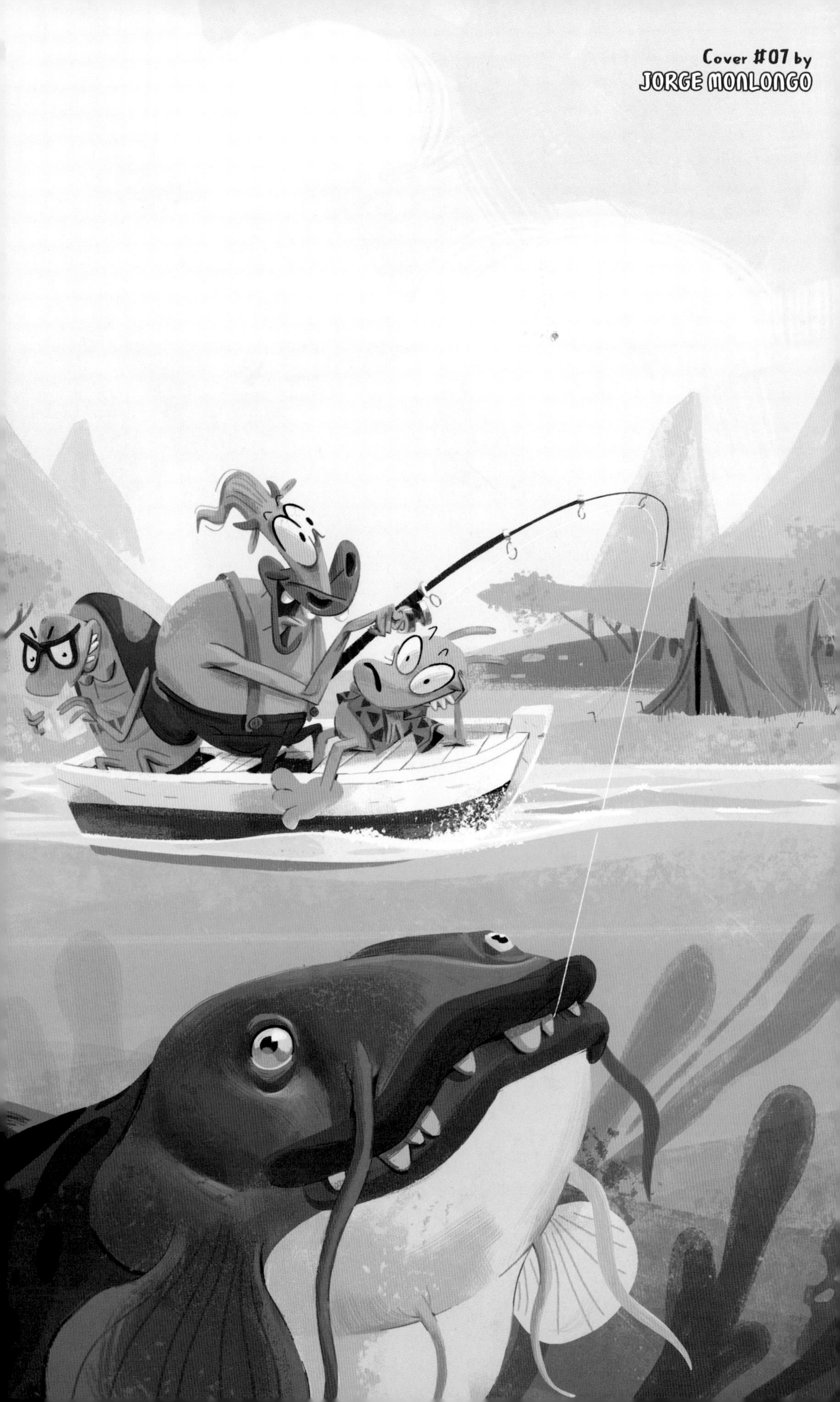

Subscription Cover #07 by
NICK CROSS

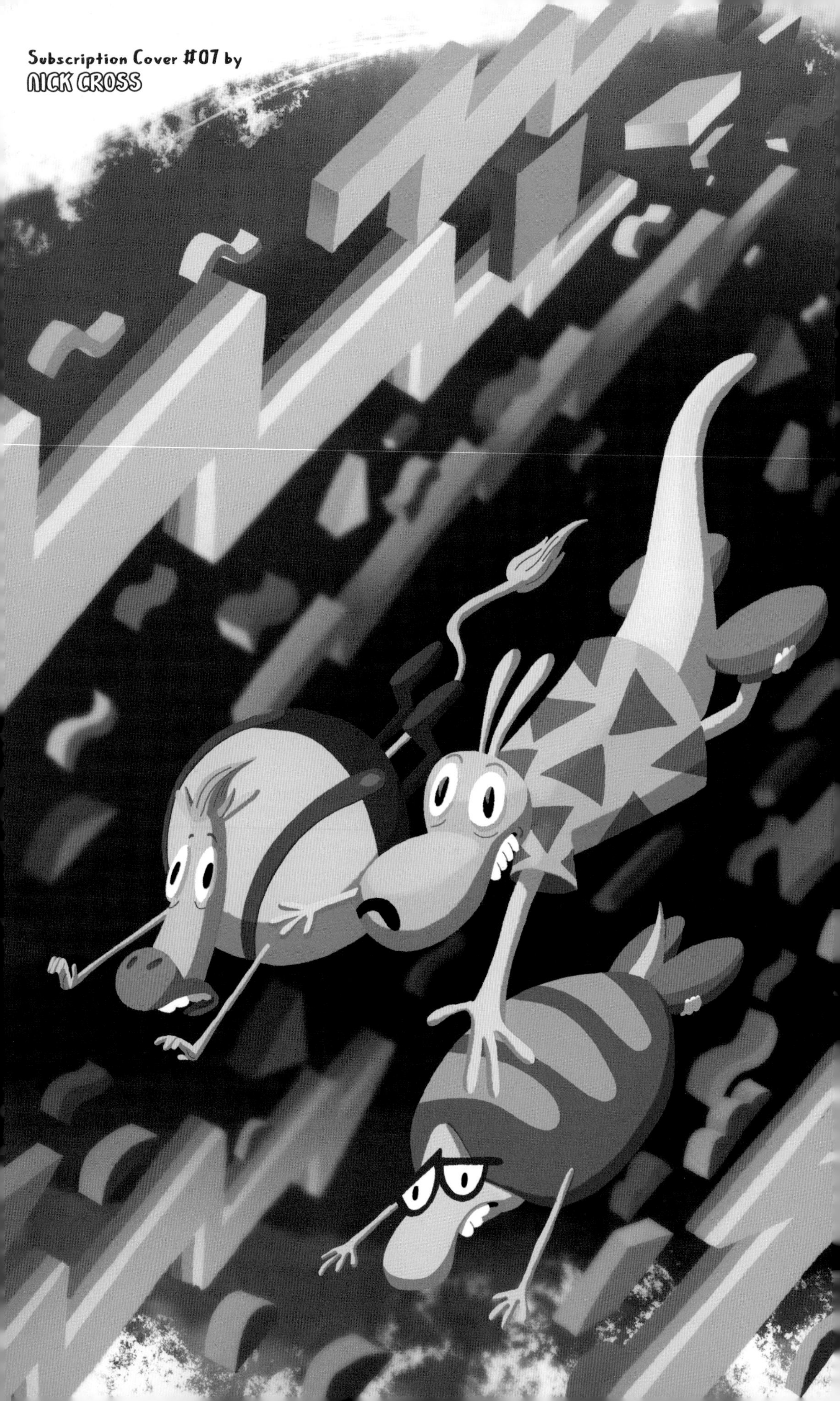

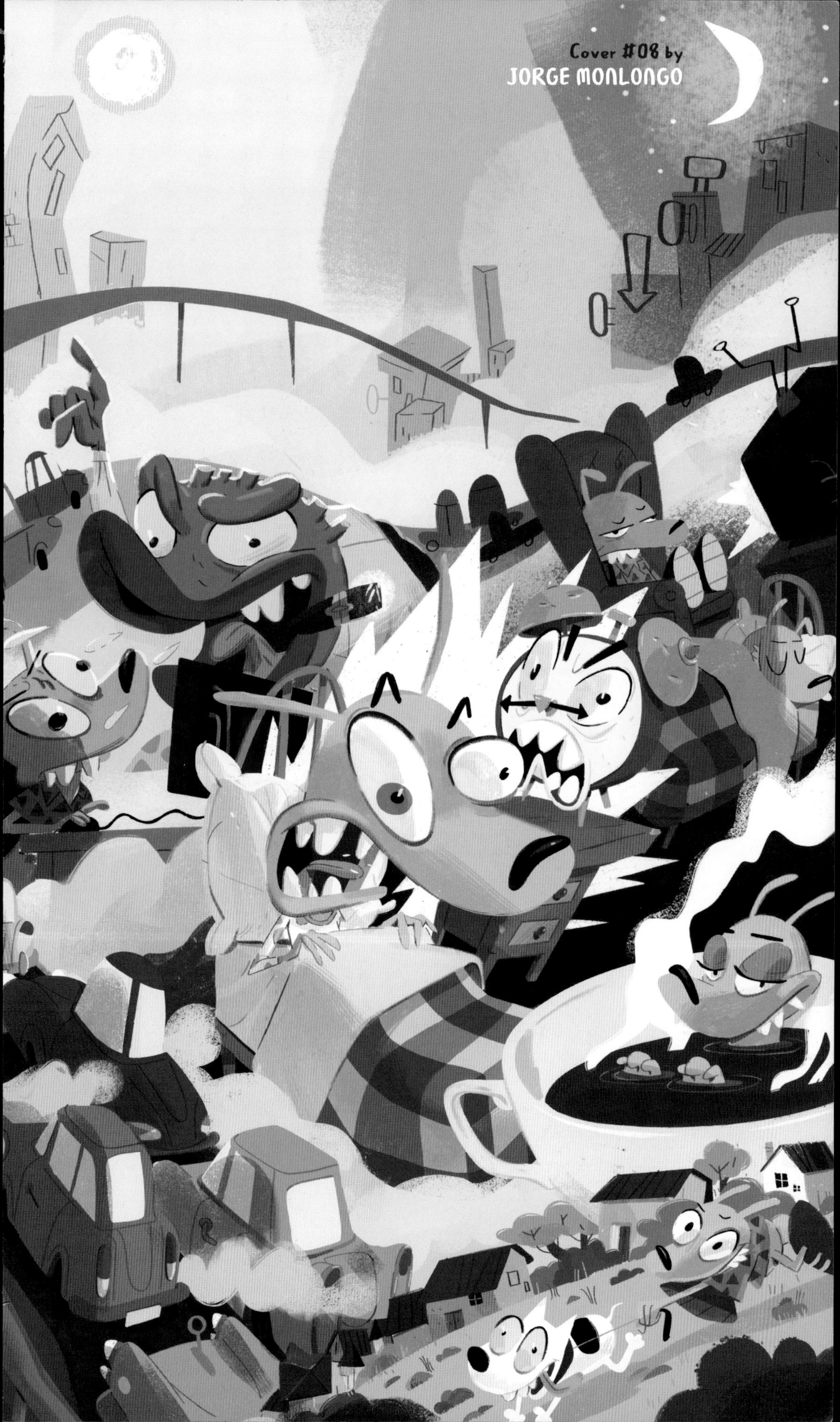
Cover #08 by
JORGE MONLONGO

Subscription Cover #08 by
DAVE PERILLO

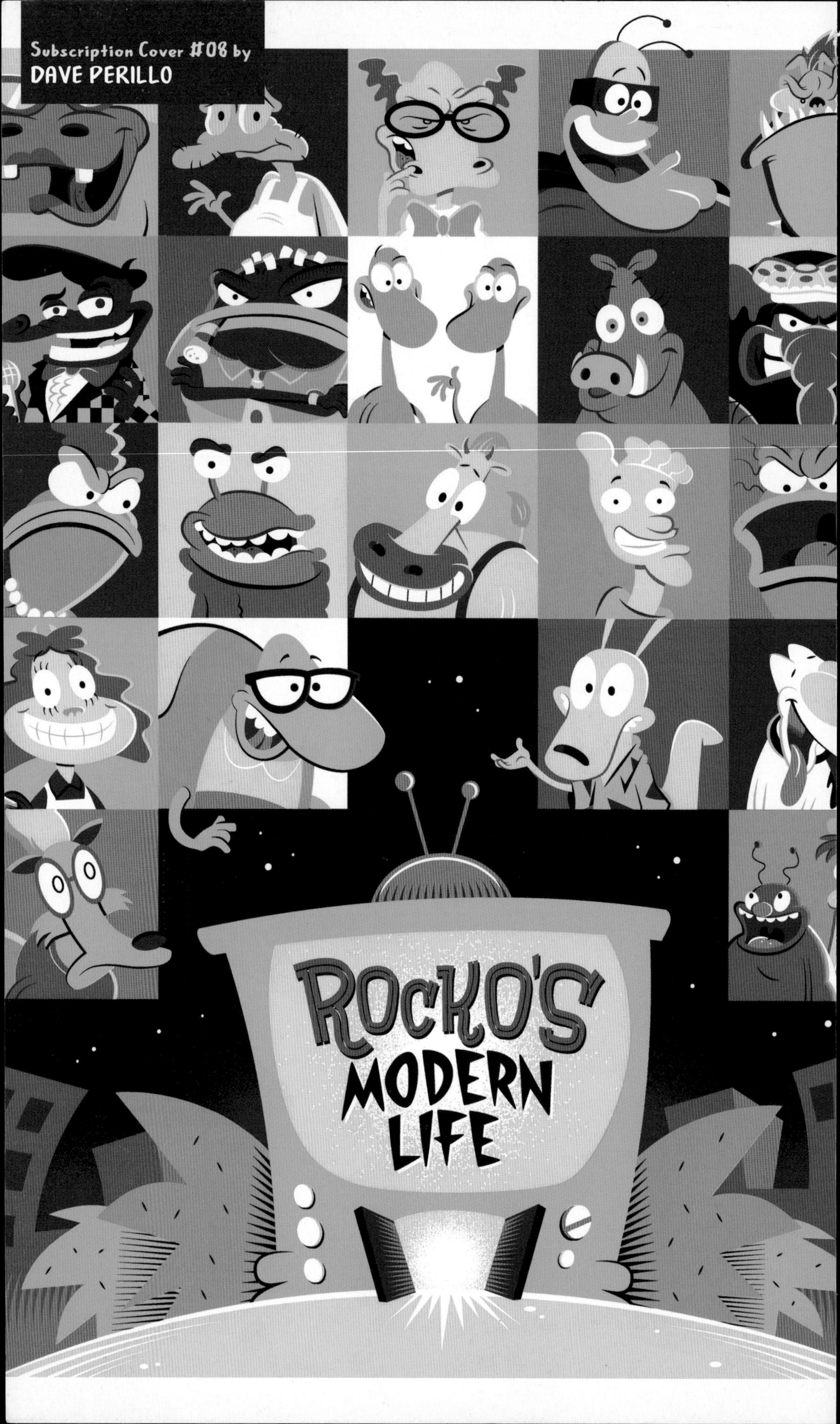
ROCKO'S
MODERN
LIFE